Whaling Captains of Color

Whaling Captains of Color

AMERICA'S FIRST MERITOCRACY

SKIP FINLEY

NAVAL INSTITUTE PRESS
ANNAPOLIS, MARYLAND

Naval Institute Press
291 Wood Road
Annapolis, MD 21402

First Naval Institute Press paperback edition published in 2022.
ISBN: 978-1-68247-832-5 (paperback)
ISBN: 978-1-68247-833-2 (eBook)

The Library of Congress has cataloged the hardcover edition as follows:
Names: Finley, Skip, author.
Title: Whaling captains of color : America's first meritocracy / Skip
    Finley.
Description: Annapolis, Maryland : Naval Institute Press, [2020] | Includes
bibliographical references and index.
Identifiers: LCCN 2020003170 | ISBN 9781682475096 (hardback)
Subjects: LCSH: Whaling masters—United States—History. | African American
    whalers—History. | Whaling masters—United States—Biography | African
    American whalers—Biography. | Whaling—United States—History.
Classification: LCC SH383.2 .F57 2020 | DDC 639.2/8092 [B]—dc23
LC record available at https://lccn.loc.gov/2020003170

29 28 27 26 25 24 23 22   9 8 7 6 5 4 3 2 1
First printing

I've learned a lot about whaling captains of color. I also learned that the time it takes to research and write a book is a gift. My wife, Karen W. Finley, provided that gift—the hours writing after work until bedtime, on weekends, and over holidays; and the many trips to New Bedford, Nantucket, and Provincetown for research. She never doubted for a moment that I can do anything—including writing a book about men of color who proved they could do anything.

I'm lucky and grateful and dedicate this book to her.

CONTENTS

ILLUSTRATIONS

PREFACE

To date there have been few concerted scholarly efforts to bring their individual or collective history to light—a situation that is particularly regrettable in light of the intrinsic drama of their stories, and the comparative success that many achieved in the face of adversity, in times when people of color were elsewhere excluded from self-realization at sea or ashore.

    —STUART M. FRANK, director of the Kendall Whaling Museum[1]

The beautiful, well-maintained homes decorating the village of Edgartown on Martha's Vineyard graphically illustrate that whaling was about money. The notion that whaling was fishing was a conceit of man. Industrial whaling—the purposeful killing of whales from the 1600s until the turn of the twentieth century—was about oil.

The Provincetown schooner *William A. Grozier* under sail past one of the Martha's Vineyard sidewheel steamboats. *Courtesy of the New Bedford Whaling Museum*

Martha's Vineyard, Sag Harbor on Long Island, Nantucket, New Bedford, and Provincetown formed the nexus of the industry for most of the time the business was pursued. Opportunity had taught Native Americans the value of whales and how to catch the "leviathans" (as white men called the largest creatures on the planet), and they passed their knowledge on to European settlers. Fortunes—and lives—were made and lost chasing whales until Edwin Laurentine Drake discovered shale oil in Pennsylvania in 1859 and the price of the difficult-to-harvest whale oil plummeted. From a high of $2.55 per gallon of prized sperm oil in 1866, the price dropped to 12 cents per gallon in 1932.[2]

The size and complexity of the whaling enterprise was immense; more than 2,700 whale ships were built. According to whaling scholar Judith Lund, 15,913 whaling trips were made from 1715 to 1928, with 954 of these conducted by "replacement masters"—experienced men who had earned the consensus of their crews to finish voyages when the original captains could not.[3]

Whaling featured an implausible cast of characters: slaves and slavers, abolitionists, Quakers, pirates, the British, killers, deserters and gamblers, gold miners, inventors and investors, cooks and crooks, and of course the whales, some with personalities of their own. That cast was accompanied by the facts and factions that conspired to kill the industry: war, weather, bad management, poor judgment, disease, obsolescence, and a "nonrenewable resource" given the zeal of the harvest.[4]

A confluence of circumstance led to men of color being involved in whaling as workers, inventors, leaders, and economic participants far out of proportion to their share of the population of America and of the New England states, the home of the industry. Indeed, whaling was the first American industry to exhibit any significant degree of diversity; but even compared with diversity today, the proportion of men of color was incredibly high.

Young America's whale ships left wakes across seas worldwide, mapping them along the way. Due to its large, deep, protected harbor and easy access to the world's oceans, New Bedford, Massachusetts—"the city that lit the world"—became the center of the industry. An annotated map at the New Bedford Whaling Museum notes: "In the 1800s, thousands of voyages, with tens of thousands of men, hunted hundreds of thousands of whales, by traveling millions of miles, for tens of millions of gallons of oil, for hundreds of millions in profits. Today, whale-watching is a multi-billion-dollar global industry." The map is highlighted with red and blue dots signifying whales and the locations of the ships that took them. The dots cover the globe. Author Lisa Norling lists forty-five whaling grounds worldwide.[5] About 3,200 logbooks (only about 20 percent of the total) remain from 15,913 whaling voyages, the total mileage of their whale trips equal to 20 round trips to the moon.[6]

The wealth of information about whaling captains of color, some of it yet to be analyzed, is extraordinary. Even by today's standards, the meticulousness of whaling recordkeeping is amazing. There are several books on whaling records, premier among them being *History of the American Whale Fishery: From Its Earliest Inception to the Year 1876* by Alexander Starbuck, which offers a 167-page history of the business and then, beginning with the year 1715, proceeds to list the name of each ship, its description, captain, owner, port of departure, whaling ground, dates, and products of the trip—along with notes retrieved from logs and shipping papers. In 774 pages Starbuck captures all of these data through 1876.

Reginald B. Hegarty's addendum to Starbuck's work, *Returns of Whaling Vessels Sailing from American Ports, 1876–1928*, was published in 1959. Judith N. Lund's three-volume *American Offshore Whaling Voyages 1667–1927* compiles and updates this work. Martha Putney (*African American Sailors: Afro-American Merchant Seamen and Whalemen prior to the Civil War*) identifies thirteen black whaling captains, Mary Malloy (*Black Sailors in the Maritime Trades*) identifies another eight, and Harold O. Lewis eleven more. Donald Warrin's *So Ends This Day* contributes the names of sixteen Cape Verdean masters to the total. In *Native American Whalemen and the World* Nancy Shoemaker identifies more than six hundred Native American whalemen from more than two thousand voyages, six of whom served as masters at least once.[7]

These sources, along with independent research (in major part thanks to databases at the New Bedford Whaling Museum Library and the New Bedford Public Library crew list), confirm the existence of these men, but the lives of only a few have been memorialized despite their unlikely success. In addition to Putney, Malloy, and Lewis, W. Jeffrey Bolster (*Black Jacks* and other publications), Jim Murphy (*Gone a-Whaling*), and

Ray A. Almeida (*Cape Verdeans in the Whaling Industry*) have added to our knowledge. *Native American Whalemen and the World*, published in 2015, was developed from a database from the National Archives in Boston, the U.S. Customs Service crew list, and others throughout New England.[8] Patricia C. McKissack and Frederick L. McKissack's *Black Hands, White Sails* was extraordinarily useful. Other authors have chronicled the more widely known black whaling captains Absalom Boston, Paul Cuffe, and William T. Shorey, who, while unlikely to become household names, are part of an elite corps of fifty-two people who, against all odds, became whaling captains.

It was not easy to rise to the level of whaling master—and it was far more difficult when harsh discrimination was the order of the day, particularly before the Civil War. Author Jim Murphy points out that "Frederick A. Lawton (who was black) shipped aboard the whaler *Charles* in 1830 when he was fourteen and stayed with the ship as a common seaman for eleven years. Any white sailor who worked on a ship for that long would have been made a boatsteerer or mate somewhere along the line. Finally, after thirty-two years of whaling, Lawton was promoted to first mate, a rank he deserved decades earlier."[9]

Paul Cuffe, the earliest of the masters and the most written about, opened the door for the rest. Although he personally captained only a few whaling voyages, Cuffe built an unequaled merchant marine dynasty. Captain William A. Martin also stands out among his peers. Although Martin rates a simple listing in each of the five principal source books of the industry (which do not mention his race), he is identified as black only in Arthur Railton's *History of Martha's Vineyard* and in Harold O. Lewis' work.[10]

Captain Martin was the inspiration for this book as a result of my research for a 2014 article for *Martha's Vineyard* magazine. Through that research I realized how rare it was to be a whaling master, much less a whaling master of color. One group stands out as an unintentional dynasty—all of them were born free, several were the progeny of slaves, some mixed by marriage to Native Americans. They were remarkably accomplished and related by blood, marriage, and kinship. Their names were Cuffe, Wainer, Cook, Boston, Pompey, and Phelps.

Whaling Captains of Color

Introduction

There is not that nice distinction made in the whaling as there is in the naval and merchant services; a coloured man is only known and looked upon as a MAN, and is promoted in rank according to his ability and skill to perform the same duties as the white man; his opportunities for accumulating pecuniary means—investing his earnings in whaling capital, is equally the same.

—PHILIP FONER and RONALD LEWIS, *Black Workers*

The Europeans who came to the New World learned from Native Americans how to row out to sea and bring back whales. But instead of using the catch for food and household goods, as the Indians did, the settlers used whale oil for smokeless candles to light their homes in the 1600s, for street lighting in the 1700s, and for lubricating the Industrial Revolution in the 1800s.

A $40,000–$60,000 investment in a whale ship could be returned several times over. When whaling ended, that money was invested in textiles in southern New England. Profits from whaling and textiles developed the railroads that supported western expansion by providing the means to move huge amounts of raw material efficiently. Finally, the money made from railroads was used to manufacture steel—the material used to construct the workhorses of the new fuel economy, oil wells.

Whaling ranked among the five largest American industries for more than two hundred years and made southern New England the Middle East of its day, because whaling was about oil. Some 175,000 people went whaling, according to one estimate; most went only once because they could not endure the lack of comfort, the mind-numbing boredom, and the potentially life-threatening danger at every turn. To black men, though, whaling was far better than slavery, and as many as 20–30 percent of all the men who participated in whaling were men of color.

While most black people before the Civil War were slaves or subject to being taken into slavery, on the sea it was different, especially for whalers, who worked freely in the waters off areas where they would be enslaved if they went ashore. Not only did black men go whaling; many were in charge of ships and earned a difficult living for themselves and their families.

Nowhere, especially in the halcyon whaling years from the mid-1700s to the antebellum mid-1800s, did any rank have more privilege than master—a term synonymous with captain of a whale ship. A black whaling captain might not risk eye contact with a white man on land, but he could flog or shackle that same man at sea.

The expression "men of color" is used here to describe those discriminated against on land because of the color of their skin, a group that included those whom today we describe as African American or Native American. Maritime historian Mary Malloy agrees with author W. Jeffrey Bolster's caution to discourage "attempting to reconstruct the black seafaring experience in entirely consistent terms." The term "African American" is not sufficiently descriptive for men of color because often neither attribute was true.[1] Whale men of color included free black men, former slaves (Africans), black descendants of slaves (Americans), Native Americans with skills and little opportunity, West Indians, and Cape Verdeans fleeing drought-induced destitution in their homeland.

Life at sea posed significant challenges, including the absence of sex and the potential for disease, with medical care left in the hands of untrained captains. Working conditions were harsh. Whalers lived in close and nasty quarters, and endured punishment swift and harsh. Virtually all literature of whaling mentions the stultifying boredom of men cramped in tiny quarters on board vermin-infested ships reeking of odors indescribable. Men on board whale ships learned to get along because there was nowhere to go. Racial prejudice had no place there. Men were judged not by the color of their skin but by their ability—and production. Nevertheless, black men, accustomed to subservience under slavery, were preferred as crew-men because they were more easily controlled and were satisfied with less pay than white counterparts.[2] For tens of thousands of black men, whaling was the lesser of two evils. For different reasons, the same was true for other men of color.

Whaling trips might last for years. The longest recorded whaling trip was that of the *Nile* of New London, which lasted nearly twelve years—from May 1858 to April 1870—during which it was captained by seven men.[3] At least another thirty-two whaling trips exceeded four years. Most trips averaged two to three years chasing whales that were very adept at fleeing. Among the few things breaking the boredom of long voyages were the vagaries of nature, among them wondrous sunrises and sunsets and sights of flora and fauna, but more often than not, wind and waves that killed indiscriminately.[4]

It is all too easy to romanticize the harpooning of a whale, made popu-lar by Herman Melville's *Moby-Dick* and fantasized by the heroic statue of a white man on board a whale ship outside the New Bedford Public Library. And there *were* moments of glory. Claude Oliviera, a boat-steerer on the *William A. Grozier*, won a competition with the *Andrew Hicks* with a mighty forty-two-foot harpoon throw. "Great Feat by Boatsteerer" proclaimed the newspaper article describing the events leading up to the whale's capture. Witnessed by "a dozen men who can prove it, the six men in the boat that secured the whale and the six in the boat that didn't get it," Oliviera's toss became the record distance for a harpooned whale. (A typi-cal throw was twenty to thirty feet.) While forty-two feet was extraordinary, that still was awfully close to an enraged animal that could measure up to one hundred feet in length.[5]

Presuming they survived the "Nantucket sleigh ride" provided by a harpooned whale that might weigh as much as fifty tons,[6] crews still had to tow the creature back to the ship, sometimes up to four miles at about one mile per hour, and then butcher it. This shipside process was made more difficult by hungry sharks in the water and the gore attendant to the task. Add razor-sharp implements and a pitching and yawing ship, and men could die in a variety of ways at any given time. The processors were brick ovens fed first by wood and ultimately by the body parts of the catch to create Stygian fires in iron pots hot enough to melt the whale's blubber for transport home in barrels. The abattoir can only be likened to a Hieronymus Bosch painting.

The harsh conditions pushed men to the edge—sometimes even to mutiny. Whaling records indicate 451 mutinies over the years—but with so many voyages, including those in which the ships never returned, who knows how many were not recorded? One gruesome statistic reveals whaling's inherent dangers—of 750 ships that left New Bedford, 231 (roughly 30 percent) were lost, a statistic consistent with other ports. (Although a lost ship did not necessarily mean the men were lost too.)[7]

And sometimes the whale won. Sperm whales, the most prized of all, had teeth. All whales had powerful tails that they used as weapons, and while the large mother ships were only occasionally sunk or damaged, the tiny whaleboats were frequently crushed by the whale's jaws or huge body parts slapped down in anger or pain. Drowning was always a part of life at sea, where the ability to swim a thousand miles or more from land was as useful as a vestigial organ.

Men of color attained the rank of captain on merit, many promoted from a larger group of first, second, and third mates; boat-steerers; and harpooners. Whaling captains of color led colored and white men on 10,000-plus-mile journeys to exotic lands and experienced foreign life as free men and then, after acquiring the sophistication of world travelers, had to return to a hostile homeland. Negro Seaman's Acts and Fugitive Slave Acts enacted prior to the Civil War thwarted their freedom. Historically, the Fugitive Slave Acts of 1793 and 1850 were enacted as federal laws under which slave owners could seek out and return to slavery people who had found ways of escaping, typically to the northern states. What is more, the law dictated that *anyone* black—free or not—could be taken against his or her will on the strength of anyone white claiming to be that person's owner, without basic due process rights like a jury trial. A special commissioner who oversaw the process was paid $10 if a fugitive was *returned* to slavery and only $5 if the fugitive was released. The law required all U.S. citizens to assist with the capture of slaves. The notorious *Dred Scott v. Sandford* decision of 1857 compounded the Fugitive Slave Act by concluding that *no black person*, free or enslaved, had constitutional rights. Northerners were generally opposed to the laws, and Quakers were outraged by them. The U.S. attorney general in 1821 went so far as to rule that free blacks in Virginia were not citizens of the United States—a ruling that lasted until Abraham Lincoln's attorney general reversed it four decades later.

Georgia law in the 1820s required a forty-day quarantine of any ships with blacks on board arriving in its ports. As a result, some captains would not hire blacks. In the 1830s South Carolina began imprisoning black crewmen, a practice followed by North Carolina and Florida. Alabama's ports were closed to blacks, and Louisiana's Negro Seaman's Act required captains to put their black crewmen in jail while the ships were in port.[8]

It was no wonder that men of color flocked to the Northeast, particularly New Bedford, where the strong support of abolition-minded Quakers created the opportunity for them to work as free men. On board a whaling ship there was little room for racial conflict. Many were the references to black whaling captains enforcing their will according to their rank—not their race—and the crew's reluctant adherence.

The talents required of a whaling captain provide an inkling of why crews would be compliant: "During the course of an average voyage he was almost certain to act as a physician, surgeon, lawyer, diplomat, financial agent, entrepreneur, task-master, judge, peace-maker, sailor, whaleman and navigator."[9] Left unsaid in the job description was management of an inexperienced crew of young men whose ranks included the dregs of early American society: former or soon-to-be prisoners, runaways, the disinherited, the mean-spirited, the adventure seeking, the poor and homeless—literally the unwanted and uncared for.

Such was the available talent pool.

Compensation took the form of a share in the net profits of the voyage. Owners spent the bare minimum on the ship, the crew, and operations: just find and kill the whale; harvest its oil; sell it on the open market; deduct the investment—and split the remainder among the investors, officers, and crew. The $35 per year average cost to feed a crewmember was substantially less, in quantity and quality, than the cost to feed a slave (one-half pound of meat and a quart or more of corn meal per day) or a soldier in the Revolutionary War (one pound of meat and one pound of bread per day). Combined, captains of color returned with revenues valued at close to $74 million in today's dollars.[10]

Some black men's efforts made them wealthy even before the end of the Civil War that officially freed them. And at the moment of freedom, most who had achieved the highest rank at sea returned to land seeking safer occupations.

Little has been written about the fifty-two captains of color discussed in this book. And there may have been another ten such captains, although there is not sufficient proof at this time to categorize them in this select, historically overlooked group (see chapter 14).

CHAPTER 1

━━┅━◆━┅━━

Dynasty
1778–1842

Come, my African brethren, let us walk in the light of the Lord.
. . . I recommend sobriety and steadfastness. . . . I recommend that
early care be taken to instruct the youth while their minds are tender;
that so they may be preserved from the corruptions of the world,
from profanity, intemperance, and bad company. . . . I want that we
should be faithful in all things, that so we may become a people giving
satisfaction to those who have borne the burden and heat of the day,
in liberating us from a state of slavery.

—PAUL CUFFE [1]

*I*t must have been stifling hot that day in 1796, with unbearable humidity and no breeze, as the 62-foot *Ranger* crawled up the Nanticoke River on its way to Vienna on Maryland's Eastern Shore. Even at full sail the *Ranger* was barely making way, giving the crew plenty of opportunity to notice slaves working the soil along the riverbanks.

Like all accomplished ship captains, Paul Cuffe knew that the sound of waves slapping on the hull meant they were getting close to the dock, the sound telling him the water was getting shallower. The *Ranger* was seeking to trade its cargo for corn—and a profit. Usually, crews heading for a port of call were loose and chatty, teasing one another about their plans for shore leave. But not that day, not on that ship—the first to land in a southern port with an all-black crew and a black captain who was also the *Ranger*'s owner. Along the way, according to author and historian Lamont Thomas, Captain Cuffe took time to warn the men to "practice exemplary conduct . . . avoid intemperate behavior and to abuse no man."[2]

Cuffe was intimately familiar with hardship and danger on the sea. He had been a whaler, after all, where occupational hazards were legion, including the predictable hostility of the weather and threats from pirates and, during the Revolutionary War, the British. This particular landing, however, was predictable only because of the familiar cruelty of white men. His own nation's Fugitive Slave Act legalized the seizure of black people accused of being runaway slaves, and putting into port south of the Mason-Dixon line posed a unique set of challenges for Cuffe. When the *Ranger* tied off at the dock, the people of Vienna were not pleased, according to Thomas' account. The whites were concerned about the example these free black men offered (might they trigger a slave revolt?) and the havoc an all-black crew could wreak on shore. This same year Maryland had passed a law allowing "suspicious" free black people to be held in servitude for up to six months.

As the ship's owner, Cuffe proudly stepped off the *Ranger* and gave his ship's documents to the local customs officer, who had no choice but to proclaim the legitimacy of the credentials and allow the crew to conduct its business. As it turned out, Cuffe and his crew conducted themselves "with candor, modesty and firmness" and "behaved not only inoffensively, but with a conciliating propriety." Several days later, the residents extended a form of respect and even a kindness—"one citizen even invited Cuffe and his family to dine in town"—before the *Ranger* set sail with a cargo of corn that would put a thousand dollars in Cuffe's coffers.[3]

Paul Cuffe is a less familiar historical figure to Americans than he should be, although several books about him are already in print and more are in the works. More than a dozen articles are devoted to his life and accomplishments. Cuffe was the first of the nation's black whaling captains.

The seventh of ten children, Cuffe was born to a former slave and a Wampanoag woman from Gay Head on Martha's Vineyard. From humble beginnings and a stint as an exceptional whaler, Paul Cuffe rose to become the wealthiest black man in the New World and the head of an extended family of black whaling and merchant captains. He consciously modeled his family after that of his close friend and mentor William Rotch, a Quaker and abolitionist who advanced the whaling industry on Nantucket and was largely responsible for establishing New Bedford as the whaling capital of the world.

Plaque commemorating Paul Cuffe. *Courtesy of the New Bedford Whaling Museum*

A life-size model of a part of Paul Cuffe's humble home in the New Bedford Whaling Museum belies his significance. Of the whaling industry's 2,500 captains, Cuffe is the only one who rates such an exhibit. Cuffe traveled the world, met the president of the United States and other American and British leaders, and led an expedition to settle black people in Africa. Cuffe founded a school for black students that ultimately became interracial and was a revered member of the Quaker religion. Cuffe fought for the freedom of his race, which he did not live to see. His storied and interesting life is summarized on a monument in the Westport cemetery, where he is buried:

In memory of Paul Cuffe—A Self-Made Man—Patriot,
Navigator, Educator, Philanthropist, Friend—A Noble Character

Whale Ship Captains

We know about Paul Cuffe thanks to his own writings and letters and the several books written about him, but we know very little about the other black whaling masters.

PAUL CUFFE SR.
(JANUARY 17, 1759–SEPTEMBER 9, 1817)

Cuffe must have been exceptional indeed to deserve Lamont Thomas' characterization of him as

> a Black, a free Black, an African, a free African, a Negro, a free Negro, a free person of color, an Indian, a native American, a Wampanoag-Pequot Native, a Black Indian, a British American, an American.
>
> He was a Christian, a Friend, a Quaker, a Puritan, God-fearing, a proselytizer, missionary, civilizer, farmer, shipbuilder, commercial trader, an entrepreneur, industrialist, a merchant, sailor, whaler, shipmaster, captain, fisherman, navigator, neighbor, a family man, a son, a father, a brother, an uncle.
>
> He was rebellious, fearless, timid, a dreamer, pragmatic, inconsistent, a protestor, petitioner, a one-man civil rights movement, an advocate, sagacious, accommodating, inflexible, conciliating, a conformist, naïve, pawn, tribalistic, a separatist, clannish, provincial, a role model, an embarrassment, "bad," a profiter, a capitalist, thrifty, a Yankee, a social climber, a name dropper, a "schmoozer," a salesman, a diplomat, a Federalist, an Anglophile, an humanitarian, a philanthropist.
>
> He was large. He was Multitudes. He was Paul Cuffe.[4]

Cuffe was born in 1759 on Cuttyhunk Island off the southern coast of Massachusetts. In mind, body, and spirit he was about as far away from slavery as one could get, remarkably so because he was born before slaves were freed. (Slavery did not end on Nantucket until 1773, in the rest of Massachusetts until 1783, and throughout America until almost fifty years after he died.)

Born to a free black/former slave African father and an Indian woman, Cuffe's mixed heritage was similar to that of other black–Native American whale masters, some of whom were born free thanks to these interracial marriages. (Under the law, the progeny of these marriages became free blacks but forfeited tribal benefits as a result. Scholars have typically interpreted this as a strategy "aimed at Indian extinction.")[5] Kofi Slocum, Paul Cuffe's father, bore the amalgamated names of an Ashanti of Akan ancestry and the slaveholders who bought him at age ten and brought him to Newport, Rhode Island, in 1728. He wound up the property of Quakers Ebenezer and Bathsheba Slocum and was sold to Ebenezer's nephew John

Slocum of Dartmouth, Massachusetts. The bill of sale, dated February 16, 1742, when Kofi (which meant "born on Friday") was about 25, indicated he was sold for 150 pounds. Slocum, following the bent of Quakers on Nantucket and elsewhere, freed Kofi in the 1740s, and Kofi—having taken the name Slocum—married Ruth Moses, a Wampanoag whose family was from Harwich on Cape Cod.

Kofi and Ruth moved from Dartmouth to Cuttyhunk Island, which had belonged to a succession of Slocums. There they pursued farming and raised a family of ten children, all of whom were given names (David, Jonathan, Sarah, Mary, Phebe, John, Paul, Lydia, Ruth, and Freelove) familiar to the Quaker religion they followed but were prohibited from joining.[6]

The Yankee concepts of hard labor, honesty, frugality, prudence, order, and humility the family also lived by helped to shape their lives. Kofi learned to read and write and keep a ledger of his activities, which included carpentry. In the 1760s he moved the family to Chilmark on nearby Martha's Vineyard, away from the white Slocums and closer to the native Wampanoags. There, according to his journal entries, Kofi built a shipping business hauling supplies and people, provisioning ships, and farming. Along with his children he hired workers to meet the goals and demands and was successful enough to acquire a 116-acre farm in Dartmouth for 650 Spanish-milled dollars in 1766; on the sale documents he changed the spelling of his name to "Coffe" to more closely reflect his African roots. He moved his four sons, six daughters, and wife to the mainland. Paul was eight years old at the time.

Paul Cuffe began whaling at age thirteen on ships belonging to the Rotch family. Whaling records were not as thorough before New Bedford took over from Nantucket as the whaling capital of the world; thus we know very little about Cuffe's whaling career, where he gained the experience in seamanship and navigation necessary to build his merchant shipping business. In those early years Cuffe sailed with experienced whalers on trips to the Gulf of Mexico and West Indies. Several sources report Cuffe was on board the *Charming Polly* on March 4, 1776, when it was captured by the British. Brock Cordeiro lists the ship as a whaler but does not specifically name it.[7]

When Kofi died in 1772 he left Paul and David the 116-acre Cuttyhunk estate (brother Jonathan had left for Chilmark on Martha's Vineyard), and the family attempted to farm the barren island. After his early whaling years, Paul went to Westport, where the family had settled, and he and David began a mercantile trade with Nantucket and other East Coast ports to help support the family.

The venture was profitable, and Paul had learned from his Quaker neighbors to save a portion of all the money he earned. Thanks to his thrift, he was able to invest in his first ship, the *Traveller*, in 1784 when he was twenty-five years old.[8] One year earlier, on February 25, 1783, Cuffe had married widow Alice Abel Pequit, a Wampanoag from Harwich on Cape Cod.[9]

In those days Cuffe was going by his father's name but by his mother's Indian identity. "Musta is my nature," he wrote, meaning he was a Mustee, or part Indian. Tellingly, his brother John, who had called himself John Slocum, changed his signature to John Cuff, the first such reference to the family name.[10]

In 1778 the Massachusetts state legislature amended its constitution to allow every adult male to vote—except "Negroes," "Indians," and "mulattoes"; Paul Cuffe and his siblings were all three. Cuffe's hometown of Dartmouth resisted because the new law deprived these people from making their own laws or disposing of their own property. Taxes were rising—Indian-owned land was not taxed, but black-owned property was—and the Coffe/Slocum family farm was burdened with black ownership. Opposed to taxation and fiercely independent, Paul grew into his African identity. It was around this time that he and the family began using Cuffe as the family name.

In 1780, irritated by the oppressive taxation and unable to vote, Cuffe and his brothers and neighbors (Adventure Child, Samual Gray, Pero Howland, Pero Russell, and Pero Cogleshell) wrote and submitted a petition to the state government: "We apprehend ourselves to be aggrieved in that while we are not allowed the Privileges of freemen of the state, having No vote or influence in the election with those that tax us, [the state has acted] . . . against a familiar Exception of power . . . too well known to need a recital at this place."

Making the point that America had sought its own freedom based on the rejection of taxation without representation, Cuffe asked a fundamental question: Why should black Americans be singled out and denied equal treatment? Although it was recorded, the petition was fundamentally ignored, failing in the House of Representatives. Trying another tack based on their Indian heritage, Paul and his brother John went to jail briefly in protest over unpaid back taxes. This time, rather than responding to the unfairness, authorities reduced the amount owed as a settlement, and the charges against the Cuffes were dropped when it was paid.

Meanwhile, the town of Dartmouth suspended trading with the hostile British, who returned the favor with a blockade that destroyed Dartmouth's economy and cut off Martha's Vineyard and Nantucket. Paul and his older brother David built a small boat and used it to outrun the British at night to get supplies to the islands. During this endeavor they were captured by pirates who confiscated the ship and its goods and then let the brothers go. Undeterred, Cuffe built another boat and continued in his new business, trading from Dartmouth with the islands on nightly trips in weather good and bad. This was the modest beginning of his entrepreneurial career.[11]

Cuffe was an excellent navigator with a natural sense of the sea. In 1792 Cuffe and his friend and partner Michael Wainer obtained the *Mary*, a 40-ton schooner that they used for a whaling trip to the Strait of Belle Isle in Newfoundland. During that season the *Mary* took six whales, two of which Cuffe captured himself. Four other boats that had declined to go out with the *Mary* because they felt it was ill-equipped wound up harvesting just one whale. Cuffe took the oil to Philadelphia, where he traded it for bolts and iron to use to build a new ship, the 69-ton *Ranger*, which he later used to buy corn on the Nanticoke River. By 1800 he had built the *Hero*, and in 1806, the *Alpha*. Because he sometimes traded the oil he harvested rather than selling it, the total value of the whale oil he brought back is impossible to determine. That notwithstanding, he was clearly the first of the black whaling captains whose skills at sea built both a dynasty and a fortune.[12] Cuffe *owned* whaling ships as early as 1780, and all of his captains were black. He often trained them himself.

After making Nantucket his first market for goods, Paul met William Rotch Sr. The two developed a long-lasting friendship that led to Cuffe's acceptance into the Westport Society of Friends (Quakers), a crucial element in his success that was denied to other black people. Even his father, Kofi, who steeped his family in the religion, was not allowed to join the

Friends. The cordial relationship bloomed into a business association said to have begun in 1783.

Paul Cuffe's leap toward equal footing with white men began with the acquisition of the *Traveller* in 1784. By 1806 he owned three brigs, a schooner, and several smaller craft—each operated by a relative and manned by an all-black crew—that traded from the United States to Africa and Europe. Despite his wide acceptance by the Quakers and his white neighbors, however, he could not serve on a jury or vote, and his children could not attend integrated schools. So, with his own money he built a school for his children and those of neighboring white families. He associated with influential Quakers and joined their church, forming relationships that eventually helped him meet a U.S. president and leaders worldwide.

Cuffe found another calling at this time, one that came through his Quaker faith. In 1792 British abolitionist Thomas Clarkson settled 1,100 former slaves in Sierra Leone—people who had supported the British during the Revolutionary War or had been confiscated from Loyalist owners in Nova Scotia. English-born Quaker William Thornton, looking for a place for his father's freed slaves, met with William Rotch Sr. and proposed the resettlement concept to him and the Free African Society in Newport. Rotch, having spoken with a merchant vessel captain just returning from Sierra Leone, thought it would be an ideal destination, a place where blacks could live safely in freedom. Rotch shared the idea with Cuffe, and he became an ardent advocate as well.[13]

As New Bedford became the center of the whaling industry, Cuffe continued to sail his ships from Westport. The port kept no records of his crews or the number of whales killed or barrels of oil he brought home. The same was true for several of the masters who were closely related to Cuffe by family or through business, including Michael Wainer and his sons. More important, Cuffe's business model was substantially different; he used his ships in both trade and whaling.

Every one of the industry's 15,000 whaling trips was a separate business enterprise: the owners invested in the equipping, staffing, and provisioning of the ship, which returned with the product. The oil was sold, and the investors shared the revenue after expenses. Cuffe's ships, however, sometimes went out whaling but returned with other cargo that could be sold at a profit. With the proceeds from his cargoes Cuffe bought more ships, acquired land, and established a retail store to sell products brought back from his mercantile missions. His enterprises made millions of dollars.

Paul Cuffe's Family

	Born	*Died*	*Married*
Parents			
Kofi Slocum	?	1773	1746
Ruth Moses	?	1792	
Siblings			
David	1747	?	
Jonathan	1749	?	Hepzibah Occouch, 1772
Sarah	1751?		
Mary	1753	1804	Michael Wainer, 1772
Phebe	1755	?	
John	1757	?	Abiah Jinny
			Bethia (?)
			Jane White
Paul	1759	1817	Alice Pequit, 1783
Lydia	1761		
Ruth	1763	1853	
Freelove	1765		
Children			
Naomi	1783		Peter Howard, 1806
Mary	1785		Alvan Phelps, 1806
Ruth	1788		Alexander Howard, 1806
			Richard Johnson, 1826
Alice	1790	?	1820, Pardon Cook, ?
Paul Jr.	1792		Mary Cook, 1812
Rhoda	1795		
William	1799	1837	Eliza Crawford

Sources: Thomas, *Rise to Be a Person*, p. 161; Nell, *The Colored Patriots of the American Revolution*.

Cuffe made a great deal of money, but his wealth dissipated rapidly. There may have been several reasons for this: a lack of foresight in investing, a lack of investment opportunities (a particular problem for men of color), or a lack of available funds for use outside of whaling. Simply put, whaling was not a transferable skill. Author Jeffrey Bolster notes that "the precarious financial stability of old black maritime families like the Cuffes collapsed quickly. Captain Paul Cuffe's namesake son spent a life at sea as a common sailor, and his granddaughter Joanna was reduced to public assistance in New Bedford by 1864."[14]

When Paul Cuffe died at age fifty-eight in 1817, "surrounded by family and friends," there was no one to assume his role in the business. Michael Wainer had died two years before. His son-in-law Alvan Phelps (daughter Mary's husband) died at sea in 1831, and Cuffe's son William was lost at sea in 1837. The Cooks, to whom he was related by marriage, were able mariners and whalers but not businessmen. The Howard brothers (Peter married Cuffe's daughter Naomi) and Alexander (who married Ruth and died) and Richard Johnson (who later married Ruth) were good partners and retailers—but not mariners. Worse, the family's Howard & Johnson retail store required the products that Cuffe's ships brought back.[15]

Ruth and Alexander had a son named Shadrack, whose son Horatio P. Howard—Paul Cuffe's

P. & A. Howard,

HAVE just received and for sale, 4800 lb. of Havana, brown, and broken loaf SUGAR, by wholesale or retail. *Also,* Hyson, Hyson-skin, Souchong and Bohea TEAS; best No. 1, Chocolate, boxes of best kind of Raisins, fresh Lemons, boxes of bar Soap, Windsor Soap, Cheese, Beeswax, Spanish float Indigo, Bengal do.; Gun-Powder, of superior quality; Richmond manufactured Tobacco; New-Orleans Cotton, cotton and wool Cards, from No. 4, to No. 10, fresh Rice, and a large quantity of Corks.

Also, an additional supply of
CROCKERY WARE,
consisting of blue printed quart and pint Pitchers, Teapots, Creampots, Sugars, Coffee-Bowls and Saucers, Plates, quart and pint Bowls; blue and green edged Tureens; cream coloured Napper Dishes, from 9 to 12 inches; short and long Pipes.

Likewise—a handsome assortment of Ladies' Morocco Shoes, of various colours, Ladies' and Children's Leather do.;—together with a good assortment of GROCERIES;—which they offer on the lowest terms for cash—and every favour gratefully acknowledged.   *May* 10, 1811.

Newspaper advertisement for P. & A. Howard (Peter and Alexander), the store owned by former slaves who married Paul Cuffe's daughters Naomi and Ruth (who later married Cuffe's partner, ship owner Richard Johnson). *Courtesy of the New Bedford Whaling Museum* great-grandson—was apparently the only other Cuffe to distinguish him-self. In 1888 he served as a clerk in the Custom House in New York. Born in New Bedford in 1854, Horatio died in 1923 and left a healthy sum ($5,000) to Hampton University and the rest of his estate to Tuskegee for Paul Cuffe Scholarships.[16]

Cuffe's legacy of land and cash, although substantial for the time, was small compared with the number of people he left behind who needed it. That was true for whaling captains of color generally. There are no lav-ish homes on Nantucket or Martha's Vineyard or New Bedford owned by their descendants. But Paul Cuffe paved the way for all the rest of the men of color who went to sea to kill leviathans. He—along with his friend and partner Michael Wainer—achieved the miraculous.

MICHAEL (MICAH) QUABEN WAINER (WANER) (1748–AUGUST 4, 1815)

Michael Waner (b. ca. 1700) and Dorcas Quebbin, Native Americans of Gay Head on Martha's Vineyard, had a daughter, Margaret Waner (b. ca. 1730), who married a Negro man named Newport Gardner in Dartmouth; they are believed to be Michael Wainer's parents.[17] Intermarriage between the two downtrodden races was common, particularly in the early Massachusetts colony, where laws put in place in 1705 prohibited blacks from marrying whites. By 1786, when the antislavery laws were being passed in Massachusetts, it was illegal for ministers to marry a white per-son to a "Negro, Indian or mulatto."

Michael Wainer married his first wife, Deborah Pequit, in 1765; she died in childbirth five years later, and he then married her sister Lydia Pequit in 1770; Paul Cuffe's wife, Alice Abel Pequit, was their sister. Michael married his third wife, Mary Slocum Cuffe (1753–1804), on October 11, 1772. Mary, who was Paul Cuffe's sister, died in 1804 at the age of fifty-one. He married his last wife, Mary Amos White, in 1806. Michael and Mary had nine children.[18]

Captain Michael Wainer was thus both a friend and partner and a relative of Paul Cuffe. His (and Mary's) sons, future whaling masters Thomas and Paul, were Cuffe's nephews. Three of the other Wainer sons worked on Cuffe's nonwhaling ships: Jeremiah (*Ranger*, 1801), and John and Michael (*Traveller*, 1811). Paul Cuffe was clearly a strong believer in nepotism.

Paul and Michael bought their first ship together, the schooner *Sunfish*, in the early 1790s and named it after its first catch, a large, unusual-looking, plankton-eating fish with a single dorsal and ventral fin. Wainer captained the *Sunfish* when the two partners went to pick up their second ship, the *Mary*, in 1792 (it was named after Cuffe's sister, Michael's wife). They sold both ships to underwrite the construction of the *Ranger* in 1796. The *Ranger* was never owned or operated by any but family members—including Michael Wainer's six sons who followed him into the business. On the return from a trading voyage to the West Indies, Michael's son Jeremiah (1778–1805), who captained the *Ranger*, and two crewmen were lost at sea.

The two friends shared other ventures, including the purchase of 70 acres of salt meadow on Horseneck Point in southeastern Massachusetts. Wainer was an investor in the P. & A. Howard retail store in New Bedford that Cuffe owned with his son-in-law Peter Howard. In 1789 Paul bought 140 acres along the Acoaxet River in Westport and placed large parcels of the property in Michael Wainer's name. Over the next fifteen years, Michael managed the farm, which grew to more than two hundred acres, on behalf of the family.

Michael Wainer's death in 1815 at the age of sixty-seven after a debilitating (but unknown) illness was a severe blow to his family and his friends. Paul Cuffe's warm letters to the Wainer family—informing some of the sons of their father's passing—showed his concern and the loss he felt after their warm friendship and partnership of forty-three years.[19]

Thomas Wainer (January 26, 1773–?)

Like his father, Thomas Wainer married a woman named Lydia Pequit, on January 16, 1800. She was the daughter of Alice Abel and James Pequit, according to Westport historian Richard Gifford.[20]

Many of Thomas' voyages were as the captain of merchant ships, not whalers. He was a master mariner whose navigational ability and ship handling made him a frequent choice of his uncle, Paul Cuffe, for trading voyages to hostile southern slave states. Wainer took Cuffe's *Ranger* (acquired from the sale of whale oil and whalebone) to Virginia, Delaware, Philadelphia, and other ports.

On April 8, 1799, a Maryland slave owner named Samuel Sloane posted a notice that Wainer had helped his slave Harry and Harry's pregnant wife escape on the *Ranger* northbound to Westport after collecting a load of corn and wooden staves. Sloane offered a forty-dollar bounty for the man he described as "a Negro man named Harry, about 23 years old—thick and well set—of a dark complexion, with thick lips and full eyes. . . . Harry has a notable scar on or near the outside of one of his ankles, occasioned by a burn, also is marked on or near the calf of one of his legs by the bite of a dog." No wonder that Thomas Wainer, twenty-six at the time, came to the aid of Harry and his wife. The *Ranger* docked in New Bedford ten days after the posting. While there is no record of what happened to the newly freed slaves, there was no better port for them to find a new life.[21]

In 1803, at age twenty-nine, Wainer was entrusted with captaining the *Hero* to Europe, expanding Cuffe's trading and merchant empire on a trip to France for a forty-three-day trip that was followed up almost immediately with a voyage to Portugal. As the third known whaling master of color, Thomas Wainer captained the *Hero* (1803) and the *Traveller* (1810) long before such a role was thought to be attainable by black men, largely because of his father, Michael (Micah), and his uncle Paul Cuffe.

In 1806 Thomas Wainer was first mate on the merchant ship *Alpha*—which Paul Cuffe had built and personally commanded on successful trips to the South and overseas bringing goods for the P. & A. Howard store in New Bedford. The Howard brothers (Alexander and Peter) were recently freed slaves who became Cuffe's sons-in-law when they married his daughters Ruth and Naomi in 1806. The retail store was a brilliant way for Cuffe and his family to monetize the products on which they risked fortune and life.[22]

Wainer's family included the whaling households of his father, Michael; John Masten (married to his sister Mary); Alvan Phelps (married to Cuffe's daughter Mary); the brothers Paul, Jeremiah, and Gardner Wainer; and Cuffe's sons, Paul Jr. and William. Thomas and Paul Wainer's brother Jeremiah was also a ship's captain but apparently never on whalers. Both Jeremiah and Thomas had captained the *Hero* and the *Ranger*. In 1805, on a trading trip hauling 250 turkeys, 500 chickens, hogs, and cattle to the West Indies, Jeremiah and two other hands on the *Ranger* were lost at sea.

Repeating a feat performed by Paul Cuffe himself, Thomas Wainer and Alvan Phelps sailed the *Ranger* and *Traveller* into the Wilmington, Delaware, harbor from Nova Scotia in 1809 on a merchant voyage. Their modest behavior must have surprised dockside observers, who left them to their business as they sailed safely and profitably into and out of the potentially hostile harbor. On an 1812 trip on board the *Traveller*, Wainer set out for Kennebec, Maine, with a largely black crew for a load of pine lumber. After returning to Westport, the *Traveller* headed out for Portugal a month later, on the way harvesting 523 barrels of whale oil to sell there. Because he sailed the *Traveller* and *Hero* from the family's home port of Westport, there is little reliable data on how many barrels of oil or pounds of whalebone Thomas Wainer may have brought back.

Thomas Wainer moved to Oneida, New York, in 1816; perhaps he had earned enough to give up whaling.[23]

ALVAN PHELPS (?–1831)

Alvan Phelps married Paul Cuffe's daughter Mary in Westport on October 11, 1806. Phelps was first mate of the *Traveller* when it shipped from New Bedford in 1810 and again in 1815, and its captain on other whaling trips.[24] He also served as captain of the *Alpha*, the *Ranger*, and the *Hammer*, although not all of these were whaling trips.

Alvan Phelps was a free black man from nearby Rochester, Massachusetts, when Cuffe appointed him captain of the *Ranger* in 1805. Phelps and Thomas Wainer were instrumental in helping Cuffe build his trading business using whale ships to transfer goods from the harbors of the South to northeastern ports. Paul Cuffe's retail business in New Bedford, P. & A. Howard, sold goods from the West Indies and southern ports such as Wilmington, Delaware. The store also offered sugar, spices, teas, coffee, lumber, leather, minerals, and earthenware from Philadelphia. Cuffe wrote to Alvan Phelps on August 24, 1816 (Boston to Wilmington), and October 7, 1816 (Philadelphia, New York, and Wilmington), with explicit instructions on what to purchase, where, and what price to pay.

Alvan captained the *Traveller* three times, twice as a merchant vessel and once, in 1822, as a whaler to the western islands in the mid-Atlantic with an all-black crew of thirteen; the ship returned early from that trip with just seventy barrels of oil due to some unexplained event that resulted in one shipmate drowning and another's arrest. Alvan's other trips had mixed crews that included, on an 1826 voyage to Canada, his sons John (age seventeen) and Milton (age fifteen). On a trip to Nantucket from Westport on the merchantman *Hammer* in 1831 Captain Phelps and his sons were lost along with all hands when the ship wrecked.[25]

PAUL WAINER (OCTOBER 17, 1776–FEBRUARY 6, 1833)

Paul Wainer was born during the American Revolution. He married Chloe Dodge Cuff (1781–1862) of Gay Head on Martha's Vineyard on September 29, 1804. They had five children: James Harris (1805), Ira Warner (1808), Uriah Varnum (1811), Asa Franklin (1813), and Adonirum S. (1815).[26]

All of the Cuffes were family oriented, taking their lead from Paul Cuffe, who had modeled his life after the Quakers generally and the Rotches specifically. Shared family values led to trust, good judgment, and sound business practices. Most captains of color tended to be family-oriented men, so much so that some, including William T. Shorey and Valentine Rosa, took their families on whale trips with them. A list of ten "whalemen's commandments" attributed to black "green hands"—crew-members new to the whaling trade—underscores the Cuffe family's values:

1. Steal, but not from a friend.
2. Lie, but never about anything important.
3. Fight anytime you think you can win.
4. Run when you think you can't win.
5. Cheat before you get cheated.
6. Swear, but never in front of a good woman.
7. Drink as much as you can hold.
8. Love as many women as you can catch.
9. Never tattle.
10. Never volunteer.[27]

Paul Wainer's Captaincies

Hero	1803 (Thomas, his brother, also served as master)
Hero	1806–7
Traveller	1807
Traveller	1810
Ranger	1810

Traveller 1815

Resolution July 20, 1816

Protection May 4, 1821–April 29, 1822 (whaling trip)

The *Protection* returned with 500 barrels of sperm oil and 6,600 barrels of whale oil with a total value (in 2016 dollars) of $122,430. The Cuffe-Wainer-Cook-Phelps dynasty steered clear of the customs officers of New Bedford and the system of crew and shipping lists, so Paul Wainer almost certainly captained more whaling trips that went unrecorded.

Paul Wainer died in Westport on February 6, 1833, and is buried in the Wainer family cemetery there.

JOHN MASTEN (1781–DECEMBER 3, 1860)

John Masten was born in Barnstable illegitimately to a woman named Hannah. He married Mary Wainer, the daughter of Michael Wainer and Lydia Pequit, on February 12, 1809.[28] Masten's first trip was on Paul Cuffe's *Traveller* in 1811, when it sailed for Sierra Leone with Thomas Wainer as captain and Alvan Phelps and Masten's brothers-in-law, John and Michael Wainer, on board.

John Masten was listed as a thirty-year-old *"Malatto"* boat-steerer on the *Sally* when it left New Bedford in 1812. The *Sally* was a Nantucket and New Bedford whaler from 1793 to 1823. It is believed that Masten was a replacement captain on the *Sally* during one of its adventures that included capture by a British warship in 1812 with Obed Clark as captain; and was a boat-steerer on the *Sally* in 1818 when William Paddack was captain. Masten was also third mate on the *Industry* in 1818 (Pardon Cook was second mate), first mate on the *Protection* in 1821 (Paul Wainer was master), and boat-steerer on the *Timoleon* in 1826.[29]

Those experiences would have more than qualified Masten as a master. For that reason I yield to Howard O. Lewis' opinion that John Masten was indeed one of a very few black masters—if even for only part of a single voyage.[30]

The 1850 Census reported that John Masten was sixty-nine years old in 1850 and living in Westport, Massachusetts, with Jeremiah W. Masten (his son, age forty-one) and daughters Mary J. Masten (twenty-four) and Amelia B. Lewis (sixteen).[31] His wife, Mary, must have predeceased him; he died at age seventy-nine in 1860.

Pardon C. Cook (1796–October 8, 1849)

"*Elizabeth* of Westport Pardon Cook Master" must have been written with a great deal of pride in 1839 when Captain Cook entered it into his logbook at the beginning of the trip. The voyage ended May 6, 1842, with 220 barrels of sperm oil. The *Elizabeth* had returned from another extended voyage to Puerto Rico and Brazil before Pardon Cook took over for his first voyage as a whaling captain on July 17, 1839, for the yearlong trip that ended on June 6, 1840. On the six recorded trips Pardon took as master of the *Almy, Elizabeth*, and *Juno*, the ships carried home sperm oil and whale oil worth almost $2.5 million today—a king's ransom for a black man to have earned in America before the Civil War.

Born to Benjamin Cook of Tiverton, Rhode Island, and Catherine Almy Cook of Dartmouth, Massachusetts (m. June 14, 1790), Pardon Cook had whaling in his DNA. Historian Martha Putney lists Benjamin Cook as the first mate on board the *Hero* of Westport, where the Cook family lived, when it sailed from Philadelphia in 1803. That is evidence that Pardon Cook and his parents were born free. Pardon C. Cook's younger brother Joseph Cook predeceased him in 1826 while whaling.

Pardon and Joseph served on the *Industry* on a voyage that left Westport on May 7, 1821, when Pardon was twenty-four and Joseph nineteen. Between 1819 and 1826 Pardon Cook sailed as first mate on the *Traveller, Industry, Almy* (coincidentally his mother's maiden name), *Two Brothers*, and *Delight* with white captains but interracial crews. John Masten was on the *Industry* in 1819, and Pardon also served with Asa and Rodney Wainer on the *Elizabeth* (1841), where they were first, second, and third mates. The records of the early Dartmouth and Westport group's voyages do not show Cook on the *Traveller* or *Delight*. He was one of the owners of the *Elizabeth* in 1841, and when he died was one-eighth owner of the whale ship *General Taylor*. Cook lost eleven of his crew when lightning struck a sail on the *Elizabeth* in 1841.[32]

Records place the eleven-person Benjamin Cook family among the black families in Dartmouth. Benjamin Cook, who died in 1815 after a fall on board a ship in Virginia, had settled there by 1791. *Fugitive's Gibraltar* by Kathryn Grover lists the Westport households: Michael Wainer, John Masten, Alvin (Alvan) Phelps, Paul Wainer, John Cuffe, Thomas Wainer, Gardner Wainer, and Paul Cuffe.[33]

The Cuffes, Wainers, and Cooks formed a whaling dynasty from Paul Cuffe's first trip in 1772 to Pardon Cook's last as master in 1844—a period lasting seventy-two years. The achievements of these men years before the Civil War ended slavery were astonishing for the time. Thanks to their ability and familial relationships they were able to excel despite their color.[34]

In April 1849 Pardon Cook's son Lysander died of typhoid fever; six months later another son, Pardon A. Cook, died as well, along with his seventeen-year-old daughter Mary Alice. Cook himself died of typhoid at the age of fifty-three.

WILLIAM CUFFE (JUNE 19, 1799–DECEMBER 7, 1837)

Paul and Alice Cuffe's youngest son, William, like his older brother Paul Jr., went to sea early—at age sixteen—with his father on the *Traveller*. Leaving Westport in early December 1815, Paul Cuffe took the *Traveller* to Sierra Leone, where he had notions of settling freed slaves from America. William Cuffe's first assignment as an officer was as first mate on the *Traveller* for the July 1816 trip.

Like most of his family and male relatives, William Cuffe spent his life at sea. In December 1837 he lost his life on the *Rising States*, which sailed with an all-black crew. No details about his death are available, but he was one of four lost on the voyage. Damaged beyond repair, the 134-ton sloop was proclaimed unseaworthy and condemned by the American consul at Cape Verde, and the surviving men were sent home.

Richard Johnson, William's brother-in-law (married to William's sister Ruth Cuffe Howard Johnson) was one of the *Rising States'* principal owners, a group that included nine other black owners. The nineteen-member crew included Shadrack N. Howard, Johnson's nephew (son of his sister Ruth from her first marriage), and second mate James Hamilton, who along with Cuffe was one of the four killed. William Cuffe's first and last trip as captain was one of only six voyages in the whaling industry's history with an all-black crew, his being the only one in which the captain did not return.

Replacement Captains

When a captain became incapacitated, another man was appointed to finish the voyage. Men of color were sometimes chosen, although it is nowhere clear who did the choosing. The widely recognized term "replacement captain" clearly indicates merit, and some twenty captains of color were accorded this on-the-job promotion.[35] There was no room for racial prejudice at sea: the man with the best chance of finding whales and getting the boat and crew home safely was the best man for the job. The dangers and difficulties of whaling made a meritocracy practical—and all actions were affirmative when lives and livelihoods were at stake. About a third of all masters (954) received shipboard promotions to captain. The rest had enough experience to be hired outright.[36]

The requirements were straightforward. The captain at minimum had to know how to navigate and keep the boat safe. Finding whales was the reason for the voyage, and the ability to kill them was mandatory. Men of color were acknowledged to be the best at harpooning whales. Those good enough to meet the challenge, black or white, had unquestioned authority. As Edouard Stackpole puts it, "Despite the fact that he belonged to a race then in slavery, on board a Nantucket whale ship he was an officer and his command coming as it did through a process of harsh elimination was nevertheless his—and he was master of his ship."[37]

PETER GREEN

Peter Green is the first-known black man to become a master following the death of his senior officers. The *John Adams* left Nantucket on June 12, 1821, with Peter Green as second mate to first mate Seth Myrick and Captain George Bunker II. Bunker died, and Myrick replaced him. When Myrick and his whaleboat crew were lost after harpooning a whale, Green became master. The *Factor*, captained by John Maxcy, reported the news at Nantucket. When he returned to port on February 28, 1825, as captain, Green reported that the men had died the previous April 2.

There is no record of the details of Green's promotion. Had the crew elected him? Had the *Factor*'s Captain Maxcy somehow participated in the decision? While no one knows, the facts are that the *John Adams* returned a year and a half after the *Factor* with Green as captain, proving he was in command as the ship continued whaling. The *John Adams* brought back 1,170 barrels of sperm oil worth $32,995 in 1825—close to $690,000 today. At 268 tons, the *John Adams* was a vessel of consequence—and the second largest (after Samuel Harris' *Phebe*, 379 tons) captained by a captain of color. The facts support Peter Green's rise as being the result of the crew trusting him to return safely and profitably.

There is no record of Green making a whaling voyage before—or after—his historic trip on the *John Adams*, which evidently went back to sea without him.[38]

CHAPTER 2

How Commercial Whaling Started

*W*haling on a commercial scale began more than a thousand years ago. The Basque people of northern Spain were apparently the first to dare the seas seeking profit from whales.

The Basques

A sunken Basque whaling ship found off the coast of Labrador in 1978 is evidence that Europeans were whaling off the North American coast at least as early as the sixteenth century. The *San Juan* went down in 1565 with a cargo of a thousand casks of whale oil with a value in excess of $6 million.[1]

The Basques settled in the area bordering Spain and France between the Bay of Biscay and the Pyrenees Mountains thousands of years ago as farmers. Hardy and independent, they were also shipbuilders. They began organized whaling sometime before the year 1000, going out in boats close to shore to catch whales for meat to market in nearby French cities. As they became proficient in capturing whales farther offshore, they found more uses for the primary by-products of the industry: the oil, of course, and then the whalebone, or baleen. Women's corsets, originally constructed of whalebone, were called "basques," in recognition of their source.

As the fifteenth century began, the Basques had developed "something approaching a modern industry."[2] Historical geographer Selma Huxley Barkham is credited with discovering key evidence of the Basque whaling industry in 1977. Archaeological research indicates that in the 1560s, a thousand mariners could produce a half million gallons of whale oil in a five-month whaling season. Compared with modern whaling, theirs was a daunting and exhausting enterprise that involved long stretches of rowing. Each 26-foot *chalupa* (whaleboat) was rowed by six men. The harpoons they used were attached to a line and a float known as a drogue. They followed the harpooned whale until it surfaced and then killed it with lances. The dead whale was towed ashore and dismembered, and the chunks of flesh were rendered down to oil in huge iron cauldrons.[3]

Whaling began so long ago in America that many Native American stories about it are believed to be apocryphal. Alexander Starbuck cites a portion of George Waymouth's journal of his voyage to discover the Northwest Passage in America in 1605. Referring to the "Indians on the [east] coast," Waymouth says:

> One especial thing is their manner of killing the whale, which they call powdawe; and will describe his form; how he bloweth up the water; and that he is twelve fathoms long [seventy-two feet]: and that they go in company of their king with multitude of their boats; and strike him with a bone made in fashion of a harping iron fastened to a rope, which they make great and strong of the bark of trees, which they veer out after him; then all their boats come about him as he riseth above water, with their arrows they shoot him to death; when they have killed him and dragged him to shore, they call all their chief lords together, and sing a song of joy: and those chief lords, whom they call sagamores, divide the spoil and give to everyman a share.[4]

In 1614 Captain John Smith, seeing so many whales off New England, predicted whaling would become a viable business enterprise in the New World. The first recorded attempt by European colonists to catch a whale was in 1620 when men of the *Mayflower* foolishly overloaded a fowling piece with gunpowder and tried to kill a curious whale that had approached the ship. The attempt failed when the weapon exploded.[5]

From the Eurocentric view, "organized" whaling in America began in March 1644 when colonists in Southampton on Long Island harvested whales that had died or been driven ashore in shallow water (drift whales). Historian John Strong argues that it was the indigenous people who taught it to the newcomers using techniques they learned from the Basques who hunted the North American coastline in the sixteenth century, camping onshore along the way and trading for furs with the inhabitants. Americans learned to excel at the craft of whaling while knowing next to nothing about the species they hunted—some of which they drove to the edge of extinction.

Sag Harbor and the Shinnecock: "People of the Shore"

There would have been no American drift-whaling fishery without Long Island's Shinnecock tribe. The Shinnecock, said to have been the best harpooners, introduced European colonists to drift whaling. From modest beginnings with shore whaling in the 1600s, Sag Harbor prospered until 1845 when fire destroyed the small village. It never recovered, especially after whalers chose prospecting for gold in California as a safer way of harvesting nature's bounty. There are few records of black and indigenous men from Sag Harbor who served on whale ships and went on to become masters, the exceptions being Ferdinand Lee and his brother William Garrison Lee.

As in other whaling ports, many of the black people who settled in Sag Harbor were runaway or freed slaves from Virginia and Maryland, a fact evidenced by some of the surnames of black whalers—Plato, Concer, and other names similar to those slave owners used in the whaling era on Nantucket. Oppression forced the black and Native American populaces together in mixed-race unions, strengthening bonds that endure today in Sag Harbor and adjacent towns.

Richard Doctorow of the Sag Harbor Whaling and Historical Museum describes whaling as "a cross between working in an oil refinery and a slaughterhouse, with the chance of drowning thrown in."[6] In an industry so fraught with difficulty and discomfort, men with other options went out whaling only once. Men of color had few options, though, in this as in so many areas of their lives.[7]

Several of the whaling masters discussed here had at least some Native American blood. Absalom Boston's mother, Thankful Micah, was a Wampanoag, and so was Paul Cuffe's mother, Ruth Moses of Gay Head. The Wainers, Haskins, Jeffers, and Belain also had Native American blood. Some of these people chose to identify as black, and others chose to identify as Native American. The Lees' father was a runaway slave, but they chose to identify as Indians regardless of how they looked or were characterized on crew lists. There were advantages and disadvantages to each. While it might seem expedient simply to label such men "men of color" and go from there, Julia Good Fox, a professor of American Indian studies at Haskell Indian Nations University, expresses the identity issue this way: "Fundamentally, it's the tribe's right to determine who its citizens are and are not. If we don't know [whether someone is American Indian], we can ask the tribe."[8]

Paul Schneider points out that

> African Americans in the eighteenth and nineteenth centuries inter-mingled extensively with the declining and equally marginalized—though still much larger—native population. There were a lot of reasons for this, including true love between individuals and greater racial enlightenment on the part of both groups. Before the aboli-tion of slavery there was also the benefit for African men, at least, of knowing their offspring with native women would remain free, which could not be said of their children by spouses of African origin.[9]

White politicians encouraged black-Indian pairings, hoping Native Americans would lose their identity—along with their rights to land and government payments. Anthony Higgins, a U.S. senator from Delaware, was blatant in advocating this insidious concept in his 1895 congressional testimony: "It seems to me one of the ways of getting rid of the Indian question is just this of intermarriage, and the gradual fading out of the Indian blood; the whole quality and character of the aborigine disappears, they lose all of the traditions of the race; there is no longer any occasion to maintain the tribal relations, and there is then every reason why they shall go and take their place as white people do everywhere."[10]

The Shinnecock tribe of Long Island, like the Wampanoags of Martha's Vineyard and Nantucket, endured racism and oppression. Finally receiving recognition as a nation in 2010, the Shinnecock are related to the Algonquian Pequot and Narragansett people. English colonists—and the diseases they brought with them—wiped out as much as two-thirds of the tribe in 1648. By 1744 only about four hundred Shinnecocks remained. After the Revolutionary War the Shinnecocks intermarried with local colonists and African American slaves who worked on farms and as craftsmen. They attempted to raise their children as Shinnecock and maintain their culture, and today many of the six hundred remaining Shinnecocks "look black but feel Indian."

In the 1700s the children of black–Native American intermarriages were considered to be free (of slavery). Strong notes that "slave status was defined by law in terms of the woman—a child becomes the property of the mother's owner. If you're a slave and you want to make sure your children are free, you marry an Indian woman." Discrimination has not disappeared with time. In local bars even today, Strong says, the Shinnecocks are spoken of disparagingly as "'monigs': more nigger than Indian."[11]

Like all the New England tribes, the Shinnecocks were known for their fishing and whaling skills; indeed, it was said that "not a ship left Eastern Long Island without at least one Shinnecock male onboard."[12]

FERDINAND LEE

Ferdinand Lee and all four of his brothers were whalers: Milton (the oldest, born in 1831), Ferdinand, Notley, Robert (referred to as James R. Lee in shipping papers), and William Lloyd Garrison Lee. William became a replacement captain on the *Abbie Bradford*, and the brothers combined served on at least twenty-five recorded whaling voyages. The Lees' father, James Lee, was an escaped slave from Maryland who married Roxanna Bunn, a Shinnecock, and he likely named his youngest son after the famed abolitionist. James was "a large, well-built man of good appearance and . . . a natural orator" who joined the Second Adventist church and became its pastor on the Shinnecock Reservation. His nickname was "Priest Lee."

Ferdinand "Ty" Lee

Ferdinand "Ty" Lee is Ferdinand Lee's great-grandson. He has continuing ties and familial land ownership in the Shinnecock Nation. "My mother's family were Walkers [Montauk Indian] which married into Shinnecock Nation," he says. "Both Montauk and Shinnecock Indians encounter[ed] English settlers [Pilgrims] in 1640 at the site known as Conscience Point in the town of Southampton, New York. The Lee family genealogy puts us at 95 percent Native American Indian . . . 5 percent is a mixture of African, Caucasian, Asian, and other Native American tribes.

"I must have been five or six in Sunday school on the Shinnecock Indian Reservation when we learned about our ancestors every Sunday. We had history night once a week after school with the elders, from the medicine man to the sachem. I was told his [Ferdinand Lee's] fishing skills weren't matched by anyone else, a leader who stood up against the oppressor and was rewarded with his own crew. A true provider for his family, he traveled the coastal seaboard in search of whalers and whales."

Born sometime between 1834 and 1836, Ferdinand Lee served on the *Young Phenix* on trips from San Francisco in 1857, and again in 1860, as second mate. The log indicated he was black and from Southampton. In 1864, again listed as black, he was the third replacement master (his first command) on the *Roman*. He was on the *Eliza Adams* as master in 1867 and again in 1876 as first mate.

Ferdinand Lee's tour as master on the *Callao* from July 1871 to September 1875 is well chronicled—and was quite eventful, according to the ship's logs. Among other things, Lee had the cook put in irons. The first mate was a bully who handled the men violently, shoving, hitting, insulting, and threatening them. It is not specified, but the log suggests that he was white. Lee discharged the man for not being able to get along. Earlier, on the *Eliza Adams* (as first mate and log keeper), he recorded, "Thomas Coring [was] put in irons and hands tied above his head for using mutinous language and disobeying of orders."[13]

Recognizing that insubordination led to anarchy, Lee, who stood at least six-feet-two, was not afraid to pull rank when necessary and wound up losing most of his men through discharge or desertion. Even with the well-kept log one cannot tell if racial tension was the reason. Native American captains were judged on both their whaling abilities and their managerial ability, an obvious double standard compared with whites, who were judged solely on performance.

There is no question these captains of color suffered prejudice on land. A travel writer who visited Gay Head on Martha's Vineyard in 1860, for example, opined that "the appearance of everything indicates a thriftless and inferior people." Historian and writer Charles Burr Todd, who visited the Shinnecock Reservation in 1882, observed, "Love of firewater, as with their fathers, is still their greatest failing. They are not industrious, despising the tilling of the soil, allowing their fine lands here to go to waste, as you see, but no better surfmen or sailors, especially whalemen, can be found. They are wandering and erratic in their habits . . . and negro and white blood being so intermixed that there is not a pure-blood Indian in the tribe." In the backhanded compliment on their whaling skills Todd managed to marginalize both their race and their heritage.[14]

What could not be marginalized was Ferdinand Lee's production. As a replacement captain he brought back oil that would be valued at almost a $1 million today. And the estimated twenty-seven whales he caught ranked him in the top twenty-five among captains of color (see appendix I).

Ferdinand Lee was second mate on the *Amethyst* when that ship left San Francisco for the North Pacific on February 21, 1885. The *Amethyst* was lost at sea with Ferdinand and his brother William Garrison Lee on board.[15]

William Garrison Lee (1848–85)

All the Lee brothers had some connection to the sea. William served as the replacement captain of the *Abbie Bradford* after its captain died on a trip during 1880–81. Lee's oldest brother, Milton, whaled for more than sixteen years; Ferdinand became a captain; Robert drowned salvaging a shipwreck; and Notley wound up a beachcomber. William told the tale, according to Charles Burr Todd, that Notley deserted a whale ship on the Kingsmill Islands in the Pacific, married the chief's daughter, and became king.

Beginning at age sixteen on the *Pioneer* in 1854 as a green hand, William Lee served on several ships in his forty-two-year career, during which he was often promoted based on his ability. On his initial voyage on the *Pioneer*, his shipmates were George Belain from Chilmark and William Belain from Edgartown, Wampanoags from Martha's Vineyard and the father and uncle of Master Joseph G. Belain. William's life at sea was eventful, to say the least. He was on the *Nassau* when it was burned to the waterline by the *Shenandoah* more than a month after the Civil War officially ended in May 1865. His brother Milton was on the *Abigail* when the *Shenandoah* burned as well. William was on the *Rainbow* in 1885 when it was crushed by ice in the Pacific Northwest and lost. He transferred to the *Amethyst*, where his brother Ferdinand was also serving, and both brothers were lost when that ship went down later that year in Arctic waters.[16]

Martha's Vineyard and the Wampanoag: "People of the First Light"

In the late 1600s the Puritans did all they could to eradicate New England's indigenous people. In what is called the Second Puritan Conquest—misnamed "King Philip's War" after the Wampanoag leader of Plymouth and

Cape Cod (Metacomet)—they killed natives until the war ended in 1678. On Martha's Vineyard, two-thirds of the Wampanoag tribe died from diseases brought by Europeans, and only a thousand remained by 1700. By 1764 that number had dwindled to 313: 86 in Edgartown (this included Oak Bluffs), 39 in Tisbury, and 188 in Chilmark (this included Gay Head and Naushon Island). Simultaneously, a plague in 1764 had just about killed off the remaining members of the tribe on Nantucket.[17]

The historian Richard L. Pease notes that "about that period they began to intermarry with negroes in consequence of which the mixed race has increased in numbers, and improved in temperance and industry." That was one view. Another, proffered by James Freeman in 1807 on Nantucket, was that "the Indians having disappeared, negroes are now substituted in their place. Seamen of color are more submissive than the whites; but as they are more addicted to frolicking, it is difficult to get them aboard the ship, when it is about to sail, and to keep them aboard, after it has arrived. The negroes, though they are to be prized for their habits of obedience, are not as intelligent as the Indians; and none of them attain the rank of endsman."[18]

Native Americans were naturally sensitive to the plight of black slaves, and Martha's Vineyard has plenty of stories of Wampanoags helping blacks escape slavery.[19] One told by Netta Vanderhoop involved "Edgar Jones," who escaped from a Charleston, South Carolina, plantation. Jones was running away for the second time and knew his master would have him killed if he were recaptured, so he was highly motivated to get away. Luckily, he was hidden by sympathetic crewmen on a ship carrying lumber north. When the ship reached Martha's Vineyard, the captain discovered Jones and, seeking reward, shared the news with the local sheriff. Warned by one of the crew, Jones left the boat and managed to hide out for the better part of a week. He was convinced to go to Gay Head, told he might even find work there. The sheriff attempted to enlist the aid of William A. Vanderhoop to capture Jones, promising him ten dollars. Vanderhoop had a Dutch father and Creole mother from Paramaribo in Suriname and was married to Beulah Salisbury, a Wampanoag. Beulah overheard her husband refuse the sheriff because the ten dollars wasn't enough to dissuade him from taking his cranberries to market. Deciding to help Jones, she dressed him in women's clothes and with help from other people of Gay

Head got him to fugitive-friendly New Bedford, where he lived for some time. He eventually left for San Francisco before the Civil War, during which it is believed he was killed. Before then, though, he made his way back to Gay Head to thank Mrs. Vanderhoop and bring her money. The 1854 story is confirmed in *The Fugitive's Gibraltar*, which indicates that his real name was Edinbur Randall.[20]

New Bedford had a large population of Mustees—the offspring of blacks and Native Americans. Businessman, abolitionist, member of the Massachusetts House and Senate, and Commissioner on Indian affairs John M. Earle wrote in 1861 that the larger proportion of these relationships involved black men and Native American women, and "at least 50 men of color (identified as 'negro,' 'black,' 'mulatto' and 'mustee') married women from the Dartmouth, Gay Head, Chappaquiddick, Mashpee, Narragansett, and Middleborough tribes, all Wampanoags of Southern Massachusetts."[21]

Shoemaker's database lists (all figures approximate) 259 Martha's Vineyard whalers who were black and/or Indian who participated in 379 whaling trips on 148 different ships from 1808 to 1894. More no doubt went unrecorded. Describing them as "the first whalemen of the new world," Martha's Vineyard author and *Vineyard Gazette* publisher/editor Henry Beetle Hough extolled the virtues of the Wampanoags, noting that their prowess as harpooners had achieved worldwide fame, in no small part due to the attention given them in Herman Melville's fictional masterpiece *Moby-Dick*. Published in 1851 during whaling's heyday, the novel is an accurate portrayal. Melville himself "went a-whaling" before writing it. One of the fictional Captain Ahab's harpooners (boat-steerers) was Tashtego, a pure-blood Indian from Gay Head on Martha's Vineyard, and the other was Daggoo, an African and a resident of Nantucket; both are true-to-life characters.

Real-life stories are as good as fiction. The June 1957 *Reader's Digest* tells of Amos Smalley (1877–1961), the Wampanoag from Gay Head immortalized as having killed a white sperm whale in 1902 while on the *Platina*. Eschewing traditional methods of harpooning, Smalley used a dart gun to catch the whale and a bomb lance to kill it. Believed for more than fifty years by Vineyard locals to be a fable, the *Reader's Digest* story finally proved it thanks to a letter to Mr. Smalley from Frank McKenzie, son of the *Platina's* captain, Thomas McKenzie. In the letter, McKenzie quoted from the ship's log in his possession that at latitude 35° north, longitude 53° east (northeast of Bermuda), Smalley had indeed killed a white sperm whale. Believed to have been more than one hundred years old, the whale was ninety feet long and produced eighty barrels of sperm oil. W. M. Davis, who wrote *Nimrod of the Sea*, registered large sperm whales at ninety feet, but modern ones are only about sixty-five feet. By any measure, Smalley's white whale was extraordinarily large.[22]

Starbuck indicates that American whaling began in 1650, with the earliest mention of whaling on Martha's Vineyard in 1652—forty years after Bartholomew Gosnold named Martha's Vineyard and ten years after Thomas Mayhew settled the island. Starbuck documented that several whales were killed off Martha's Vineyard in 1702–3 and suggested that deepwater offshore whaling began in 1738. *In Pursuit of Leviathan* uses the year 1712 as the start of commercial whaling there. Starbuck opined that whaling thrived better on Nantucket than on Martha's Vineyard because there was little arable land on Nantucket, and food had to be obtained from the sea.

Native American Whalers

Martha's Vineyard historian Richard L. Pease notes "in Dukes County in 1764, 313 Indians, 86 in Edgartown, 39 in Tisbury and 188 in Chilmark [and] . . . about that period, they began to intermarry with negroes in consequence of which the mixed race has increased in numbers and improved in temperance and industry."[23] With blacks unable to own land (Indians could) and their progeny becoming free as a result of their Indian heritage, there were positive incentives—in addition to love—to mixed-race relationships. In 1820 Native Americans constituted up to one-eighth of Nantucket whalemen, and black–Native American Mustees accounted for more than one-fourth. Indians not living on reservations were sometimes classified as "equivalent to blacks, as colored people, thus removing any entitlements specific to Indians."[24]

It is telling that a white man from Edgartown, Henry A. Davis, was unable to find—or unwilling to record—a single Native American on Martha's Vineyard when he conducted the 1870 census for the entire island, including in the town of Gay Head. This was rectified in 1900 when

Edwin D. Vanderhoop, the first Indian to collect the data, recorded most of the people of the town as Native American.[25]

Amos Jeffers Jr. (1818–July 5, 1847)

Thomas Jeffers ("half Indian, one quarter white and one quarter negro") and his second wife, Sarah Sepit (an Indian from Mashpee), had a son, Amos Jeffers, who served on the whaler ships *Industry* (1801) and *Hero* (1802–4) at the same time as Thomas Wainer and Paul Cuffe, its owner.[26] In 1816 he served on the *President*. Amos and his second wife, Bathsheba Occouch Haskins, had a son whom they named Amos Jeffers Jr. Another son, Thomas Jeffers, sailed on the *Splendid* from 1849 to 1851 during the Gold Rush and—joining his brother Henry Hubbard Jeffers and Samuel Haskins—helped rescue survivors of the *City of Columbus* wreck in 1884.[27]

Amos Jeffers Jr.'s history as a captain is a story of misfortune. After six whale trips, beginning in 1835 on the *George Porter*, then on the *Mary* from 1836 to 1844, he was appointed captain of the *Mary* in 1847. After serving successively as green hand, second mate, and first mate, Jeffers was certainly qualified to lead a whaling expedition. Alas, Jeffers drowned in a fishing accident while waiting for the ship to be outfitted.[28]

The *Vineyard Gazette* for July 15, 1847, reported the accident under the headline "Two Men Missing":

> Two men (Indians) natives of Gay Head, named Amos Jeffers, Jr., and Jeremiah Weeks, proceeded in a Vineyard sailboat on a sword fishing expedition off Noman's Land. Nothing has since been heard of them, and as the boats mainsail was picked up on Tuesday, the 6th, on Gay Head, the supposition is, the boat was stoven by the sword of a fish, and sank from under them. It is barely possible they were picked up by some vessel; but the impression is general that they have found a watery grave. They were both men of uncommon promise. Mr. Jeffers lately returned from sea, as first mate of the whaling bark *Mary*, of New Bedford, and was soon to have sailed from that port in the capacity of master.

So many masters received shipboard promotion to replacement captain that it seems fair to include Jeffers, who had already received his appointment at the time of his death, among our whaling captains of color. It is ironic that Jeffers died reportedly chasing a swordfish instead of a

The *Eliza* was captained by Joe Belain in 1889–90. *Courtesy of the New Bedford Whaling Museum*

whale, and bad luck that he is remembered for losing his life before officially captaining a whale ship.

Joseph G. (S.) Belain
(November 27, 1848–October 20, 1926)

Joseph G. Belain was the last known whaling master with Native American blood. His obituary in the *New Bedford Standard* ("Indian Chief's Scion Is Dead") notes that he was a lineal descendant of Chief Mattark (Mittark/Mattack), a Gay Head sachem born in 1620, and a descendant of Nohtooksaet, born in 1590.

The Belains were an extensive family of Martha's Vineyard whalers believed to be descended from Pierre Belain d'Esnabuc, who founded a colony in Martinique in 1635. The first of the American Belains was Peter Belain (1777–1833). Born in the West Indies, Peter served as a cook on the whale ship *Eagle* in 1805. He married Sarah Johnson that year in Chappaquiddick and moved there from Rhode Island. The 1823 census described Peter as "half negro, half white," and Sarah as "half Indian, one fourth negro, one fourth white." Their son George Johnson Belain

(1810–95), who whaled on the *Hercules, Adeline, Pioneer, Samuel and Thomas*, and *Massasoit* and reached the rank of first mate, was Joseph's father. He married Sophia Peters, whose parents, Johnson Peters and Mary (Cooper) Ephraims, were "three fourths Indian, one eighth negro, one eighth white" and "half Indian, one fourth negro and one fourth white" respectively. This delineation of genealogy is a good example of the practices the newcomer whites used to enforce their superiority over the native inhabitants.[29]

Joseph Belain, born in Gay Head, first went whaling at age seventeen on the *Cape Horn Pigeon* in 1866. On that three-year voyage to the Atlantic and Indian Oceans, which returned with 1,397 barrels of sperm oil, Belain would have seen a good piece of the world and learned a great deal about whales. He whaled from San Francisco from 1886 to 1905, three times as a boat-steerer, once as second mate, fifteen times as first mate, and once as replacement master of the *Eliza* from December 21, 1889, until it was lost on October 11, 1890 (Joe survived). Joe Belain's uncle Thomas (*Mercury*, November 19, 1844) was a whaler as well, a steward who as a result of indifference to his own health and a beating by his captain died on the trip. Shoemaker lists dozens of Belains who served on multiple whale trips, some during the same period—indisputable proof of how valuable the Martha's Vineyard whalemen with native ancestry were.

Joe Belain was living in Gay Head when he shipped on board the *President* in 1879 as first mate. After that he captained the *Eliza* from San Francisco as a replacement captain (1889–90). He was a contemporary of the colorful William T. Shorey from that West Coast port.[30]

Crew lists for the *Cape Horn Pigeon* (1866), *Palmetto* (1875), and *Arthur V. S. Woodruff* (1912) identified him as "dark" or "brown." He was listed as black on a trip on the *Wanderer* in 1882 at age forty. Whether he considered himself black or not, Joseph was certainly counted as being so. Based on her research, Putney considers his relatives George, William, Peter, and Thomas to be black as well.[31] That Belain was competent, however, was never at issue. Twenty whaling trips are proof. He once advised another Vineyard Wampanoag whaleman (Napoleon Bonaparte Madison) to take enough money with him, as well as his own boots and foul weather gear, so he wouldn't be caught miles from home penniless or have to pay the exorbitant shipboard prices for clothing.

Probably due to his experience as first mate on the *Navarch* in 1892, Belain again became a replacement master in 1893. Whaling for baleen in the Pacific Northwest toward the end of the whaling days added additional terrors to the business, hull-crushing ice not being the least of them. When the *Navarch* hit the ice, the ship's captain, Joseph A. Whiteside, panicked and screamed, "Every man for himself!" even though his own wife was on board. It was Belain who led Mrs. Whiteside across the ice to safety. (One can only hope that Mrs. Whiteside divorced her husband afterward.) Whiteside became relief captain for John Atkins Cook on the next voyage of the *Navarch* (1893–96), again with Belain as first mate.

In a 1944 *Vineyard Gazette* newspaper article editor Henry Beetle Hough remembered Belain: "In 1889 he was master of the *Eliza* of San Francisco. Not many Indians went as captains, but their skill and prowess as harpooners cannot be overemphasized."[32]

How competent was Belain? Shoemaker studied Belain's logs as first mate on the *Palmetto* (1875–79) and the *Arthur V. S. Woodruff* (1917–18) and determined that his entries were, on the one hand, "the most professional," and on the other, "the least interesting." Belain, like many masters, used the log for basics: course, locations of whales caught, and crew accidents. Whaling captains generally did not add too much information that might later be taken out of context and preclude another trip, and captains of color were particularly careful in this regard.[33]

Belain died at age seventy-seven, one month before his seventy-eighth birthday. Bedridden at his niece's (Mrs. Bessie James) home at 51 Smith Street in New Bedford for the prior nine weeks, his death on October 20, 1926, was due to "shock and hardening of the arteries." His extensive obituary in the October 22, 1926, edition of the *Vineyard Gazette* entitled "Pigeon from Sea Alights on Hearse" acknowledged Belain's fame and skill as "Champion of Gay Head Whalers" and noted his career of more than a half century of whaling, which ended eight years before his death. He left behind his brother, John W. Belain of Gay Head, his aunt Anstress G. Webquish of Chappaquiddick, Mrs. James, and several other nieces and nephews. "When his funeral was held in the Gay Head church," Henry Beetle Hough wrote, "a carrier pigeon flew in from the sea and alighted on the hearse, and stayed until the service was done. . . . [Sixty] of his years had been lived on the far oceans."[34]

Captain Joseph Belain. *Painting by Elizabeth Whelan. Tintype from the collection of the Martha's Vineyard Museum*

The obituary included a much lighter version of the story crediting him with saving the crew and life of the hapless captain of the *Navarch* and his wife (but mistakenly giving the name *Belvedere*). After his whaling career Joseph Belain bought a small boat that he used for fishing and lobstering between the Vineyard and New Bedford. In his last days, the *Gazette* reported, Belain returned to Gay Head for the annual cranberry picking, during which "he picked far more berries than the average person in his prime." Reverend George A. Furness officiated at his funeral service.

Belain was accomplished enough to have two stints as captain, was in much demand as an officer, and was literate. One trip of the *Navarch* was modestly successful, bringing back whale oil and baleen worth $911,850 in today's dollars. If the cost of the voyage was $60,000 and Belain's share was a one-fifteenth lay, the trip would have been worth more than $50,000 to him. Besides selling their land, whaling was essentially the only way Native American men of color could receive such financial windfalls.[35]

WILLIAM H. HASKINS

William Haskins was not related to Amos Haskins but was among several other Haskinses who went whaling at about the same time, all described in records as "black," "mulatto," or "Indian." A number were from Martha's Vineyard. Given his identification by Shoemaker, William H. Haskins was probably Mustee. Haskins obviously did not begin his career as a third mate, but there is a logical progression to all of his merit-based promotions. He was not particularly lucky—other than the fact that he survived all three trips he captained, trips in which two of the ships were condemned and the third one was lost (see appendix B).

CHAPTER 3

Nantucket to New Bedford

*T*he history of whaling in Nantucket is tied to the history of the Quakers who established a thriving industry there and provided an opportunity for men of color and Native Americans to become involved. In 1647 George Fox (1624–91) founded the Religious Society of Friends, who espoused the doctrine that people should work hard, live thriftily, and conduct their affairs with honesty. Gambling, music, art, dancing, and playing cards were frowned upon. The Friends were called "Quakers" after Fox told an English judge, "You should quake at the word of the Lord," just as Friends tended to do during their meetings.[1] Persecuted because of their peculiar (at the time) beliefs, the Quakers relocated to America in search of freedom to practice their religion.

Even in the New World, though, the Quakers faced persecution from the Puritans. With such firsthand knowledge of prejudice, the Quakers ardently believed all humans should be treated with dignity and respect. Opponents of taxes, the death penalty, and slavery, the Quakers were the first organized abolitionists, and they maintained that position to slavery's end. In 1758, Quakers in Philadelphia excluded from membership anyone who bought or sold slaves. The Quakers were thus key to the ability of whalemen of color to fully participate in the whaling industry first on Nantucket and then in New Bedford. The Native Americans on Nantucket, thanks to the island's offshore location and excellent fishing, possessed the skills and expertise that perfectly suited them for the new industry the Quakers were building.[2]

A large, sandy island with no industry or agriculture and an indigenous population of about eight hundred, Nantucket was acquired in 1659 by ten Englishmen led by Tristram Coffin, with Edward Starbuck, Thomas Macy, and Isaac Coleman among them. There was no established religion on Nantucket until Mary Coffin Starbuck (Tristram's daughter) and her oldest son, Nathaniel, promulgated Quakerism after her conversion from Puritanism in 1701. Her daughter (also named Mary) was the first white person born on Nantucket.[3]

By 1686 the Quakers had established meetings (congregations) on the mainland that, while spreading their religion, also created the foothold they would need to expand their whaling business. Over the next one hundred years the Quakers built whaling into one of the largest industries in the New World.

While the Quakers were accommodating of black and Native American people—and far more racially tolerant than other Americans—they were not saints; whaling was business, first and foremost. Early in the game they understood that Indians and blacks had skills useful for whaling, and they also recognized that few other avenues were available to either group. "For those whose ships required cheap and bountiful labor," as Nathaniel Philbrick puts it, "the growth of the black community was a matter of business rather than the result of lofty social ideals."[4]

Indeed, while they abhorred the violence often associated with racism, Quakers rarely associated with blacks or Native Americans, and did not encourage them to become Quakers until late in the game; Paul Cuffe was probably the first, no doubt due to his relationship with William Rotch (pronounced "roach").

The Rotches

William Rotch (1734–1828), son of Joseph Rotch, was an abolitionist leader and Quaker who owned the *Friendship*. By 1795 the Rotch family had left behind Nantucket's shallow waters for New Bedford's deep, protected harbor and miles of surrounding forest ideal for shipbuilding. The success of their venture is suggested by Samuel Rodman's (related by marriage) boast: "There is not a ship in the harbor but what belongs to our family."[5] Renowned as the father of the American whaling industry, Joseph and his brother Francis utilized their political and diplomatic skills domestically and internationally to grow the business. By the 1790s, along with the Samuel Rodman family, they had established New Bedford as the

William Rotch Sr., Paul
Cuffe's associate, portrayed
from the side, the Quakers'
preferred position. *Courtesy of the New Bedford
Whaling Museum*

capital of the sperm oil
and spermaceti candle-
manufacturing business.

The Rotches and
Rodmans were found-
ing members of the
rather fulsomely named
Providence Society for
Promoting the Abolition
of Slavery, for the Relief
of Persons Unlawfully
Held in Bondage and for Improving the Condition of the African Race.
William Rotch was known for buying the indentures of men of color for
his ships, and in 1785 he wrote his son William Jr. and son-in-law Samuel
Rodman to do just that when preparing a ship to go from Nantucket to
London. The senior Rotch, although a pragmatist, derived his abolitionism
from his belief in God and the tenets of his religion. His son William Rotch
Jr.'s antislavery notions were even more deeply rooted as a matter of character. Rotch Jr. fought slavery with his money and in the courts and gained
freedom for several black men.

William Rotch Jr., born on Nantucket on November 29, 1759, was ten
months younger than Paul Cuffe. It was fortuitous that the two became
friends—largely due to Cuffe's having met and impressed William Rotch
Sr., who became his friend and business associate. The younger Rotch and
other Quaker families further developed the financial system necessary to
concentrate the resources needed for shipbuilding and investing in whaling.[6] They also had something to do with ending slavery on Nantucket.

ABSALOM BOSTON (1785–JUNE 6, 1855)

May de enemy of our celebration and of African freedom, hab 'ternal itch and no benefit scratch so long as he lib.

—ABSALOM BOSTON's toast upon the return of the whale ship *Loper*[7]

Absalom Boston made money on at least five whaling trips, one of them as the captain of *Industry* (May to November 1822). Earlier, he sailed on the *Thomas* to the Pacific in 1809 as a crewman, and on the *Richmond* as an ordinary sailor in 1817 on a voyage to Patagonia.[8] Later he was part owner of (and may have sailed as first mate on) the *Loper* (June 21, 1829–1830), which is probably the trip that made him rich. In today's dollars, the trip produced $1,417,385. Boston's one-twentieth lay would have amounted to $67,869, a relative fortune.[9]

Boston's ownership interest was probably even more valuable. It is believed that Boston, Samuel Harris, and Edward Pompey were all shareholders in the voyage. That trip was the *Loper*'s most profitable and was notable because its entire crew was black (except for its captain, Obed Starbuck). After the successful voyage the ship's owners gave the crew a dinner preceded by a joyous parade through town led by Absalom Boston and Samuel Harris.[10]

Absalom Boston must have been a good leader. After the *Industry*'s trip, a crewmember was inspired to write:

Here is health to Captain Boston
His officers and crew
And if he gets another craft
To sea with him I'll go.[11]

Absalom Boston probably could have been described as middle class—if such a thing were possible for blacks in the early 1800s. His grandparents and parents had been born into slavery, but Absalom was born free on Nantucket.

The patriarch of the clan, Absalom Boston's great-grandfather, was simply named "Boston." He and his wife, Maria, had eight children, one of whom was Prince Boston, born in 1750 (Absalom Boston's uncle). William Swain and his family were owners of the Boston family in Nantucket between 1739 and 1760.[12] Swain planned to gradually free the Bostons through manumission, a legal process that provided for servitude until a certain age. Indeed, when the canny Swain freed Boston, Maria, and their youngest child in 1760, he put the older children on a schedule according to which each would be freed at age twenty-eight, keeping them as his slaves for their most productive years.

Prince Boston was scheduled to be freed in 1778, so in 1772, Swain hired him out for a whaling trip on the *Friendship*, planning to receive his wages, as was customary. Prince's performance was good enough that the *Friendship*'s captain, Elisha Folger, paid the lay directly to Prince. As boat-steerer Boston's earnings were equal to "28 pounds for the three-and-a-half-month voyage, which," as the historian Daniel Vickers points out, "was equivalent (on a monthly basis) to the wages earned by the captain of a British slaver!"[13]

Swain died before the *Friendship* returned, and his son John Swain sued for Prince Boston's wages, but the jury determined that Prince had earned the money. The decision by the Nantucket Court of Common Pleas granted Boston not only his wages but his freedom as well. When Swain threatened to appeal, William Rotch let it be known that he would enlist the services of none other than John Adams to argue Boston's case. Prince in turn filed for and was granted immediate freedom five years ahead of schedule. The ramifications of this case in 1773 were extraordinary, first because it ended slave owners' practice of shipping slaves out on dangerous whaling voyages, but it also heralded the end of slavery on Nantucket. The state of Massachusetts followed in 1783. Prince Boston became the first slave to sue for his freedom (and win).[14]

Nantucket's native Wampanoags had been dying in epidemics caused by white settlers during these years—ironically giving blacks experience in whaling as they replaced the Indians. The diphtheria, smallpox, and measles brought by the Europeans may as well have been the bubonic plague to the Indian population, which had largely disappeared by 1764—and was completely depleted by 1854–55 when the last two full-blooded Nantucket Wampanoags, Abram Quary (November 25, 1854) and Dorcas Esop (January 12, 1855), died.[15]

The year after gaining his freedom, Prince Boston's brother Seneca married a Wampanoag woman named Thankful Micah. They named their first child Freeborn Boston. Absalom Boston, the fifth of their six children, was born fifteen years later. Seneca, a weaver, bought the family home on

Nantucket on September 13, 1774, and it remained in the family until 1919. A white person purchased the house and owned it for just one year before it was acquired by Frances Higginbotham, a black woman trained at the Boston Cooking School in 1920. She also bought the African American Meeting House next door (29 York Street, Nantucket) in 1933.[16] After Mrs. Higginbotham died in 1972, her family donated the property to the city. It is now the site of the city of Boston's Museum of African American History.

Absalom was known to have been more than just literate, and as a whaling captain he knew navigation. Since there were no public schools in Nantucket then, it was probably the Quaker Macy family (Obed Macy was the captain of the *Loper*) who assisted with young Absalom's reading skills and handsome penmanship during the time when he worked in the family's gardens.

Seneca Boston and his oldest son, Freeborn, died at the same time (causes unknown, but disease is presumed), and the family's assets were left to Absalom and his sister Mary, since Thankful had developed dementia.[17]Absalom Boston married Mary Spywood (or Sayword) on January 7, 1808; after she died, he married Phebe Spriggins.

Boston had the benefit of being free on an island in a state where slavery had been abolished, so he was spared some of the hardships other men of color had to face. Much of his early life was spent on the water learning the sea, navigation, and whaling (interrupted by the devastating—to the whaling industry in particular—War of 1812). He whaled on the *Thomas* in 1809 and rounded Cape Horn (a benchmark for sailors). He also was able to sign his own name on the ship's crew list instead of just making his mark as the others did. His is said to have been an elegant signature that appeared on several documents.[18]

In 1822 Boston became master of the *Industry*, which was owned by a black man named Richard Johnson. At the end of a six-month voyage (May–November 1822) to the Cape Verde Islands with an all-black crew Boston brought the *Industry* back to Nantucket with seventy barrels of whale oil, probably barely making expenses.[19] Although that voyage was widely heralded as the first time a black whaling captain sailed with an all-black crew, Paul Cuffe had actually been the first on the *Traveller* in 1815.[20]

In 1826 Phebe Spriggins-Boston became sick and died, and Absalom married again, this time to Hannah Cook. The two had another five children: Phebe Ann, Absalom, Oliver, Thomas, and Sarah. Charles (from Boston's first marriage) and Henry (from his second marriage) also both died, having followed their father's footsteps to the sea.

Nantucket Historical Association records indicate that in 1826 Absalom invested in the *Independence* by buying a quarter share of the lay from one of the crewmembers who chose to stay home with his sick wife. This proved to be a shrewd decision when the *Independence* returned with 2,044 barrels of sperm oil—and a big payday for Absalom without the dangers of a Pacific Ocean voyage. Indeed, there is no record of him going back to sea after the *Industry* voyage.

Boston invested his whaling earnings and his inheritance in Nantucket. He acquired land, a store, and an inn, and helped build a church and a school. He ran for public office after his daughter Phebe was prohibited from attending the public high school. He brought suit against the school in 1845, and with the introduction of twelve new school committee members achieved his goal of integration. By 1850, partially thanks to Boston, public schools in Salem, New Bedford, and Nantucket were open to blacks.[21]

In a portrait by an unknown painter said to be his likeness, the clear-eyed Absalom Boston appears well dressed in a white shirt and tie, with a gold earring in each ear. He wears a look of pride and accomplishment— and a confidence unexpected in a black man of the times. His clothing suggests the picture dates back to between 1835 and 1845.

When Absalom Boston died, he left cash, property, and assets with a value of $1,351.50 (about $34,400 today), tangible proof of a productive life.[22] At the time of his death he was a successful businessman who had worked tirelessly to integrate the island's communities. He was buried in a segregated cemetery.

The Absalom Boston Household (1850 Census)

Absalom F. Boston, 65

Hannah C. Boston, 53

Caroline D. Boston, 32

Oliver C. Boston, 14

Thomas S. Boston, 13

Amelia B. Clough, 8

Mary C. Cuff, 57

Thomas S. Boston, Absalom's youngest child with Hannah Cook, apprenticed as a barber, but his love for music led him to become a violinist instead. Described as "a dandy but not a fop" he enjoyed the company of whites and was reported as saying that he would have been gladly skinned alive if he could survive as white himself. After the Civil War he married Anna Wilson, daughter of a cashier at the Freedman's Savings and Trust Company in Washington, D.C. The lavish wedding at the Wilson's home was attended by Gen. Oliver Otis Howard, founder of Howard University. Described in the *Inquirer and Mirror* as Professor Boston because he taught music, Thomas was also employed by the Freedman's Bank, which failed three years later as a result of embezzlers—one of whom was Thomas Boston himself. Anna stood by him through his lesser employment as a laundry worker and a move to Chicago, where he again taught music and worked as a clerk. Thomas died leaving no children and was the last of the Boston family.[23]

Today, Absalom F. Boston is revered in Nantucket's historic whaling community as a symbol of extraordinary success.

Edward J. Pompey (1800–October 6, 1848)

Absalom Boston's contemporary Edward J. Pompey (locally pronounced "Pompy") is remembered as a man of commitment. The English who settled America in the 1700s did not bother giving surnames to their human property—any more than they did to pets or the domestic animals they raised for food. On Nantucket in those days, "blacks" or "negroes" more often than not were listed as having only one name. The earliest Pompey was a slave of Ebenezer Gardner.[24]

Pompey resided on Nantucket through much of the 1700s, and when he died in 1791 the selectmen directed that a coffin be made for "Old Pompey" at the town's expense. Another Pompey was a blacksmith who adopted the name Pompey Nailor. Pompey Nailor's sons chose to be called George and John Pompey rather than George and John Nailor. Edward Pompey is believed to have been a member of this family.

Like his friend Absalom Boston, Pompey was a freeman and a whale ship owner. Pompey's only known voyage as master was at the helm of the *Rising States*, from November 1836 to June 1837 on an Atlantic expedition. There are no references to his prior whaling experience, but it seems reasonable to believe that he served with Boston or others earlier. In 1836 black ship owner Richard Johnson convinced Edward Pompey to come to Westport to captain the *Rising States* with a crew of several other experienced mariners, including William Cuffe as first mate and James Hamilton as second mate, each with sixteen years of whaling experience. Henry Champlain, who served on the *Diana* in 1815 and the *Abigail* in 1821, was the oldest recruit at forty-seven. Abraham Gooding, who had been at sea since 1829, was another member of the all-black enterprise. The ship returned with only 87 barrels of sperm and whale oil worth about $2,700, which did not cover the $4,000 investment (not including insurance, bonds, and other incidentals). Having probably decided that serving on board a whaling vessel was less productive than owning one, Pompey became a partial owner of the *A. R. Smith* and the *Highland*.

Throughout Edward Pompey's entire life and career, he, like Absalom Boston, Samuel Harris, and almost half of all the captains of color, could have been thrown into slavery thanks to the Fugitive Slave Act of 1793. Discrimination was institutionalized in details large and small. For example, the state of Virginia adopted a law in 1804 that no more than one-third of ships' crews could be black—and none could have a black captain.[25] Maryland required all-black-crewed ships to have a white pilot on board, and South Carolina prohibited even free black men from leaving ships when docked at its ports on the threat of being sold as slaves.[26]

After an unknown number of trips leading up to his one known trip as master, Pompey returned to Nantucket for good when the *Rising States* completed its voyage on January 29, 1837. Pompey opened a store and sold subscriptions to William Lloyd Garrison's newspaper, *The Liberator*, and became a prominent abolitionist. He also sold Garrison's *Thoughts on African Colonization*. Unlike well-meaning black men like Paul Cuffe and some whites who thought settlement in Africa was the best option for the free black population, Pompey sided with Garrison in believing that blacks belonged in America—as free citizens.

Garrison wrote a letter to Pompey on August 11, 1832, saying, "I have forwarded to you by the schooner *Eagle*, 12 copies of my *Thoughts on African Colonization* which I hope you will be able to sell as the work has very deeply involved me in debt, and unless I can get out of the same, the *Liberator* must stop." Garrison told Pompey he could have "the dozen for five dollars," which would barely pay for the printing but allow Pompey to make some money. "Every colored man," wrote Garrison, "ought to own a copy, as the book contains the sentiments of his brethren in all parts of the country on the subject of colonization, and fully exposes the wickedness of the American Colonization Society." In closing, Garrison said he looked forward to visiting Nantucket, "when I shall be able to tell you, face to face, how much I appreciate your efforts to promote the circulation of the *Liberator* and also to thank my colored brethren for their patronage." Garrison did indeed visit Nantucket in 1842. Pompey was president of the Nantucket Colored Temperance Society and had attended the New England Anti-Slavery Convention of 1834 as a representative of Nantucket.[27]

When he died in 1848, Pompey's estate included three copies of the autobiography of Frederick Douglass and one of the *Narrative of William Brown*, published in 1847. William Wells Brown, born into slavery, had been active in the cause of abolition since 1836 and had been hired in 1847 as a Massachusetts Anti-Slavery Society lecture agent.[28]

When Eunice Ross, who was black, was denied admission to the local public high school in 1838, the island's black population took a stand. The controversy attracted quite a bit of attention, and in the 1840s the Massachusetts Anti-Slavery Society held conventions in Nantucket. Frederick Douglass delivered his first address to a multiracial audience at one of these conventions in 1841, launching his career as a civil rights spokesman.

In an attempt to open the schools to black students, ten black men—including Pompey's friend Absalom Boston—ran for the school board in January 1842, but the segregationists prevailed. The situation worsened the following year, when black community leaders wrote an address printed by William Lloyd Garrison's *Liberator* asserting their rights for their children to have the same access to town schools given to white children. The statement to the "inhabitants of the Town" received no response.

On August 10, 1842, the Anti-Slavery Society returned, featuring speeches by Garrison denouncing the Constitution as "an agreement with Hell" and by the fiery abolitionist Stephen S. Foster, igniting a riot that lasted several days. It was on this occasion that Foster delivered his well-known "Brotherhood of Thieves" address. Slavery, he claimed, consisted of five distinct crimes: "theft, or the stealing of a man's labor; adultery, the disregard for the 'requisitions of marriage' involved in holding women as 'stock' and prostituting them; man-stealing or kidnapping, the act of claiming a man as property; piracy, the illegal taking of slaves from the coast of Africa; and murder, the firm intention of masters who could hold slaves only by the 'threat of extermination.'"[29]

The Quakers of Nantucket were no doubt embarrassed when Foster held them indirectly culpable for the situation. "Because members of the Southern clergy in the Methodist, Episcopalian, Baptist, and Presbyterian churches held slaves, and Northern members of those denominations kept fellowship with slaveholders, they were all, by extension, guilty. The church, Foster proclaimed, was the 'Bulwark of Slavery,' its clergy 'a designing priesthood,' and its membership a 'Brotherhood of Thieves.'"[30] Nevertheless, segregation lasted a few more years.

Edward J. Pompey and 104 others submitted a petition to the Massachusetts Senate and House of Representatives in 1844 that described the "insults and outrages upon their rights." Another followed, signed by more than 200 white Nantucketers—mostly Unitarians and abolitionists—in support of the petition, and in 1845 Massachusetts legislators passed the first law in the United States guaranteeing equal education.[31]

His headstone in Nantucket's "New Guinea" cemetery identifies Pompey as "Capt. Edward Pompey." He died in 1848 at age forty-eight, leaving behind neither wife nor children, and was buried in the same cemetery as Samuel Harris. His estate included his one-thirty-second-part ownership of the schooner *Highland*, which was probably a merchant vessel. Other substantive possessions in his probate dated November 4, 1848, included his store, barn, and land; cash and loan notes; and books on the life of Frederick Douglass, geography, Daniel Webster (probably a dictionary), English grammar, and the history of Nantucket.

Born free, of free parents on Nantucket, the first place to end slavery in America, Pompey ascended to whaling captain. While his sole trip as master yielded only about $62,000 in today's dollars, it was enough to invest in a store, books, and the cause of abolition.

The Fight for Freedom

The early whaling community played a huge role in freeing blacks many years before the Civil War, leading by example and supporting abolition efforts with money and literature. James Forten, William Peter Powell, and Frederick Douglass were among the most influential of these people.

JAMES FORTEN:
SAILOR, INVENTOR, ENTREPRENEUR, ABOLITIONIST
(SEPTEMBER 2, 1766–MARCH 4, 1842)

James Forten was an unlikely character for his time. He was born free to Thomas and Sarah Forten in Philadelphia. Forten's great-grandfather had been brought from Africa to be a slave, and his grandfather was born a slave but gained his freedom. His father was sailmaker before he drowned in 1776. When Forten was fourteen he served in the army as a powder boy on board a privateer, the *Royal Louis*, during the Revolutionary War. Like his friend Paul Cuffe, he was captured by the British ship *Amphyon* and imprisoned for seven months.[32]

After developing a friendship with the British captain's son, Forten was offered the opportunity to live with the family in Britain but chose to stay in America. Thanks to the captain, Forten was not sold into slavery, as were many blacks captured while fighting on the side of the revolutionaries. Transferred to a British prison ship, Forten befriended a white boy named Daniel Brewton. Forten had a chance to escape but allowed Brewton to take his place, and they remained friends for life after Forten was released. Forten taught himself to read and write and went to London to learn shipbuilding. When he returned to Philadelphia, he worked for sailmaker Robert Bridges and rose to be foreman. When Bridges died in 1798, Forten took over the company. At age thirty-two he was worth more than $100,000 and employed more than forty workers, blacks and whites. Forten became the leading sailmaker in Philadelphia and one of the wealthiest black people in the country, with a fortune listed in his estate amounting to a million in today's dollars. Over the course of his life he used his money to buy the freedom of slaves; formed the Free Africa Society to help unemployed blacks; bought and financed *The Liberator*, William Garrison's abolitionist newspaper; used his home as a stop on the Underground Railroad; and opened a school for black children when his own could not attend the better white schools. Important to whalers, in 1800 Forten was one of the petitioners who attempted to have the Fugitive Slave Act modified to protect free blacks—an effort that was unsuccessful for many years.[33]

Initially a supporter of Paul Cuffe's American Colonization Society, which advocated relocating blacks to Sierra Leone, Forten later opposed resettlement in his *Letters from a Man of Colour* in 1813. He became president of the Anti-Colonization Society in 1817, a group that opposed sending blacks to Haiti or Sierra Leone. Forten strongly believed that blacks should claim their right to live free in America instead of migrating. Brought here by force, black people were entitled to the same protections of the Declaration of Independence as everyone else. Further, he believed "colonization as a panacea for the amelioration of the Negro race [to be] impracticable."[34]

Forten married Charlotte Vandine, with whom he had eight children, several of whom became active in the abolitionist cause. Forten died on February 24, 1842. His funeral was one of the largest in the history of Philadelphia.

WILLIAM PETER POWELL,
ABOLITIONIST AND PUBLISHER
(CA. 1807–CA. 1879)

William Peter Powell, a prominent abolitionist, was the publisher of the *National Anti-Slavery Standard* from 1840 to 1871. Born free in New York to a former slave and possibly an Indian mother, Powell married Amos and Bathsheba Haskins' daughter Mercy Orker Haskins on December 23, 1832. Powell was widely quoted in several abolitionist papers, fought the Fugitive Slave Law of 1850, and opened seamen's homes in New Bedford and New York. William Lloyd Garrison's American Anti-Slavery Society met in his home, and he championed civil rights all his life.[35]

FREDERICK DOUGLASS
(AUGUSTUS WASHINGTON BAILEY)
(CA. 1818–FEBRUARY 20, 1895)

Frederick Douglass' story involves the three early whaling centers of Martha's Vineyard, Nantucket, and New Bedford. Rented by his owner to another slaveholder as a ship caulker (much as Prince Boston was hired out) and treated like chattel in a Baltimore shipyard in 1836, Douglass was attacked and beaten unmercifully by four white men while more than fifty other white men looked on, cheering, "Kill him, kill him, kill the nigger" when he fought back. His owner brought him back to work in another shipyard, where Douglass came to the realization that the slave owner had no right to benefit from Douglass' labor:

> He did not earn it—he had no hand in earning it—why, then should he have it? I owed him nothing. He had given me no schooling, and I had received from him only my food and raiment, and for these, my services were supposed to pay from the first. The right to take my earnings was the right of the robber. He had the power to compel me to give him the fruits of my labor, and this power was his only right in the case. I became more and more dissatisfied with this state of things, and in so becoming I only gave proof of the same human nature which every reader of this chapter in my life—slaveholder, or non-slave-holder—is conscious of possessing.[36]

In 1838 (after an earlier attempt in 1835) Douglass escaped from slavery using Seaman's Protection Papers borrowed from another man. Dressed as a mariner, he took a train to Wilmington, Delaware, then a steamer to Philadelphia and a train to New York, where he married his fiancée, Anna Murray. After a steamer trip to Newport, Rhode Island, the couple took a stagecoach to New Bedford, where Douglass initially found work at a candle works. During his time in New Bedford Douglass formulated his thoughts on slavery, wrote, and prepared to speak publicly on the subject. A meeting with William Lloyd Garrison helped to frame Douglass' thoughts. In 1841 Douglass addressed the Anti-Slavery Society convention—his first speech to a mixed-race group—and was "warmly received."[37]

In 1857 Douglass traveled to Martha's Vineyard to speak. The *Vineyard Gazette* announced the event:

> While upon this subject, it may not be out of place to state that Frederick Douglas [*sic*], the colored gentleman and orator, will lecture before an "Association of gentlemen," at the Town Hall on Saturday evening next. We are not advised as to his subject, but suppose from his antecedents, that he will treat mainly upon this subject of slavery in our country. We hope the learned lecturer will aim more to enlighten his audience than to excite their prejudices against the South; that he will disappoint the expectations of those who can see good in nothing but agitation, by endeavoring to allay rather than

excite hatred among the members of the States of the Union. Let peace and concord, and brotherly love, be his watchword, rather than that which leads to strife and all manner of evil. We learn that he will give two lectures or addresses next week.

The *Gazette's* review of the lectures the following week was less than enthusiastic.

Frederick Douglas [*sic*], the colored orator, addressed a very respectable, though not large audience, at the Town Hall, on Saturday evening last, on the Unity of the Races (The Unity of Man). His arguments in favor of a common origin of mankind were very logical, and doubtless deemed conclusive by the great majority of his hearers. He is a fluent and powerful speaker, and commands uninterrupted attention. On Sunday evening, he lectured at the Congregational Church, to a full house. His subject was slavery, or the slave power in the United States. He failed to handle his subject with the power and ability he displayed in his former lectures, and hence some little disappointment was manifested by the public at the close of the performances. We think Mr. D. is entitled to great respect and to the best wishes of all true lovers of the colored race.[38]

Douglass' use of Seaman's Protection Papers led him to the whaling capital of the world, where freedom was the law and success was based on merit.

From Nantucket to New Bedford

The decade from 1820 to 1830 was Nantucket's most important as the world's leading whaling port. The business was thriving, and the whale ships got bigger as longer voyages became essential to finding the whales. Unfortunately, Nantucket's harbor was too shallow to handle the larger ships, limiting its ability to compete effectively with other ports. The island's superb Native American harpooners had been decimated by disease, and the black whalers who closed the talent gap followed the fleet elsewhere. By 1840 Nantucket was home to 578 black people, many of them mariners who were part of a community with its own churches and shops—and who were self-segregated in a section of town called New Guinea or Newtown.[39]

The 1849 Gold Rush had a deleterious impact on whaling generally. In one estimate, Nantucket lost 25 percent of its voting population to California within a nine-month period. The discovery of shale oil in

Pennsylvania in 1859 presaged the end of the industry. The epidemics that caused the extinction of the Wampanoag tribe on the island, a lack of natural resources (timber), the emigration of the whales farther offshore, and the shallow harbor all conspired to reduce whaling on Nantucket to insignificance. By 1874 it was no longer a viable whaling port.[40]

Black Population of Nantucket

Year	Number
1764	44
1776	133
1790	110
1800	228
1810	300
1820	274
1830	279
1840	578
1857	242
1870	85

After years of creating wealth on Nantucket, the Quakers moved their whaling operations to New Bedford.

New Bedford: Oil City, or the City of Light
Lucem diffundo. (We light the world)[41]

Once upon a time, the rank smell of whale oil permeated the air of New Bedford, which rose from humble beginnings to become the prosperous world capital of industrial whaling. New Bedford was created as part of the colonial town of Dartmouth in 1787 and was incorporated as a city in 1847, more than a hundred years after the introduction of whaling as an American industry. New Bedford emerged as a whaling colossus because of its physical attributes. Most obvious were its deep, protected harbor close to the Atlantic and its access to the other oceans of the world. Another reason was not as readily apparent—the miles of nearby forests yielded timber ideal for shipbuilding. While New Bedford was not the ancestral home of whaling, for the majority of the time the industry lasted, it was Emerald City for an unlikely cast of escaped slaves, Cape Verdeans, and Quakers.

By 1928, the year that marked the end of the industry, New Bedford exhibited a diversity seen nowhere else on earth. Elmo Hohman described New Bedford whaling crews as "Portuguese and mulattoes from the Azores and Cape Verde Islands, Spaniards, Swedes, Norwegians, Danes, Dutchmen, Germans, Frenchmen, Englishmen, Scotchmen, Irishmen, Gay Head Indians, negroes from the United States, Africa, and the West Indies, Maoris from New Zealand, Kanakas from the Sandwich Islands, natives from other South Sea Islands and half-breeds who represented the crossing of many different stocks."[42]

Along the way New Bedford had become the third-largest textile-manufacturing city in the United States, as measured by the number of spindles in its factories, and was the largest manufacturer of fine cotton goods in the world.[43] It is ironic that whaling, which provided so much opportunity for former slaves and other men of color in a city built largely by abolitionists, would wind up processing cotton in the North that was harvested by slaves in the South. New cranberry bogs provided work for Cape Verdeans displaced from whaling. And the railroad boom from 1869 to 1873 demonstrated a final irony as the machines initially lubricated with whale products became a better investment than whale ships.

CHAPTER 4

⸺ ⊰⊱ ⸺

Whaling

Awaite pawana! (Here is a whale!)

—Call of the Nattick Indians on spotting a whale
(Hohman, *American Whaleman*, p. 50).

"*Thar she blows!*" may have been the three most terrifying words a whaler ever heard—the second time he heard them. The first time surely fueled the adrenaline of excitement rather than fear. Several sources indicate that the plaintive cry romanticized by Herman Melville's *Moby-Dick* may have been dramatic license. "*There blows,*" wrote William Fish Williams, junior officer of the whaleship *Florence*, "I never knew why most writers of whale stories insist upon using the words, 'There she blows,' because there is no reason for saying 'she' any more than 'he' and either would be a word too many. The cry was always 'There blows' with the last word long drawn out."[1]

Whale hunters were always on the lookout for that "blow," a sign that a whale had breached the surface and spouted. Surfacing whales empty their lungs of warm air, which condenses in the colder air and creates steam that appears to be a waterspout rising from ten to forty feet into the air.[2] With experience, whalers learned that a single forward-slanting spout was a sperm whale and a double spout was a right or bowhead whale. They also learned that a whale that remained above the surface for twenty minutes would dive and submerge for twenty minutes, always swimming in the same direction it had been heading when it went under. With that knowledge hunters had a good idea where it would be when it resurfaced. Under the right conditions a whale might be spotted four to

Whaleboat from the *Pedro Valera*. Frank Lopes was lost on the *Valera* with all hands. Anthony Benton, Theophilus M. Freitas, Antonio José Senna, and Ayres J. Senna also sailed on the *Valera*. *"Whaling 038" image from* In the Giant's Shadow *exhibit, Martha's Vineyard Museum, 2016, Collections of the Martha's Vineyard Museum*

five miles away from the ship. Taking into consideration the wind speed, the whale's heading, and the likelihood of overtaking it, the captain would call for the ship's three (or four) 30-foot whaleboats to be lowered into the water to give chase. Sometimes these six-man boats would be rowing after several whales, since many species traveled in pods. Often crews pursued the whale into the darkness of night—and rowed back in the dark after the chase.

Finding whales had more to do with luck than skill—and once spotted they had to be caught. Everyone on board the whaleboat—except the boat-header—rowed after the prey backward, blind to whatever peril might await them. The boat-header (facing forward) steered the whaleboat with its single steering oar.[3]

The boat-steerer (harpooner) in the bow directed the crew in order to get the boat to a spot where he could harpoon the whale. This catching up to and successfully embedding a harpoon in the whale was the only glamorous part of the business; the rest was sheer hard work. Blacks and Native Americans were generally accepted to be the best boat-steerers. Many captains (black and white) were former boat-steerers. Seamen and green hands were the rowers; a mate or the captain generally played the role of bowman. One of the bowman's responsibilities was to cut the line of an embedded harpoon if the whale dove so the whaleboat would not be dragged below the surface. It was the boat-header's place to actually kill the harpooned whale once it had tired. More often than not, the harpooned whale dragged the boat across the sea for many miles attempting to escape—the famed "Nantucket sleigh ride"—at times out of sight of the ship. When the sleigh ride ended in the whale's death, the whale had to be towed back to the ship for processing. Rarely was a catch quick; at times more than one harpoon was needed to secure the beast, which could be many times the length of the fragile whaleboats pursuing it. A harpooned whale thrashed about trying to get free of the harpoon, and this was the most dangerous part of the enterprise. A fragile whaleboat was no match for a furious whale fighting for its freedom.

When he was certain that the harpoon was firmly embedded the boat-steerer would shout, "All fast." When the opportunity presented, the boat-header would plunge a razor-sharp lance into the whale's mortal spot—the heart and lungs behind the whale's left flipper. The dying beast churned the sea in its death throes (called a "flurry"), and the spouting of its blood (the "red flag") coloring the water indicated its end was near. The exultant cry, "Fin out" was made when the whale rolled onto its side, its fin sticking out of the water, signifying its death.[4]

After the excitement came the real work: six tired men rowing tons of dead whale as much as eight miles back to the ship—sometimes in the dark—and the bloody slaughter that followed.

"Showcase of Terrors"

Once the whale was brought back to the ship, it was lashed to the side with chains while the men stripped the meat, or blubber, from it in a process called "cutting in"; the blubber was then melted into oil, called "trying out." A scaffold was lowered alongside the ship so the crew could use various razor-sharp, specially constructed cutting devices to carve the whale meat. The whale was rolled about and sliced into big pieces, which were cut into smaller "blanket pieces" that were then winched on board. Unwound spirally "like the skin of an orange," these pieces were lowered onto the ship where they were cut into smaller, more manageable "horse pieces." These one- or two-foot-wide parts were pitched back on deck and sliced with a mincing knife into smaller "bible leaves," which were put into two (sometimes three) try-pots and boiled down into oil. Try-pots were squarish brick ovens with iron cauldrons that sat atop wood fires that kept the cauldrons hot enough to boil the blubber. Whale ships had to carry

The *John R. Manta* showing the gory and dangerous "cutting-in" process, believed to be removing the head of a sperm whale. The *Manta* was captained by Joseph Lewis, and sailed on by Julio Fernandes and August P. Gomes. *Courtesy of the New Bedford Whaling Museum*

spare bricks to replace those that had degraded from use because the pots were kept fired for twenty-four hours at a time. The middle part of the whale's head, the "junk," was also cut into smaller pieces and boiled down. Sperm whales' teeth were harvested too. Sharp utensils cut the teeth at the bottom and winches were used to strip them from the jawbone. Flensing knives were used to cut the remaining flesh into pieces small enough for boiling. The oil was stowed in barrels (or casks) for the trip home. The uncooked remains and skin were used to restoke the hot fires beneath the try-pots and were sometimes eaten like pork cracklings.

Sperm whales were decapitated, and the "case" in the whale's head was bailed out by hand. The best whale oil—the clear, snow-white sperma-ceti—was located in the whale's head. A mate standing waist-deep inside the head would scoop it out with a bucket, and it was immediately put into barrels without "trying" it. If the head was too big to bring on board, the crew would perform this part of the operation in the water.[5]

Paul Cuffe Jr. never became a captain, but he had many years of experience as a whaler and seaman. He offered a colorful first-person account of catching a whale on a trip in about 1812:

I harpooned all these, and assisted in taking and towing them along side the ship. After we get a whale along side, we hitch our blubber hooks into the head, after severing it from the body, then, with our windlass, draw it aboard, and dip the oil out, which sometimes amounts to more than fifty barrels. After this, we commence cutting the whale in a circular manner with our spades; then we hitch the blubber hooks into the commencement next to where the head was taken off, and by pulling at the windlass, take off a large piece which will usually when tried and strained, produce ten barrels of oil. Before heaving on board this piece, another hook is fastened below the one to be taken off; when this is done with a cross blow from the spade, the first piece is separated from the rest of the whale. Then the cutting is continued in the same manner as before mentioned, and another piece torn off and swung aboard. This operation keeps the whale constantly rolling over until the mass of the flesh is stripped from the carcass, which is then permitted to float off, or sink, and it becomes the sport of sharks, who feed upon the little flesh which remains after it has gone through the hands of the whalemen.[6]

How Bad Was It?

Twas on the briny ocean
    On a whaleship I did go.
Oft times I thought of distant friends,
    Oft times I thought of home
Remembering of my youthful days.
    It grieved my heart full sore
And fain I would return again
    To my own native shore.
Through dreary storms and tempest
    And through some heavy gales
Around Cape Horn we sped our way
    To look out for sperm whales.
They will rob you, they will use you
    Worse than any slaves.
Before you go a-whaling boys

> You had best be in your graves.
> If ever I return again
>   A solemn vow I'll take
> That I'll never go a-whaling
>   My liberty to take.
> I will stay home
>   And I will roam no more
> For the pleasures are but few my boys
>   Far from our native shores.
>   —From *Whaleman's Lament* and *Songs the Whalemen Sang*,
>   logbook of the *Catalpa's* voyage, 1856[7]

Whaling was certainly a better choice for a black man than slavery, but it was often a faster track to the grave as well. Most men who went whaling found no inherent romance in brutal working conditions on strange seas that rarely cooperated with the perils that constituted whaling, including, in Stuart Sherman's words, "castaways, mutinies, desertions, floggings, stowaways, drunkenness, illicit shore leave, scurvy, fever, collisions, fire at sea, stove boats, drownings, hurricanes, earthquakes, tidal waves, shipwrecks, ships struck by lightning, falls aboard ship, hostile natives, Confederate raiders and ships crushed by ice."[8]

The whaling life "was likely to appeal only to three classes of men: those who had been compelled to leave the land to avoid gaol or starvation, those who thought they were going to see the world and gain adventures, and those who were determined to work their way up until they owned a whaling ship of their own."[9]

THE PAY

Frederick Douglass explained one reason why black men chose whaling: "There is not that nice distinction made in the whaling as there is in the naval and merchant marine services; a coloured man is only known and looked upon as a MAN, and is promoted in rank according to his ability and skill to perform the same duties as the white man; his opportunities for accumulating pecuniary means—investing his earnings in whaling capital, is equally the same."[10]

From 1780 to 1800, wages were higher on the sea than ashore in Massachusetts. The system of compensation was based on the lay—a profit-sharing arrangement under which, presuming a profit per voyage (which was not always the case), crewmen were paid on a merit system using an often-arbitrary combination of experience and seniority. Whalers averaged $18 monthly until after 1812, when it dropped to $12. After 1830 the pay declined to $8.12 per month on average. From 1840 to 1860, according to Hohman, the average daily wage for unskilled workers was about 90 cents per day, while 156 hands from 3 whaling ships (*James Maury*, *Marcella*, and *Minerva*) made what amounted to 19 cents per day over 10 voyages between 1840 and 1860.[11]

Crew of a Whale Ship
HOHMAN, *Federal Writers Project*

Title	Responsibility	Lay	Lay
Captain (Master)	Senior officer	1/12–1/17	1/8–1/15
First Mate	Second in command	1/20–1/25	1/18
Second Mate	Boat-steerer	1/25–1/30	1/28
Third Mate	Boat-steerer	1/45–1/60	1/36
Fourth Mate	Boat-steerer	1/60–1/65	1/60
Boat-steerer	Harpooner	1/75–1/90	1/80
Cooper	Barrel maker	1/50–1/55	1/60
Seaman	Experienced sailor	1/140–1/160	1/150
Steward	Supply officer	1/100–1/150	1/90
Cook		1/140–1/160	1/110
Carpenter		1/165- 1/180	
Blacksmith		1/185	
Green Hand	Rookie seaman	1/180–1/190	1/175
Cabin Boy		1/90–1/350	

Cape Verdeans, who came late to whaling, were paid even less than black and Native American whalers of similar rank. During the period 1795–1885, the lay for green hands (the starting shipboard rank) ranged from 1/175th to 1/190th, substantially more than the 1/200th lay Cape Verdeans were often paid.

We have detailed records for a specific voyage on the *Morning Star* by Valentine Rosa (a Cape Verdean) that isolates gross revenue (about $46,000) from the sale of about 25,000 gallons of sperm oil, less expenses of about $28,000, giving a profit of about $18,000—a profit margin of 39 percent. Thirty-nine percent of $3,696 (for the sale of the 2,800 gallons yielded by one sperm whale) is $1,446. A lay of 1/200th of $1,446 paid the crewman $7.23 for each whale; a 1/275th lay paid $5.26 per whale.

What justified that insultingly low lay? Cape Verdeans were easy targets, unfortunately, refugees who were subjected to discrimination based on their color and their differing ways and language. Melville described them as "descended from Portuguese convicts and an aboriginal race of negroes, ranking pretty high in incivility and rather low in stature and morals."[12]

Theophilus M. Freitas (1878–?)

Born in 1878 on Sao Nicolau, one of the Cape Verde Islands, Theophilus Freitas came to America on the *Rosa Baker* in 1895 at age seventeen.[13] Freitas was one of the few black masters to sail from the port of Fall River. He was a master three times, twice on the *Sullivan*, when he replaced Captain William Hegarty, and once on the *Pedro Varela*. Freitas served on thirteen whaling voyages from 1899 to 1921, most often as a boat-steerer, boat-header, or officer. Records indicate that he was paid a total of $6,969.48 on six of the thirteen known trips—the equivalent of about $170,000 today (see appendix C).

Freitas' brothers, Antone and Frank, and his uncle Benjamin were also whalers.[14] Freitas played the part of the harpooner in the silent movie *Down to the Sea in Ships*, a 1922 production about whaling starring Clara Bow. The film shows him performing duties he had performed on real whale ships and remains one of only a few filmed portrayals of a whaler at work. Most whaling wives would have agreed with his wife, Theodolinda, who said after seeing the movie, "I never would have slept had I known how dangerous whaling voyages were," according to a New Bedford Whaling Museum exhibit. A May 2015 photograph from the film that shows Freitas about to harpoon a whale leaves little doubt that he was black.

The Ships

In spite of her slowness, her breadth of beam, and her broad-ended wallowing, the typical whaler was the vehicle of a life which merged adventure and exploitation, courage and brutality, abandon and niggard-li-ness, as fully as any occupation in America, past or present.

—HOHMAN, *The American Whaleman*

Life on a whale ship was no vacation cruise. Five different types, or rigs, of ships were used for whaling, each with a specific objective. Schooners, sloops, and brigs were smaller vessels for closer whaling grounds; the larger barks and ships were used for longer voyages. Larger vessels were needed when a ship spent long periods at sea (trips averaged three and a half years from 1842 to 1857), not just to carry home the cargo but also to carry enough for provisions for the crew.[15]

America's only whale ship still in existence, the *Charles W. Morgan*, is docked at Mystic Seaport in Connecticut and was restored to operable condition for its historic voyage in 2014 with stops in New London, Newport, Martha's Vineyard, New Bedford, Boston, and returning to Mystic, where it is today a living exhibit. I watched the *Morgan* sail into the Vineyard Haven Harbor and was able to board it on the historically significant voyage, its thirty-eighth after thirty-seven whaling trips, the last ending in 1921. That the *Morgan* even exists as the sole memorial of a two-hundred-year industry is a brilliant testament to the work of a handful of individuals led by Matthew Stackpole.

The fifteen or so minutes I spent on board were more than enough. The *Morgan*, 351 tons, nearly 107 feet long, and 27 feet wide, is tiny indeed in comparison with Royal Caribbean's *Allure of the Seas* and *Oasis of the Seas*. Each cruise ship is 225,200 tons, 1,181 feet long, with a beam of 208 feet. On the *Morgan*, a vessel eleven times smaller, thirteen to thirty-six seamen would spend about three and a half years together capturing and processing whales.

The Forecastle (Foc'sle)

The best forecastles were bad while the worst were truly vile.

—DOLIN, *Leviathan*

The forecastle was where rookie whalers (called "green hands" due to the color they turned while finding their sea legs) made their home. It was often self-segregated, with black, white, and Cape Verdean crewmembers staying on particular sides of the bunking area. Innocent young boys shared the cramped space with "immoral and unprincipled wretches" who "attempted to elude the Ten Commandments . . . confirmed drunkards, vagrant ne'er-do-wells, unapprehended criminals, escaped convicts and dissipated and diseased human derelicts of every description."[16] In this area below the main deck men slept on coffin-sized bunks with mattresses made from straw or cornhusks called "donkey's breakfast."

Granville Allen Mawer colorfully referred to the forecastle as "a space the area of a bedroom and the height of a chicken coop":

> In that repulsive hole . . . not high enough to allow a tall man to stand upright, with little or no light or ventilation but what comes down the narrow hatchway (and even this must be closed in rough weather), here some twenty or five-and-twenty men are to eat, and sleep, and live, if such a state can be called living; here, in sickness and in health, by day and by night, without fire in the rigours of the polar regions, or by cooling appliances under the equator, these men, with their chests and hammocks, or bunks, are to find stowage. After again and again examining this feature of their arrangements, and comparing it with the cells prepared for and enjoyed by the felons in all our principal prisons in more than half the states of our Union which I have visited, the latter would be pronounced princely, enviable even in all the requisites of roominess, light, ventilation, and facility for seclusion![17]

Wind and Weather

While the relatively tiny whaling vessels pitched and bobbed like tops in a tub in the wind, "greenies" provided entertainment for seasoned crews in much the same way that pledges amuse frat men. Joseph Gomes of the *Pedro Varela* was seasick for eight straight days. "Oh, no," he begged a shipmate. "Please, I am so sick. I've got nothing else to throw up. The water stinks, the food stinks, everything stinks. Please! I forgive you, and the Lord will forgive you. Please! Just kill me and throw me overboard!"[18]

Jim Murphy wrote about a new whaler: "Robert Weir became ill almost as soon as the whaling bark *Clara Bell* left port. Five days later he was still seasick. 'And oh! How dreadfully sick I was. Saw two sharks, one about 12 ft. long and the other 5 or 6 ft. I felt very much tempted to throw myself to them for food.' Called up to the crow's nest for the first time, Weir said that 'the ship was almost on her beam ends by the wind, and the spray dashing nearly to the fore-top. Often a big lurch of the ship will knock half the ideas out of one's head.'"[19]

Typically, first-time whalers were fourteen to eighteen years old (although many were younger) with duties ranging from cabin boy to ordinary seaman. They were rapidly trained in the language and operation of the ship, with the expectation that when the ship reached the whaling grounds, each crewmember with an assigned role would be in a position to contribute to the mission in a rapidly moving scenario where mistakes made the difference between life and death.

The *Canton II* docked in New Bedford. It wrecked and sank while under the command of Valentine Rosa and was also once captained by Theophilus Freitas. *Courtesy of the New Bedford Whaling Museum*

Lost at Sea

There is no accurate tally of whale ships wholly lost—those that sailed and never returned. Of 750 ships that left New Bedford, 231 were lost. With each ship carrying an average of thirty men, almost seven thousand men left port and were never heard of again. And that is just from New Bedford. Some 265 captains died at sea for one reason or another.[20]

It was almost never clear what had happened when ships did not come back. For example, no one really knows what became of Alvan Phelps, William Cuffe, Amos Haskins, Henry Lewis, Joseph Lewis, Amos Jeffers Jr., the Lee brothers, and Collins Stevenson, all of whom were "lost at sea." But it was weather that killed Valentine Rosa (who had survived a shipwreck earlier in his career) and Frank Lopes.

Valentine Rosa (1874–1915)

Valentine Rosa was born on Maio in the Cape Verde Islands. He was about eighteen years old in 1892 when New Bedford whaling captain Thomas McKenzie hired him in Cape Verde to sail on the *Platina*. Starting at the very bottom of the command structure, Rosa worked his way up to become a whaling master.[21]

Rosa served on the *Josephine* and the *Clara L. Sparks* (with Joe Benton) as boat-steerer and first mate. On Rosa's voyage as first mate on the *Josephine* in 1903, Marian W. Smith, the *Josephine*'s navigator and the wife of Captain Horace Perry Smith, took it upon herself to pass along her knowledge to him. A story in the *Boston Herald* aptly summarizes the remarkable relationship: "In 1903, the white wife (of a white Master), herself the navigator of a whaleship, taught a black officer navigation, allowing for his rise to become Master of a whaleship."[22]

Tall for a whaler at six-feet-one, Rosa sailed on the *Canton II*, *Clara L. Sparks*, *Josephine*, *Morning Star*, and *Platina*. He was master on four whaling trips—two on the *Canton II* and two on the *Morning Star*, between 1907 and 1912. The oil he brought back would be worth about $4.5 million today. The last two voyages of the *Morning Star*, in 1910 and 1912, each brought back a million-dollar-plus cargo. When Rosa shipped out as master on the *Morning Star* on May 16, 1910, his 1/13th lay earned him $3,075.45 (about $72,000). Fifty-four other seamen served on the trip:

thirty-four began the voyage in New Bedford, and others joined at stops in Fayal, Cape Verde, and as far as away as Dominica as replacements for those who left. Captain Rosa's net pay after deductions for shipboard expenses was $2,520.85 (about $59,000 today), almost a third of the entire crew's pay.[23]

Not all his voyages went so well.

Captain Rosa left New Bedford on the *Canton II* on October 7, 1909, bringing along his wife, two daughters, and a son. His wife was the navigator for the trip, just as his teacher Marian Smith had been for her husband. The *Boston Herald* noted that Mrs. Rosa was listed "in the shipping articles as assistant navigator." Fate and the lack of wind on November 26, 1909, brought the aging whale ship to grief on a reef, where it broke up and sank, although all hands were saved.[24]

The original news account said only that the vessel was lost on the Cape Verdean island of Maio, coincidentally Rosa's birthplace. When two seamen, Walter J. Flagg and Thomas Williams, both nineteen when the voyage began, got back to New Bedford January 14, 1910, on a steamer from Cape St. Vincent, they reported to the ship's owner that they had just gotten out to sea that fateful morning when at 4 a.m. the ship was caught in a strong current in dead calm weather. When it became apparent that the current would drive them onto the reef, kedge anchors were put out to pull it off. (Kedges were smaller anchors generally used to help steer a ship by attaching them to fixed objects [like a reef] to have the wind or current change the ship's direction.) When the attempt failed, it only remained for those on board

Valentine Rosa. *Courtesy of the New Bedford Whaling Museum*

to leave the boat safely, and over the next few days they watched it get "pounded to pieces."[25]

Valentine Rosa got back to New Bedford on Wednesday, April 7, 1910, almost five months after the accident. A newspaper interview with him on April 11 confirmed the earlier details, with the additional information that the watch at the time had failed to see land due to the fog. Driven by the strong current, the ship struck the reef so hard that it was filled with water within two hours. All provisions were lost along with the ship, and almost nothing of value was saved, according to another newspaper report.[26]

The *New Bedford Mercury* described the *Canton II* as the oldest ship of the fleet. It was built in Baltimore in 1835 and had been used for twenty-three whaling trips, beginning November 9, 1841. It had whaled successfully from New Bedford to the Pacific, Indian, and Atlantic Oceans as well as in Hudson Bay; several newspaper reports claimed it may have traveled farther (in miles) than any other whale ship. During its sixty-five-year life more than seven hundred men had served on its decks, in addition to the thirty-six who sailed on the *Canton II*'s last voyage. Of the last crew, three were of indeterminate race, five were white, six were black (including Rosa), and the other eighteen were listed as "dark." Virtually all of those eighteen were from Cape Verde or New Bedford. It would be safe to conclude that, including Captain Rosa, at least twenty-four of the crewmembers were black or men of color. Of the crewmembers specifically listed as black, Manuel Arceno was a boat-steerer and assistant cooper, Joaquim José Gabrilla was a boat-steerer, Joaquim D. Silva was a seaman, and Alexander Samuels was the steward. Samuels, the oldest on board at forty-two, was listed as having taken at least ten whaling voyages, quite a few in a business where most men only went once or twice.

Rosa's last whaling trip was the subject of a remarkably biased newspaper article after he returned. The article misidentifies him as "Antonio G. Roza" and takes pains to note that the large crew of forty-one was "manned entirely by Portuguese, with a scattering of Maho and few other island people, not a white man being on board" (newspaper articles on whaling rarely identified whalers by race).[27]

Four whaling trips left New Bedford in 1912 and came back in 1914:

Ship	Sailed	Returned	Months	Barrels	Barrels/month
Carleton Bell*	5/7/1912	8/19/1914	28	1,695	60.5
A.E. Whyland	7/28/1912	8/21/1914	25	2,170	86.8
Valkyria	9/28/1912	6/10/1914	24	1,025	42.7
Morning Star	10/10/1912	9/17/1914	27	2,650	98.2

Source: Hegarty, Addendum to "Starbuck."

* Joseph H. Senna owned the Carleton Bell on this trip, which was captained by Antone Sylvia.

Had the article's author meant to imply that ships with "not a white man being on board" were poor whalers, the figures in the table, especially those for the *Morning Star*, prove him dead wrong.

Over the course of Valentine Rosa's career, his ships killed more than 130 whales during his 4 known trips as master. After he returned on the *Morning Star* in 1914, it was sold as a coal barge. Rosa bought a coastal schooner that made trips between New York and Nova Scotia. Valentine Rosa was lost at sea off the coast of Nantucket in 1915, "likely in a gale." He was forty-one.[28]

FRANK M. LOPES (1884–1919)

Frank M. Lopes, Captain Louis Lopes' younger brother, was master of the *Pedro Varela* three times. Only one of those trips was successful—the voyage from October 1917 to February 1918, returning with a modest 320 barrels of oil (valued at $184,000 today). He took the *Varela* to sea again in July 1918, but the results and return date are unknown. Earlier in his career he served as the boat-steerer on the *A. E. Whyland* in 1915, when his older brother Louis was master, as well as on the *Bertha* in 1916.

The *Pedro Varela* along with its master, Frank M. Lopes, and all hands disappeared in an Atlantic hurricane that lasted from February 9 to February 11, 1919. The storm caught five other ships in its path. The *Ellen A. Swift*, with white master George L. Denham and a crew of nineteen (of whom fifteen appear in a newspaper photo to be black), was also destroyed. Captain Henry Mandly of the *William A. Graber*, one of the ships that survived, wrote to his brother that the barometer had dropped to 28.90, far below any reading he had ever seen. With the water flat calm at 3 a.m. on February 9 he called the crew on deck to reef the sails and prepare. The *William A. Graber*, built in 1900, was a 137-ton schooner probably only about 100 feet long. What must the crew's thoughts have been as they waited? Mandly wrote:

> At 4 a.m. it commenced to blow. I never knew the wind could blow so hard before. After daylight the seas began to climb until they were at least thirty feet high and when they would break it was a good imitation of a clap of thunder. At 9 a.m. a big sea took the schooner and hove her over on her beam end and there she stayed for about ten minutes and the biggest part of that time I and the steward were under the water. When she righted again I had lost one boat off the larboard cranes. I tell you then things began to look pretty blue. It was impossible to look into the wind as the spray from the seas as they broke and also the rain from the squall stung a person's face just like a lot of hailstones.[29]

That this account was written by an experienced whale captain makes it even more chilling. The *Ellen A. Swift* and Frank M. Lopes' much smaller *Pedro Varela* had no chance in such weather.

Henry A. Lewis (Levin) (1859)

There is a lot of information on Henry Lewis' whaling career, which lasted more than twenty-five years until he was lost with his ship in 1859. Identified as black by Martha Putney, Lewis was a boat-steerer on the *Washington* in 1838. Prior to becoming master he served as third mate and then first mate on the *William Hamilton* (June 17, 1848, and June 20, 1850). Capturing perhaps seventy-nine whales whose oil was valued at $7 million in modern dollars, Lewis served as master on board the *Rodman*, *March*, *Euphrates*, *Bolton*, *Charleston Packet*, and *Friendship*; and as an officer or crewmember on the *Oliver Crocker* (third mate), *Stephania* (seaman), *Zephyr* (first mate), *Hercules* (cooper), *Washington* (boat-steerer), and *Newark* (boat-steerer). The data on these trips are confirmed by Lund and Hegarty and largely corroborated by the New Bedford Whaling Museum and New Bedford Public Library crew lists. There is no record of why Lewis served in so many roles, several of which were in lower ranks, long after having served as captain. Lewis is listed as master of the *Rodman* on an 1833 voyage from New Bedford, with a crew that included other black men.

The *Newark*'s trip that left New Bedford in 1859 may have been Henry A. Lewis' last. Alexander Starbuck writes that the ship, captained by Nathan S. James, was "lost on Sandal Wood Island (Malay Archipelago) on April 11, 1863: crew in boats 9 days and 10 nights, with but little bread and water, sent home 76 sperm." No log of the voyage exists, and there are no references to Henry A. Lewis/Levin afterward. When whale ships were lost, only conjecture remains.[30]

Time of Year

June, too soon.
July, stand by.
August, look out you must.
September, remember.
October, all over.[31]

Of all the variables conducive to whaling, the weather was one of the most important. Availability of whales was another important variable. "Their habits seem to have been somewhat migratory," Starbuck notes, "as the boat-whaling season usually commenced very regularly early in November and ceased in March or April." Whalers from Provincetown sailed for the Caribbean from February to June, then docked for the summer and the hurricane season. On the East Coast, hurricane season lasted from June until November—and many a ship was lost. By the mid-1800s the whale fishery had spread to the Pacific Ocean, with boats sailing from the Northeast in the fall to round Cape Horn during the southern summer and arrive at the Bering Strait by October or November. They had to complete the work before the winter freeze, and whale ships that missed that deadline were subject to being crushed in the ice.[32]

Differing from the rhyme and more consistent with Starbuck's observation, twelve of Collins Stevenson's trips began after November, including his last, which started January 27, 1904.

COLLINS A. STEVENSON (1847–1904)

Born in St. Vincent in the West Indies in 1847, Stevenson immigrated to the United States in 1865 as a young widower. Little is known about his early life, but at age thirty-four his occupation was sailor and he had remarried. It is thanks to a video by George Bryant, a local Provincetown historian, that we know Stevenson was black. Provincetown's whale fleet owners exhibited a cash-motivated racial tolerance. Reports suggested Collins A. Stevenson was light-skinned, and whaling documents list him as "mulatto." In what I believe to be his picture on board the *Carrie D. Knowles*, he does appear light-skinned.

Laurel Guadazno wrote in a 2015 *Provincetown Banner* newspaper column that "Captain Stevenson was well respected and considered more knowledgeable about the whaling grounds then most captains. He was 57 years old, and although he lived in Provincetown, he was born on the island of St. Vincent in the British West Indies. Because he would be able to call at St. Vincent and visit with his daughter and other relatives who still lived on the island, Captain Stevenson was probably looking forward to the ill-fated voyage, which began on January 27, 1904."

The *Carrie D. Knowles* was lost at sea in February 1904 under Stevenson's command. Under the headline "Whaling Vessel Believed Lost," the *Boston Herald* reported in April 1904: "The word 'missing' must, it is felt, be recorded against the name of still another of Provincetown's shrunken whaling fleet. This time it is the *Carrie D. Knowles*, newest and best of the handful representing the town's once mammoth whaling squadron." The ship left port on January 27, 1904, according to the newspaper, which described correspondence from Dominica inquiring about the schooner's whereabouts when it had not arrived by March 30 after a trip that should have taken twenty days. The article named the twelve-member crew, all presumed to have been lost.

A newspaper report five years later gave hope, though fleeting, to their families. An article now in the scrapbook files at the New Bedford Whaling Museum Library bears the headline "Lost American Crew in Venezuelan Jail." Datelined Kingstown, St. Vincent, B.W.I., the story appeared in newspapers throughout the whaling world, including the *New York Times* and Sag Harbor's *Corrector*, in May 1909. An American seaman named Elisha Payne who had escaped from a Venezuelan prison claimed that

The *Carrie D. Knowles*. The man at right is believed to be Captain Collins Stevenson. *Courtesy of the Provincetown History Project Archives*

Collins Stevenson and his crew (whose names Payne repeated) were being held prisoner there. The credible-sounding story created quite a bit of excitement, particularly in Provincetown among the surviving families. By May 13, however, the *Provincetown Advocate* was reporting, "At this writing few Provincetown people give credence to the story told by Payne at Kingstown, St. Vincent. It is quite generally regarded as a hoax, the most cruel, most anguish exciting bit of deceptive work ever visited upon this community."[33]

Perhaps the one most affected was Collins' wife, Hannah (1846–96), who had been making plans to remarry when the story broke. She canceled the wedding and never married again.[34] Senator Henry Cabot Lodge conducted an official inquiry with no results—and Elisha Payne disappeared.

Captain Collins A. Stevenson's whaling legacy is impressive. On 16 trips as captain across 15 years, he averaged 358 barrels of oil per trip (killing about 95 whales) with a value today of $3.3 million. Stevenson must have been remarkably focused: it appears that all but two of the whales he harvested were sperm whales. When he (evidently) died at age fifty-seven he had been a captain for fifteen years. His barrel average at the end of whaling was dwarfed by the early years when thousand-barrel trips were not uncommon, but few captains had such consistent careers.

Stevenson was a member of the predominantly white King Hiram's Lodge, founded when the Pilgrims landed in Provincetown in 1620. It officially became a Masonic lodge with Paul Revere's approval in 1795, according to its website. The lodge retained meticulous records in its archives and has devoted a section to fellow lodge member George O. Knowles, the owner of the *Carrie D. Knowles*, the ship that failed to return with Captain Stevenson and his crew. The lodge's website has a picture of the *Carrie D. Knowles* with Captain Stevenson on board.[35]

CHAPTER 5

How Hard Was Whaling?

*W*halers on board ship put up with discomfort in every aspect of their lives. They were cold (or hot), their food was monotonous and vermin infested, and theirs was the second most dangerous American occupation after mining.

Clothing

A whaler wrote in 1856: "Everything is drenched in oil. Shirts and trowsers are dripping with the loathsome stuff. The pores of the skin seem to be filled with it. . . . You feel as though filth had struck into your blood, and suffused every vein in your body. From this smell and taste of blubber, raw, boiling and burning, there is no relief or place of refuge." What was used to clean the whale grease on the deck? None other than urine, contributed in a communal bucket over time by the crew.[1]

Food

Until on board kept on such filthy fare
It has often times caused me to stamp and to swear
For we have nothing fit for a Christian to eat
For most of the time it is old stinking meat
Sometimes meal and maggots mixed up in a tub
One of our great messes some think it good
With the sweat that ran down the old negro's face
All mixed up together Oh Lord what a taste
We have some potatoes half rotten to eat
Mixed up by the negro with poor stinking meat

> Not fit for a hog without (rine) like a boar
> And after one eating would never want more.[2]

The casual racism is to be expected considering the times, and traditionally many a whale ship cook was black. The "negro" was not being blamed for the quality of the food in this case. That was largely the result of poor-quality food and poor storage practices. Shipboard food, which ranged from unpleasant to revolting, could even cause mutiny. Long whaling trips were difficult to provision, and even with frequent stops for resupply, parsimonious owners rarely bought the best quality. Flour and hardtack—an unleavened biscuit—became wormy. Even whale blubber made its way to the menu; the "crisp bits" of tried-out scraps apparently tasted like pork cracklings. "Duff, a mixture of flour, lard and yeast boiled in a bag in equal parts of fresh and salt water until it was quite hard, like an old fashioned plum pudding," was another staple, often served with molasses. "Salt horse" was what corned beef, the main meat diet, was called, and at times may indeed have been horsemeat. Lobscouse, a stew made of hardtack and chopped salt meat sprinkled with pepper, was by contrast a delicacy.[3]

When food stores ran low, the cook served whatever was at hand. Often the meat was "locally sourced." Edwin Pulver, on the *Columbus*, was served polar bear after all else had run out:

> I hope when we get more fresh meat
> It'll be of a kind that we can eat
> I care Not weather [*sic*] it be cow or hog
> Nor would I run from a well-cooked dog
> So here I vow likewise declare
> I neer will Eat more polar bear.[4]

Galapagos tortoise was a delicacy and a blessing for whalers in the Pacific. The tortoise was its own storage container (for several months!) that yielded not just food but the substance (fat) with which it could be cooked. Said one whaler: "Their flesh, without exception, is of as sweet and pleasant a flavour as any that I ever eat. It was common to take out of one of them ten or twelve pounds of fat, when they were opened, besides what was necessary to cook them with. This was as yellow as our best butter, and of a sweeter flavour than hog's lard."[5]

Crews were subjected to a number of other unappetizing sounding recipes:

- *Whale Balls*, made from fried sperm whale brains and flour
- *Whale's Lip*, the gelatinous outer lip edge of a right whale placed in hot oil for six hours until it reached the consistency of jelly (resembling pig's feet)
- *Dandyfunk*, four buckets of hard bread combined with two pounds of salt pork fat and molasses, boiled
- *Whale Steak a la Melville*, steak cut from sperm whale's back: "Hold the steak in one hand and 'show it a live coal with the other,' wash down with a pint of whale oil. For a rare steak, omit the oil" (this is no doubt meant to be a joke).[6]

Belowdecks on a whale ship was a repulsive, rat- and roach-filled place without light; the forecastle was "black and slimy with filth, very small and hot as an oven." And this was the crew's quarters, not the storage area. The drinking water, stored for months at a time in subtropical heat in wooden barrels, was "gooey and stringy" from the microscopic organisms that thrived in the closed casks. Whalers rarely drank it, preferring instead "longlick, a mixture of tea, coffee and molasses."[7]

Vermin

Reports of "cockroaches as large as mice, bug infested food, and deadly epidemics" (no doubt the result of some of the former) were commonplace on whale ships. Ernest Dodge wrote: "One can throw a saddle on the cockroaches." Rats abounded due to the "profusion of blood," and "nothing could cope with the cockroaches." "It's a horrible experience to awaken at night, in a climate so warm that a finger ring is the utmost cover you can endure, with the wretched sensation of an army of cockroaches climbing up both legs," William Davis wrote. And whaleman Antone Fortes observed that shipbound rats searching for water were able to dislodge the bungs of water casks and often fell in and drowned.[8] When the try-pots were fired up, the heat caused the rats and cockroaches to "march, like armies from hell, over the fitfully sleeping men" off duty.[9]

Harsh and Cruel Captains

Whaleman J. Ross Browne wrote in 1840, "There is no class of men in the world, who are so unfairly dealt with, so oppressed, so degraded, as the seamen who man the vessels engaged in the American whale fishery."

Englishman Samuel Johnson compared a ship with a jail, and the ship came up lacking: "A ship is worse than a jail. There is, in a jail, better air, better company, better convenience of every kind."[10]

The master of a whale ship had complete authority; he was to be obeyed without pause, even if he was cruel, crazy, or drunk. It was largely due to the treatment of whaling crews that flogging was outlawed. The captain of the *Arab*, Benjamin Cushman, had a mean streak that was evidenced when, in 1830, steward Michael Ryan unlawfully gave crewmembers liquor. Cushman beat him until he bled, punched and kicked him, stripped him naked, and flogged him. When Ryan lost control of his bowels he was made to clean it up with a shovel. When he moved too slowly, he was flogged again and made to stand naked in the rain for two hours. He was later awarded $150 for the "excessive" punishment "disproportionate to the offense." Small recompense, it would seem.[11]

Highly exploited and underpaid, whalers were often characterized as "the very refuse of humanity, gathered from every quarter, escaped from poor houses and prisons or gleaned from the receptacle of vagrancy and lazar-house corruption."[12] Obviously, this included some of the captains.

HENRY JOHN (GONSALVES) GONZALES (1883?–)

It is both ironic and disappointing that Henry John Gonzales was the last known of the captains of color.[13] Certainly he knew his job. Gonzales was a tough, experienced whale ship captain. On board the *Gay Head II* as third mate in 1909 to the Arctic from San Francisco, he saw an enormous whale—the biggest he had ever seen. The whale proved to be a match for the whalers. From a whaleboat, First Mate Joseph Baptiste fired his harpoon at the whale, which in a rage used its head to flip the boat and the men into the air, sending the captain thirty feet. The whale's tail then sent them all flying again—including Gonzales' boat. No one was badly injured, and the second mate's boat picked up the men in the water. Luckily for all, the whale escaped.

Gonzales was born Henry John Gonsalves in Cape Verde around 1883; his name was hispanicized to Gonzales sometime between 1910 and 1912. Described by explorer Harold Noice as "tall, handsome and servile to the captain—but domineering to everyone else," Gonzales spent much of his career in the Northwest ocean passages. He served as boat-steerer on the

Andrew Hicks from San Francisco in 1903 and on the *Gay Head II* in 1909. Gonzales showed his true colors when he became captain of the schooner *Polar Bear*, a former whaler sold to the explorer Vihljamur Stefansson in 1915 for the Canadian Arctic Expedition that lasted from 1913 to 1918. The expedition, initially sponsored by the National Geographic Society and the American Museum of Natural History, was taken over by Canada because of the prospect of discovering new land. George H. Wilkins, the expedition's official photographer, said of Gonzales in a racially charged comment: "He is probably quick tempered, quick to decide, but rather unstable in purpose. A good man, no doubt, in charge of Latin people, but unsuitable for the more methodical Europeans."[14] Gonzales would show that he was as ruthless as he was "quick tempered."

Captain Louis L. Lane, known as one of the best of the "ice pilots," was employed to lead Stefansson's group with the *Polar Bear* but was forced to return following weather-related problems. At that point Lane left the expedition. Stefansson decided to buy the ship outright and hire Henry Gonzales, the mate, as captain after Lane left. Stefansson took the role of commander of the three-ship group that continued the expedition.

Henry Gonzales with part of the Canadian Arctic Expedition house behind him, Walker Bay, Victoria Island, June 1917. *Courtesy Canadian Museum of Nature*

With a multinational crew (Scandinavian, Samoan, Inuit, Anglo-Saxon, Swiss, and Portuguese [Cape Verdean]) of all colors, clashes quickly broke out. According to young Noice, Gonzales believed himself better than the Inuits and could not help showing it—and that almost cost him his life. He and Storkerson, one of Stefansson's trusted men, also clashed. Behind Gonzales' back, Storkerson and many of the crew referred to him as "that Nigger" because of his insolent bearing.

Gonzales and some of the Inuit members of the expedition were sent to the Inuits' village to trade for supplies; two of the guides spoke no English. The travel inland required sleds and dogs, and when the guides clambered on board with Gonzales, he angrily threw them off. They mistook the action as playful and tried again, and the enraged Gonzales turned the sled over and again hurled the Inuits off. Insulted, the two went ahead of the others for the four-day trip to the village, so the chilly welcome Gonzales received when he arrived could have been expected. The two Inuits who remained with Gonzales told him the villagers were probably conspiring to kill him. Indeed, they stole all of the goods Gonzales had brought to trade.

According to Noice's account, Gonzales' companions told the villagers Gonzales was a powerful shaman, and to convince them Gonzales dipped his fingers in alcohol, lit them, and turned so the villagers could see his hands blazing in blue flames. It had the desired effect, and the visitors lived through the night. The elders reached the conclusion that while their actions may have been justified, Gonzales' magic called for a more reasonable course of action. They brought out supplies and food to replace the barter items they had stolen from Gonzales. Although the supplies did not equal the stolen items in value, Gonzales returned to the expedition with a story framing himself as the hero. Gonzales departed with the *Polar Bear* after that, leaving Stefansson and his group to continue their explorations with dogsleds and on foot while Gonzales promised to meet the party at the next planned juncture with fresh supplies. Noice's colorfully descriptive book about the expedition's tribulations is laced with stories of Gonzales' deceit, ego, and inflated sense of importance:

> Gonzales was a pretty good whaler, a fair seaman, brave enough in the face of danger, particularly when danger called upon the Congo strain in him for the picturesque pose and the melodramatic gesture.

He was kind to dogs, and soft-hearted to children—and women. But new islands north, soundings, currents, sea-bottoms, meteorological observations, were to him only the childish diversions of a fool. He looked upon Stefansson more or less as an easy-going fellow, whom he had to humour to a certain extent for the sake of his pay, of course, whose orders he was justified in discounting when he pleased.[15]

"What dat kin' of man doin' in de Nort' anyways?" Noice quoted him as saying. "He better stayed home where dey look after him."

It was no doubt that attitude that left Stefansson's party, near starving, shocked to arrive at the rendezvous and find that one of the three ships (the *Sachs*) had been wrecked and stripped by Gonzales and his crew from the *Polar Bear*, which was nowhere in evidence. Gonzales' plan was to maroon Stefansson and his expedition for a year, leaving them to die while he took ownership of the *Polar Bear*. The plan failed when another ship, the *Challenger*, arrived. Stefansson purchased the *Challenger*, which carried them to safety near Herschel Island. When the *Polar Bear* was spotted, the captain of the *Challenger* raised a distress signal to lure in the *Polar Bear*. Stefansson and his party remained hidden until the two boats grew closer. Loyal crewmen on the *Polar Bear* were happy to see Stefansson and their other comrades safe. Henry Gonzales was summarily dismissed without pay and abandoned on the island with the Inuit woman he had taken as his wife. At the conclusion of the expedition, young Noice, now an experienced Arctic explorer himself, bought the *Challenger* from Stefansson to continue exploration on his own. He tracked Gonzales down to get the only sextant available—and traded it for some dainty teacups that Gonzales' wife, Violet Mamayauk, the teenaged daughter of a whaler and an Inuit, fancied.

Beginning in 1919, Gonzales served on a series of other ships: the diesel schooners *Herman* and *Carolyn Frances*, the schooners *Arctic* and *Nanuk* as first mate, and then on the *Carolyn Frances* (renamed the *Charles Brower*) as captain for voyages in 1926 and 1927. In 1930 Gonzales was said to be living in Berkeley, California, with a Portuguese wife, Candida, and working as a deckhand on the Golden Gate Ferry.[16]

Clearly, not all of captains of color were heroes—and it would be difficult to describe Gonzales as anything other than a scoundrel.

Blubber on the deck of a ship believed to be the *Arthur V. S. Woodruff. Courtesy of the New Bedford Whaling Museum*

Odors

Many writers describe one aspect of processing whales as among the worst: the disgusting smells from the blood and gore. And it was not just the odor of dying whales and boiling blubber. During its "flurry" before dying the whale regurgitated the contents of its stomach, which, for sperm whales, was squid.[17] The "trying out" could sometimes take three days, and "the stench of processing whales was so strong a whale ship could be smelled over the horizon before it could be seen."[18] Even processed whale oil—available for sampling today at the New Bedford Whaling Museum—is at best an odor to be avoided.

Desertion

If a ship were bound for heaven and should stop at Hell for wood and water some of the crew would run away.

—CAPTAIN THOMAS WILLIAM WILLIAMS, the *Florida II*[19]

Whale ships carried crews of thirteen to thirty-six, depending on the size of the vessel and the availability of seamen. Most whale ships were staffed largely by men with few or no other employment options. While few men made more than one trip, not all who signed on even managed that. Men deserted because of the relentless dangers of the job, the squalid living conditions, and the boring and seemingly interminable voyages. A notable example is the *Montreal*, which left New Bedford in November 1857 with a crew of 30 and returned 4 years and 7 months later with 158 total crewmen having served at various stages of the trip: 79 were dismissed; 30 deserted; and 15 died, left, or were transferred to other ships. Dismissals and desertions accounted for close to 70 percent of the entire crew, desertions alone for close to 20 percent. Only five members of the original crew returned on the *Montreal*. On average, two-thirds of original whale ship crews changed during the course of the voyage. By the middle of the nineteenth century, "whaling vessels never returned to New Bedford or Nantucket with the same crew that they shipped."[20]

Captains of color were no luckier than white captains when it came to crews deserting. Amos Haskins, William A. Martin, Ferdinand Lee, Anthony Benton, and others all had to deal with desertions.

AMOS HASKINS (SEPTEMBER 25, 1815–1861)

Amos Haskins' parents, Amos and Bathsheba Occouch Haskins, were "free colored persons." The senior Amos (1789–1837) was a boat builder from Rochester, New York, and Bathsheba (c. 1793–1853) was a Wampanoag from Gay Head; they married in 1812. After the elder Amos Haskins

died, Bathsheba married Amos Jeffers' father, Amos (1785–1872), a widower, making the younger Amos Haskins and whaleman Amos Jeffers Jr. stepbrothers. Bathsheba moved back to Martha's Vineyard when she married Amos Jeffers Sr. on October 4, 1849.

Portrait of Amos Haskins. *Courtesy of the New Bedford Whaling Museum*

Amos Haskins grew up as one of nine children of the combined marriages, five of whom died in or before their teens, and one, Arnold, who died the same day as his father in 1837, perhaps as a result of accident or epidemic.[21]

In a picture of him said to have been taken in 1855, Haskins looks black. He is wearing a double-breasted captain's uniform jacket over a waistcoat and a neat white tie. Unsmiling, with hands in pockets, Haskins looks like he means business.

Like many, he advanced through the ranks as a result of his skill with a harpoon. Interestingly, the name of one of Haskins' ships, the *Massasoit*, means "leader" in the Algonquin language. Massasoit was also the name of the sachemship (tribe) associated with Pockanocket (Pokanoket), Rhode Island, in 1621 that included Martha's Vineyard and Nantucket and was known collectively as Wampanoag. In an oral history at the New Bedford Whaling Museum Library, Edith Andrews of Martha's Vineyard claims Haskins was her great-great-grandfather. Mrs. Andrews' oral history mentions that Amos Haskins' "son" Samuel was instrumental in the rescue of passengers on board the ill-fated *City of Columbus*. Both *Native American Whalemen and the World* and *Wampanoag Families*, however, report that Samuel was Amos' brother; Amos and his wife had only daughters.[22]

Samuel served on the whale ships *Palmyra* in 1856, *Elvira* in 1858, and *Sarah* in 1865. When the 275-foot steamship *City of Columbus* sank at Devils Bridge at the foot of Gay Head Cliffs on Martha's Vineyard on the icy night of January 18, 1884, 103 people died. Twelve men in three whaleboats managed to rescue twenty-three of those on board. Samuel Haskins was in the first of the three boats launched. Another rescuer was Henry Hubbard Jeffers, a former whaler and, coincidentally, the son of Amos Jeffers Jr. and stepbrother of Samuel (and Amos) Haskins.[23]

Haskins was identified in local newspapers as an Indian of the Narragansett tribe and classified as "mulatto" or "black" in the census. His wife, Elizabeth Farmer (m. October 31, 1844), is believed to have been of African descent, and two of his daughters are believed to have married men of color; one of them, Mary L. Emerson Haskins, married Hiram I. Tilghman, a great-grandson of Paul Cuffe.[24] While it is possible that Captain Haskins was 100 percent Wampanoag, more than likely he was of mixed blood.

Amos Haskins is believed to have taken at least twelve whaling trips during his twenty-seven-year career, beginning at age eighteen on board the *Dryade* in 1834 and ending in 1860–61 on the ill-fated *March*. There is an unexplained four-and-a-half-year gap after Haskins' first trip that could have been due to a reluctance to pursue that difficult occupation or perhaps a lack of opportunity. Or he may have been serving on trips for which we have no records. He earned rapid promotions to second mate on the *Chase* in 1841, first mate on the *Annawan II*, and on the *Elizabeth's* 1849 trip was named replacement captain at age thirty-two. That enterprise was eminently successful; the ship came home with more than one thousand barrels of oil (see appendix D).

Although his rapid rise indicates that he was a talented seaman, Haskins' captaincies were not without drama. Haskins was an investor and partner in his first official assignment as master on the *Massasoit*, a remarkable achievement in 1851 for a man of color. George Belain (Joseph G. Belain's father) also owned shares of the *Massasoit* on this trip—Haskins owned an 8/64 share (12.5 percent) and Belain, 1/64. That voyage brought a modest return with just 325 barrels of oil and saw an extraordinary number of desertions or discharges (firings) of the largely white crew (more than half). While the reasons are not clear, race rather than managerial deficiencies may well have been the cause. It is difficult to argue against that. Shoemaker's substantive research of shipboard comings and goings left her believing that

> racial prejudice may have been Amos Haskins's undoing, however. The Massasoit's crew in 1851 was almost entirely white. They deserted at every opportunity. Did he think race was behind his crew troubles? The only clue to that possibility is that, when he next took the *Massasoit* to sea, men of color had more than doubled to become a majority, and he had as first and second mates George and William Belain, Wampanoags from Martha's Vineyard. Because illness cut this voyage short, we cannot know whether the change in composition secured him a more loyal crew. Ferdinand Lee also lost most of his men to desertion and discharge in the four years the *Callao* was at sea, but whether this had anything to do with racial tensions over his command is indiscernible in the logbook [of the *Callao*, not the *Massasoit*].[25]

The crew list indicates that Haskins was thirty-four years old on this trip, born in Rochester, a five-foot-ten-inch "mulatto" with black hair. Shoemaker points out that as captain it would have been Haskins providing this information. Typically, masters did not include their own racial characteristics on crew lists, but at least this time Haskins did. According to Shoemaker's detailed list of crew changes on the *Massasoit*, the trip started with twenty-three crewmembers (including Haskins), only seven of whom were "mulatto," "black," or "yellow." Many of the replacements occurred in the Azores; others in Barbados. The substantial change in the crew's racial makeup seems to support racial motivations behind the defections.[26]

Unfortunately, the drama on Haskins' ship continued, this time with Mother Nature prematurely ending the trip after six months. Following a provisioning stop on an island off West Africa, seven members of the crew contracted something Shoemaker calls "African fever," and two of them died. Only two more deserted after that, but this voyage marked the end of Haskins' career as whale captain.

We may never know why it took four years for Haskins to take another trip. Shoemaker suggests shame or depression, but it may have been just the money. In 1857 he signed on as first mate of the *Oscar*, headed for San Francisco. This was the *Oscar*'s last trip and for a time appeared to be Haskins' last as well: someone sent Haskins' wife, Elizabeth, a bill for his funeral after a report that he had drowned. This turned out to be inaccurate—he had left the trip early in Honolulu—but it must have taken several months for her to find out. He again went to sea on the *March* in 1861, which went down with all hands, including Haskins.[27]

In a twenty-seven-year career including three voyages as master and owner, Amos Haskins was responsible for bringing home oil valued at close to $3 million. He left his family with what was described as "a cozy New Bedford house."[28]

WILLIAM A. MARTIN
(JULY 17, 1827–SEPTEMBER 5, 1907)

The town of Edgartown on Martha's Vineyard has never looked the same to me since I completed an article for *Martha's Vineyard* magazine about black whaling captain William A. Martin, an assignment that ultimately prompted my research on captains of color. For the first time I realized

The *Golden City* was commanded by William A. Martin for two of his whale trips. John T. Gonsalves and Ayres J. Senna were also captains of the *Golden City*. *Courtesy of the New Bedford Whaling Museum*

the importance of whaling in American history—although I was an adult before I discovered that whaling had more to do with oil than food. Now, as I walk through the town in the dead of winter, largely absent of tourists, the white Federalist-style homes with black shutters and white picket fences stand out in the bare landscape. Above the doors are dates from the eighteenth and nineteenth centuries boasting of their antiquity—and marking an important part of American history. During those two centuries black people were enslaved in America and then freed. The simple elegance of these wooden homes belies their cost in the sacrifices their owners made thousands of miles away at sea to pay for them. Looking at the widow's walks on their roofs, one wonders what a captain's loved ones must have felt—longing? joy? dread?—when a ship appeared on the horizon, not knowing whether he had survived a voyage that could have taken several years.[29]

Records identify forty-one free black people on Martha's Vineyard in 1830: in Edgartown (twenty), Tisbury (twelve), and Chilmark (nine).[30] One of them, Captain William A. Martin, was born in Edgartown. Martin's first listed whale trip, on the *Benjamin Tucker*, began the day before he turned nineteen in 1846. As a green hand he earned $189.70 for the twenty-eight-month voyage. Later he shipped as an officer on board the *Almira* and the *Clarice*.[31]

On board the *Waverly*, which returned to port in 1854 after a three-year trip, the 1/37th lay he earned as cooper and boat-steerer was extraordinary; typically coopers earned 1/50th–1/60th lays, and boat-steerers 1/75th–1/80th. (Martin earned the equivalent of almost twice as much.) His promotion to boat-steerer made him one of the officers. Thereafter, his promotions were normal, except for rising to master at the relatively old age of forty-eight.

Other than newspaper articles referencing his great-grandmother, grandmother, and mother as a slave, former slave, or colored, respectively, there are few public acknowledgments that Martin was black. The announcement of his fiftieth wedding anniversary in the July 11, 1907, *Vineyard Gazette*, for example, does not mention Martin's race. Although Martin is included in Harold O. Lewis's private research, his life was first brought to public attention in 1997 by Elaine Weintraub and Carrie Tankard, founders of Martha's Vineyard's African American Heritage Trail. Martin has since been referenced in Robert Hayden and Karen Hayden's *African Americans on Martha's Vineyard and Nantucket* (1999), Arthur Railton's *History of Martha's Vineyard* (2006), Donald Warrin's *So Ends This Day* (2010), and Nancy Shoemaker's *Native American Whalemen and the World* (2015).

The crew list for the *Rebecca Sims* in 1857 lists Martin as "light"-skinned. The *Emma Jane's* 1881 crew list describes him as "dark," but these seem to be the only references in whaling records to his racial characteristics.

With a whaling career that extended from 1846 to 1887, Martin was well respected in his hometown of Edgartown and apparently received a good public education. It is unknown what kind of discrimination he might have faced growing up.

Martin's roots on Martha's Vineyard date back to colonial days, when his great-grandfather, Sharper Michael, became the island's first casualty of the Revolutionary War, killed by a wayward musket ball from the British privateer *Cerberus*.[32]

Born to a troubled and unwed mother, Rebecca Ann, in 1827, he was raised by his grandmother Nancy Martin. "Black Nance," according to the

The *Eunice H. Adams*, captained by William A. Martin and also John T. Gonsalves and Jasper M. Ears. *Courtesy of the New Bedford Whaling Museum*

Vineyard Gazette report of her death in the January 1857, was fond of children and attentive to their wants—and "few among us . . . at some time have not been indebted to her." Black Nance was thought to be a witch, and many believed that her incantations provided "good or bad luck to those bound on long voyages." The *Gazette* article added that "her strange power and influence over many continued till the day of her death."

Although she never saw her grandson become captain (she died in 1856 and his first captaincy was in 1878), one could speculate that her powers contributed to Martin's success. He was well known through the activities of his mother and grandmother, and his education at the Edgartown School no doubt helped him get chosen as log keeper on several early trips to sea. Black people who could read and write almost twenty years before the Civil War were rare.

Martin made at least fourteen voyages, from the first one at age sixteen until 1890, when the *Eunice H. Adams*, his last command, was damaged in a storm and Martin was injured.

Martin's voyage as master of the *Eunice H. Adams*, which left New Bedford for the North Atlantic on October 16, 1887, was difficult and ended badly. The ship's log offers some details of the trip.

The inscription "Remarks of a Whaling Voyage on Board . . . Brig *E. H. Adams*, W. A. Martin Master,"[33] is written across the top of each of the two facing log pages and appears to have been written at one time, probably at the beginning of the trip.

October 16, 1887: "Took our anchor from port of New Bedford at 9 O'clock AM and shaped our course for sea with a company of 25 all told. At 12m [noon] discharged the Pilot. Wind blowing strong from South west. At 3 O'clock PM kept off and steered for Tarpaulin cove. Came at anchor at 6 PM in eight fathoms of water. So ends this day."

The concise and legible log generally records only what was important: the date, weather, and sometimes location of the ship. Entries finish with "So ends this day"—exceptions sometimes include the information that he saw nothing, no other ships or creatures. It appears the first mate, Arthur O. Gibbons, was the writer.

Incessant high winds and bad weather hampered the trip: "the wind blew so that we could not lower the boats"; "strong winds"; "heavy" and "continuous gales"; "squally with rain" were the expressions most commonly used from October 1887 to January 1890, the last month of Captain Martin's time on board.

There were plenty of accidents (men falling, sometimes overboard) and illnesses, some specified as diarrhea and mumps. This had become a bad luck voyage, although the log gives no indication that Martin was distressed about it or felt sorry for himself.

A storm that began December 1 was bad enough to damage one of the whaleboats, and although not specifically indicated in the log, Hegarty says the brig was damaged on December 6. The damage caused severe leakage that continued for the next year with notations of up to 400 strokes per hour (strokes referring to a seesaw-like pump manned by two men); the number represented how many strokes were necessary in a twenty-four-hour period to keep the ship from filling with seawater and sinking. There are two log entries of "4,000 stroke days," indicating full-time pumping (every twenty seconds). The crew wanted no part of this. When the ship came into Port Royal, South Carolina, for repairs, a crewman jumped ship, hoping to escape to land, but was returned by a passing boat. The crew (excepting three men) "sent a letter on shore to the authorities stating that they considered the vessel unseaworthy. And that they did not wish to go to sea in the vessel again."

On December 21, some members of the crew deserted and others refused to work. One crewman jumped ship, went to Beaufort, and returned with a lawyer who interviewed the crew. Evidently nothing came of it because the ship raised anchor and headed for sea on January 3 with a full crew of twenty-five, the crew apparently having agreed to return to work.

By the end of the voyage, forty-seven men had served on the crew (including Martin and his replacement captain, Thomas E. Fordham), and between eight and fourteen men had deserted.

Captain Martin was diligent in reporting the food he "broke out" to feed the crew, including bread, water, flour, molasses, vinegar, sugar, butter, and, alternately, beef and pork. And there are no indications of crewmen being punished. The captain provided for occasional leave for the entire crew. The crew several times refused to work, but in each instance Martin was able to reengage them, so his managerial skills seemed adequate. The constant references to the ship leaking, harpoons breaking, major and minor accidents—and miserable weather—certainly reflect conditions that did not contribute to the happiness of the crew.

Martin's part of the log ends mysteriously on page 172—January 6, 1890. After a blank page, page 174 bears the inscription: "Remarks of A Whaling Voyage on Board Brig *E. H. Adams* T. E. Fordham, Master." The entry says only: "Remarks on board Thursday, Feb 20 arrived on board about noon and find all hands dissatisfied with everything brig leaking bad and provisions bad and long lays. So ends this day."

There is no indication of what happened to Martin, other than that he was replaced because of illness by Thomas E. Fordham, who returned the ship to Edgartown two months later.

It is unlikely that race played a factor in the crew desertions; it was more likely the condition of the ship and the bad weather. Several of the original crewmembers were black, with no doubt others hired at stops in the West Indies and Cape Verde. On this, William A. Martin's last whale trip, the *Eunice H. Adams* traveled from New Bedford to Cape Verde, St. Eustatius, Dominica, Monserrat, St. Michaels, Barbados, Norfolk, Virginia, and Beaufort and Port Royal, South Carolina. Oil prices had dropped by this time, and the value of the two dozen whales killed on the trip in today's dollars was a modest $238,000.

The *Eunice H. Adams* made one more whaling trip three years after its return to Edgartown, from August 1893 to September 1894, under the command of Clarence J. Silvia—and his replacement, Captain John T. Gonsalves.

On July 2, 1857, Martin had married Sarah G. Brown of Chappaquiddick, who was mostly black but part Wampanoag. (Her father, Abraham

Photograph of William A. Martin's headstone, by Jeanna Shepard. *Author's collection*

Brown, the son of a former slave, married Lucy Wamp [or Wayman], who was "half Indian, one fourth negro, one fourth white.") Martin and Sarah celebrated fifty years of marriage two months before his death at age seventy-seven. The *Vineyard Gazette*'s announcement of the event starkly contrasts his failing health with his prowess as a captain: "Captain Martin has been a paralytic for the past seven years, and is now practically helpless. . . . To those who remember Captain Martin as he appeared some twenty-five years ago, and recall his quick, alert movements and crisp, decisive speech, qualities which went far to make him a successful whaleman, it is difficult to realize his utter helplessness at the present time, and he has the deep sympathy of all in the community."

There is little information about the two decades of Martin's life after his last whale trip other than his paralysis for the final seven years, but it is likely he had earned enough for a modest retirement.[34] There is plenty of evidence that Captain William A. Martin was a competent master, but despite a note in the May–June 1999 *Footsteps: African American History*, it seems unlikely that Martin had "amassed a considerable fortune." Martin's home was modest in scale, design, and location compared with those of white captains of the time, almost all of whom had homes with water views in Edgartown. Of course, any black man owning a home in those days was unique. William and Sarah's house still stands on Chappaquiddick, an island across the harbor from those gleaming captains' homes in Edgartown on Martha's Vineyard. Captain Martin and Sarah are buried nearby. Little else remains of this man's legacy.

Anthony P. Benton (1843–?)

Anthony Benton, born in 1843 in Maio, Cape Verde, was Master Joseph Benton's older brother. He captained whale ships from 1876 to 1899 and was responsible for capturing about forty-five whales with a value today of $2.7 million. From the time of his first command on the *Pedro Varela* in November 1878 until September 1886 he spent all but six months at sea whaling.

The log keeper on board the *Ohio* (1881–85) under Benton's command wrote, "I think we Have gut forward the meanest Set of men that Ever sailed from New Bedford, as Ever will again Thay [*sic*] is some of them in hot water all the time. We Have English Dutch Irish Germans and Portugeas [*sic*] French. And a number of different Nations."

The *Ohio's* log indicates that the second mate ordered a crewman named Ignacio Gomes to learn how to steer the boat. When Gomes refused, the mate pushed him; Gomes responded by stabbing him in the back. Captain Benton struck Gomes twice with a belaying pin, strung him to the rigging, and later put him in irons in the hold for two weeks, letting him out during the day to scrub try-pots.[35] The punishment could have been worse, including lashes. Although flogging was outlawed in America in 1850, at least sixty-two incidents were recorded in logs afterward.[36]

Benton took the *Wave* to Hudson Bay in northern Canada in June 1885 to catch migrating whales at the end of winter, just as the Basques used to do. When cold weather came, a house was erected on deck, and snow was used to buttress it against the cold. Over the winter, temperatures plunged to 40° below zero; one crewmember died of scurvy and another eight almost died as well. Finally, sailing with the thaw, they caught a whale in July but due to the weather had to cut it loose. They managed to catch it again three days later; it was the only one they caught on the trip, but it was a big 150-barrel whale.

Skippering the *Tamerlane* out of New Bedford in 1888, Benton headed for the North Pacific intending to relocate to San Francisco, the leading whaling port of the day. Whalebone (baleen) had become the primary product by then. In the South Atlantic the ship's steering failed, and they put into the Falklands for repairs. The first, second, and third mates all deserted ship there; writer Donald Warrin concludes it was due to racism.[37]

Benton hired replacement officers, and the *Tamerlane* made Cape Horn and turned into the Pacific. Benton was writing the log by then and reported the ship was out of medicine, with seven men sick with scurvy. They "could not whale it if we saw the chance," he wrote, and the *Tamerlane* reached San Francisco with oil valued at only $63,312. New Bedford was listed as the home port for two more trips, then the *Tamerlane* used San Francisco as home port for its final three voyages, the last of which saw it wrecked off of Hilo, Hawaii, on February 2, 1892.[38] One may assume that there were survivors, and there is no indication Benton was lost, but there is no further information as to his fate.

Mutiny

I sincerely believe that the captains of whaleships at the present day are the most cruel and unfeeling men (at sea) of any class of people on the face of the Earth.

—JOSEPH EAYRES of the *Gratitude*, November 1841[39]

In his introduction to Philip Purrington's *Anatomy of a Mutiny* Charles Batchelder notes that "during the century and a half before 1906 . . . about 2,600 American vessels made some 15,000 whaling voyages. Seventy-one of these voyages, less than half of one percent, are recorded as having had mutinies or other more surreptitious acts against the 'establishment.'" Sometimes, though, men could take no more—of bad food, harsh discipline, boredom, and life at close quarters—and mutiny was the result. Men of color were involved in some of these cases. Joseph Roderick had an entire ship revolt against his leadership, and John T. Gonsalves relieved an entire crew on board the *Charles W. Morgan* as a way of avoiding one. Frederick Hussey was on board the *Cape Horn Pigeon* when the steward stabbed the captain. Because mutinies were so rare, and often so violent, they became worldwide news when they did occur.

THE *CAPE HORN PIGEON* (1854)

The *Cape Horn Pigeon* sailed in 1854 under the command of Captain William Almy. Eleven of the thirty crewmembers were black, including a boat-steerer and Frederick Hussey, who became a captain years later when he replaced Almy on another trip. On this voyage, the steward (identified in the New Bedford crew list as John Pimmg Coleman) stabbed Almy following a disturbance. The incident may not have been an actual mutiny, but the steward *did* attack the captain.[40]

THE *JUNIOR* (1857)

On Christmas Eve 1857, after 157 days at sea without catching a whale, the crew of the whale ship *Junior* awoke to a mutiny. Conditions on board were terrible. The men had to eat rotten food described by crewmen as "beef that was soft and discolored and possessed a terrible odor. Bread that was old and moldy and full of weevils, so full, said one witness, that its own maggoty strength sufficed to move it across the table."[41]

A substantial amount has been written about the causes and effects of the mutiny on the *Junior*. An inexperienced captain left management to an insensitive first mate, Nelson Prevost, who treated the crew like cattle, addressed them with insulting names, and subjected them to frequent floggings. He was at least consistent in his xenophobia, calling various men among the multinational crew "damned Mickey," "damned Indian," and the probably not well-received "black Arab." At least twelve of the thirty-two crewmen (and possibly three others) were men of color—including the black third mate, John Smith. It is likely that Charles H. Stanley (black) was one of the mutineers. According to the New Bedford Whaling Museum's crew list, no one present on that voyage ever went whaling again.[42]

THE *PEDRO VARELA* (1910)

The *Pedro Valera* was captained by three captains of color: Anthony Benton in 1876; Antone José Senna in 1891; and Frank Lopes for trips in 1917, 1918, and 1919 when the ship and all hands were lost at sea. On its voyage of 1910, with a white captain, five men were arrested for mutiny after damaging the boat in order to get off the ship. The story in an August 1910 newspaper article titled "Prisoners Tell Thrilling Story" indicates that only one had ever been whaling, and the others were apparently unprepared for conditions on a whaling expedition. The five—all white—complained about everything: the rough seas, the food, the constant work, only a pint of water for shaving and a bucket to wash clothes in, and being upbraided by the captain for playing cards and disturbing crewmen trying to sleep. One was quoted as saying, "From the very start the conditions on the schooner were not pleasant. The afterguard and many of the others of the crew were Portuguese Negroes (Cape Verdeans) and they made it mighty unpleasant for us." The entitled crewmen were ultimately charged with plundering and disabling the ship.[43]

John Theofilo Gonsalves
(December 16, 1858–1928)

Don't sink the vessel. We are poor fishermen looking for sperm whale.
—Captain John T. Gonsalves to a German submarine captain, 1918

John Gonsalves was one of the more productive whaling captains of color, if the number of voyages he took (at least 32) and number of whales he killed (calculated at about 189) are any indication.

There is some dispute over whether Captain Gonsalves was actually a man of color, at least according to his grandson Dan Rodrigues. Mr. Rodrigues said his late older brother's research on Gonsalves' genealogy indicated John T. Gonsalves' father was from Barcelona, Spain, and his mother was from Portugal. Gonsalves' racial characteristics are also widely questioned in the accounts of other whaling researchers such as Mary Malloy and whaling descendants from New Bedford such as Carl Cruz of the New Bedford Historical Association and James Lopes of the New Bedford Whaling Museum. Author Donald Warrin and a Cape Verdean exhibit at the New Bedford Whaling Museum both indicate Gonsalves was born on Brava in the Cape Verde Islands. Described as "dark" on the *Amelia*'s crew list, Gonsalves appears to be Cape Verdean and would thus be considered a man of color. He became a naturalized U.S. citizen on November 11, 1882, and was successful enough to own property in New Bedford, Fairhaven, Harwich, and Provincetown.[44]

Many of Gonsalves' trips began in Provincetown. He was one of about a dozen of Provincetown's famous masters and was a contemporary of Collins A. Stevenson and William T. Shorey, who whaled from Provincetown before moving on to San Francisco.

He was a cabin boy at age eleven on the *Roman*, which hunted elephant seals. Over his colorful fifty-year career Gonsalves served as master of twenty-four whaling voyages on a dozen different ships. Promoted along the way, Gonsalves was cook of the *Laetitia* for three years and boatswain on the *Sea Queen* for another three. He was second mate on the *Quickstep*, the *Amelia*, and the *Rising Sun* of Provincetown; second mate and navigator on the *Fannie Bond*; and at age thirty-two finally became a master on the *Rising Sun*. Being treated as a man of color may have had much to do with it taking Gonsalves a long twenty-one years to become master.

Crewmembers from the *Eleanor B. Conwell* (captained by John T. Gonsalves) and the *Sunbeam* (Theophilus M. Freitas and John Z. Silva) "gamming." *Courtesy of the New Bedford Whaling Museum*

The headline of an article in an unnamed newspaper dated August 9, 1905, reads: "*A MODERN LOG* Happenings on a New Bedford Whaler of 1905 an Exciting Day aboard the Schooner *Eleanor B. Conwell.* A Cuban Machete in a Red Handkerchief Remains as a Memento."[45] "Exciting" is a bit of an overstatement. Based on one of Gonsalves' logs, the article summarizes a successful trip whose sole excitement seems to have occurred when a bored or angry crewman threatened other crewmembers for some unstated reason and was lashed to the rigging for a ten-minute time-out.

Families of whalers saved scrapbooks of loved ones' escapades, and many of these have found their way to the New Bedford Whaling Museum Library. Often lacking dates or even names of publications, these clippings leave much to the imaginations of researchers. The August 9 article does include some extremely useful information. Noting that there had been hundreds of New Bedford whale ships fifty years earlier (compared with twenty-five at the time), the article indicates that most of the crew were Cape Verdeans, including the captains, and states that "nothing eventful" occurred on the thirteen-month trip. At least two men died (no causes referenced), however, another five deserted (all replaced by Gonsalves), and many suffered illnesses (one had rheumatism, the rest had unknown ailments). The ship reprovisioned at several ports and made contact with other whale ships, including the *Sunbeam*, *Golden City*, and *Adelia Chase*. It returned with 550 barrels of sperm oil, about all that the relatively small schooner could hold.

Another unidentified newspaper article, dated March 4, 1917, recounts Captain John T. Gonsalves' record at sea, describing him as one of the "big bodied" masters of the time. The article's opening sentence—"Captain John T. Gonsalves somehow can't keep away from the water"—was no exaggeration. Gonsalves spent fifty-three of his seventy years as a whaler. The story ends: "He has had many boats stove up by whales and has been aboard of the boats too, but he never lost a man"—a remarkable achievement.

One of the more entertaining whaling stories involving Gonsalves occurred on the *A. M. Nicholson* in June 1918, when a German submarine surfaced and fired a shot across the whale ship's bow. One of the German officers ordered them to heave to, disembark, get into their whaleboats, and come alongside the submarine for questioning. When they explained that they were whaling, the officer inquired if they were doing any other type of fishing. Gonsalves replied no and implored: "For God's sake . . . don't sink this vessel. I am a poor man and it will ruin me, as I am a big owner in her." The German laughed and sent word down to his own captain, who came topside and told Gonsalves, "Don't you know that this is a poor time to buy vessel property when people are at war?" As Gonsalves was telling him that the boat had been acquired prior to the war, the *Ellen A. Swift* came into view, and Gonsalves confirmed it was also an American whaler. Satisfied, the German captain told him to get back on board his boat and get home as quickly as he could, and to not let them catch him or the other ship again. Cursing their bad luck—but thankful they were not sunk—both ships sailed home. Gonsalves had 625 barrels of oil on board at the time, and the *Ellen A. Swift* returned with 200 barrels of sperm oil—and a harrowing tale.[46]

Even as geezers, whaling captains were tough guys. An undated *Boston Herald* "special dispatch" from the New Bedford Whaling

Museum archives, dated October 24 (likely 1922), reports ex–whaling master Henry A. Morse's sneak attack on Gonsalves after a yearlong dispute. Morse socked Gonsalves in the face hard enough to knock him into the Acushnet River. Morse and Captain Joseph Senna had to jump into the river to save the sixty-five-year-old Gonsalves, who was taken to a local hospital. Morse, a small man of middle age, was arrested and charged with assault and battery.

A March 15, 1928, article in the *New Bedford Standard* reported that "word came to relatives in the area that Captain John Theophilo Gonsalves had passed away in the Cape Verde Islands." He was sixty-nine.[47] Captain John T. Gonsalves was inducted into Providence's Cape Verdean Hall of Fame in 2008.

FREDERICK HUSSEY (1828?–?)

Frederick Hussey was born in 1828 or 1829 in the Western Islands of the Pacific (New Guinea), where the people are variously described as Melanesian, Papuan, Negrito, Micronesian, or Polynesian. The official language, Tok Pisin, is a creole language. Hussey is described as "Dark" on one crew list.

Hussey must have had several voyages by 1854 when, at age twenty-six, he was a mate on the *Cape Horn Pigeon* when it sailed for the Indian Ocean from South Dartmouth with William Almy as captain. Eleven of the thirty-two crewmembers on the voyage were black, including another officer and a couple of boat-steerers.[48]

The crew list identifies them as:

John Pimmg Coleman, New York, steward
Peter Minge, Boston
Joaquin Antone Da Goaz, Cape Verde
Francisco Penale, Cape Verde
Francis Ferguson, cook
*John Smith, green hand
Frederick Hussey, first mate/master
William A. Taylor, boat-steerer (1/47)
Simmons Kanaka (the generic name given to Polynesians),
   boat-steerer (1/75)[49]

*"John Smith" was the name given by 363 whalers, from which I deduce several may have been aliases of men who could have been runaway slaves.

On this trip, for reasons unrecorded, the mulatto steward John Pimmg Coleman stabbed Captain Almy, an assault that provided Frederick Hussey with his first command as a replacement captain.[50] Although badly injured Almy did not die—that time. Hussey again served with Almy as his first mate on the *Roscoe* in 1859. On that trip he became the replacement after a whale killed Captain Almy and seven others in two whaleboats.

Hussey was master of the *Stella* from 1860 to 1864, first mate of the *Gazelle* in 1866, and served twice in unnamed positions on the *Benjamin Cummings* in 1871 and again from November until December 1875 when the *Benjamin Cummings* was lost at Fogo in the Cape Verde Islands. The 305-ton bark, built in South Dartmouth in 1854, had a whaling career half as long as Captain Frederick Hussey's, who, not pressing his own luck, served his last trip on the *Benjamin Cummings* at age forty-six.[51]

JOSEPH RODERICK

Joseph Roderick, the forty-nine-year-old first mate of the *Charles W. Morgan* (1908–10), was illiterate and had no navigational skills. Apparently, though, he was a good whaler, because when Captain Arthur O. Gibbons got sick in June 1909 and the *Morgan* was taken to South Africa, Roderick was officially appointed as his replacement.[52] Recognizing Roderick's limitations, the crew refused to raise anchor until a navigator was chosen as well—and the *Morgan* finally departed on June 22. Less than two months later, on August 2, the ship returned and one Charles A. Church assumed command of the ship. No doubt anticipating his reduction in rank, Roderick, according to the log, spent the last night of the trip drunk in his cabin—and was summarily discharged when the ship reached port.

His career appears to have begun on the *Bertha* in 1887 when he was twenty-seven. He crewed on the *Navarch* when he was thirty-two and is listed as "dark" on the crew list. After the *Charles W. Morgan* fiasco, he signed on for trips with the *A. E. Whyland* in 1910 and the *Margarett* in 1921 at age sixty-one.[53]

Being a good whaler—probably an excellent harpooner—did not make a man a good captain. Getting the crew home safely was just as important as returning with a full hull. Joseph Roderick did have a short stint as captain, but he was not competent enough to get a crew home safely. And in this case the crew seemed prepared to mutiny as a result.

Cannibalism

Cap, what's the news of the *Nancy Ann*?
Tell me the news mister, if you can.
We are just in from around Biscay
But there ain't no news for you today.
Our ship was blowed on the rocks by squalls,
And the crew was et by cannibals.
But there ain't no news.[54]

Cannibalism is rarely cited as an occupational hazard, but men stranded at sea without food have been known to take desperate measures to survive. The euphemism "lifeboat strategy" for cannibalism is attributed to whaling. "The custom of the sea" is another euphemism for cannibalism: sailors left on board disabled ships miles from shore or help would draw straws to see which would sacrifice his life so the others could live. More often than not, survivors waited until others had died before partaking of the grisly solution.

Walter Noble Burns sailed on board black master William T. Shorey's bark the *Alexander* in 1890 with shipmate "Nels Nelson, a red-haired, red-bearded old Swede" he called the best sailor on board. Nelson was also a good yarn spinner. Among his stories was one about the time he had been cast off in an open boat with three others and survived by eating the flesh of a dead shipmate.[55]

More than several islands in the South Seas whaling grounds were home to tribes and cultures that practiced ritualistic cannibalism—that is, not for sustenance. Whalers had to be wary when they stopped to resupply at these way stations. More often than not, as in the story of the *Essex*, the "lifeboat strategy" was something to be feared.

CHAPTER 6

──── ⚜ ────

Sometimes the Whale Won

*T*here were hundreds of ways to die on a whale ship. Robert R. Newell identifies some of them in *The Grisly Side of Whaling*.[1] Crewmen fell to their death from the ship's rigging, were slain by Native Americans, died from scurvy or other ailments, were dragged underwater by fouled lines, were killed while cutting in (including Captain Brown of the *Ontario*) or while fighting whales, and drowned or died from other accidental causes. Newell claims that 71 mates and 242 crewmen were killed by whales, although there is no indication of his source or the time frame or location. He also indicates that a Captain Holmes and two of his mates on the *Sea Fox* were killed by a powder explosion.[2]

The *Essex*

On November 20, 1820, the *Essex* of Nantucket was more than a thousand miles from land in the Pacific Ocean when First Mate Owen Chase's whaleboat was "stove" by a whale—for the second time that week. While returning to the *Essex* to repair the boat he saw an eighty-five-foot whale

> lying quietly, with his head in the direction of the ship. He spouted two or three times, and then disappeared. In less than two or three seconds he came up again, about the length of the ship off, and made directly for us. . . . His appearance and attitude gave us at first no alarm, but . . . observing him a ship's length off, I ordered the boy at the helm to put it hard up, intending to sheer off and avoid him. The words were scarcely out of my mouth before he came down upon us with full speed and struck the ship with his head, just forward of the fore chains. He gave us such an appalling and tremendous jar as

nearly threw us on our faces. The ship brought up . . . violently as if she had struck a rock and trembled for a few minutes like a leaf.[3]

The angry whale hit the *Essex*, crippling her and forcing the crew to abandon ship. The 238-ton, 100-plus-foot-long *Essex* sank about 10 minutes later. The 85-foot whale probably weighed about 70 tons, could swim between 21 and 27 miles an hour, and had a rock-hard head that could withstand the pressure of depths of up to 2 miles below the surface of the ocean. That day, the whale won.

The survivors sat in the small whaleboats for two days amid the wreckage as the realization sank in that no help was coming and they were on their own. Thus began the grisly story of the last of the nine trips of the *Essex*, the single most tragic and deadly whaling trip of them all. The chilling story, said to be the model for *Moby-Dick*, is recounted in Nathaniel Philbrick's *In the Heart of the Sea: The Tragedy of the Whaleship* Essex and depicted in the 2015 movie of the same name.

Seven of the *Essex's* twenty-one crewmen were black. Four were cannibalized by the survivors, one was buried at sea, one went missing but probably died, and one (Henry De Witt) had the luck (or the foresight) to desert beforehand. Only nine survived the four months at sea in tiny, open boats. It took nearly a year for the last survivors to make it back to Nantucket.[4]

Essex Crew

Name	Rank	Result
Bond, William (Negro)	Steward	Missing
Chappel, Thomas	Boat-steerer	Survived (Henderson Island)
Chase, Owen	First mate	Survived
Coffin, Owen	Sailor	Shot, body eaten for food
Cole, Isaac	Sailor	Died, body eaten for food
De Witt, Henry (Negro)	Sailor	Survived (deserted)
Hendricks, Obed	Boat-steerer	Missing
Joy, Matthew	Second mate	Died, buried at sea
Lawrence, Benjamin	Boat-steerer	Survived
Nickerson, Thomas	Cabin boy	Survived
Peterson, Richard (Negro)	Sailor	Died, buried at sea

Pollard, George	Captain	Survived
Ramsdell, Charles	Sailor	Survived
Ray, Barzillai	Sailor	Died, body eaten for food
Reed, Samuel (Negro)	Sailor	Died, body eaten for food
Sheppard, Isaiah (Negro)	Sailor	Died, body eaten for food
Shorter, Charles (Negro)	Sailor	Died, body eaten for food
Thomas, Lawson (Negro)	Sailor	Died, body eaten for food
Weeks, Seth	Sailor	Survived (Henderson Island)
West, Joseph	Sailor	Missing
Wright, William	Sailor	Survived (Henderson Island)

Source: Philbrick, *In the Heart of the Sea*, pp. xvii, 69.

The *Essex* was not the only whale ship defeated by whales, whether by accident or intent. On December 24, 1847, the *Acushnet* harpooned two whales—a cow and a calf. The two injured whales destroyed two whaleboats, damaged another, and killed six of the crew before they got away. On September 29, 1807, the *Union* from Nantucket struck a whale at night and promptly sank. On August 20, 1851, the *Ann Alexander* was rammed by a whale in the Pacific and sank. Martha's Vineyard captain Joseph Dias reported that on December 12, 1851, his ship *Pocahontas* was hunting a school of sperm whales when one turned on the *Pocahontas* and rammed it; the blow broke several planks in the ship's side at the waterline, causing "the vessel to leak at once at the rate of 250 strokes per hour." In March 1902 the bark *Kathleen* from New Bedford was attacked and sunk by a sperm whale in the South Atlantic, but the crew was rescued after a time afloat in the small whaleboats. August Paul Gomes was on board the *Kathleen* as a cabin boy.[5]

August Paul Gomes

Born in Cape Verde, August P. Gomes had a clear path to the post of master, beginning at age seventeen on the *Kathleen*, which left New Bedford on October 22, 1901. That trip must have been one of the more interesting ways to gain experience, because a whale sank the 206-ton bark on March 17, 1902. Young Gomes earned $21.50 for the five months. Widely reported as black, he signed on as a seaman on the *Greyhound* (1903–7)

The *Kathleen*. It is unclear what these men are doing. The *Kathleen* gained fame after being sunk by a whale in 1902. *Courtesy of the New Bedford Whaling Museum*

on an Atlantic trip that returned with an amazing 4,625 barrels of sperm oil. August Gomes went to sea again from July 15, 1907, to 1908 on the *John R. Manta* from Provincetown. In the successive years from 1912 to 1919, Gomes served on the *Arthur V. S. Woodruff*, *Greyhound*, and *A. M. Nicholson* as an officer, earning his way from third mate to first mate before becoming a master himself on the *Woodruff* on November 6, 1919. The *Woodruff* was lost at Barbados on April 19, 1920.

From November 1920 to September 1921 Gomes captained the *A. M. Nicholson*, returning with 400 barrels of sperm oil. On this trip he endured two hurricanes off Bermuda in which he lost three whaleboats and one man. His final voyage was again on the *Nicholson*, which left on April 10, 1922, before it was sold as a Brava packet ship and used to haul goods to Cape Verde—and Cape Verdeans on the return trip seeking new lives in the United States.[6]

The *Wanderer*

The *Wanderer*, known to have had mostly crews of color, may have been the last whale ship to narrowly escape disaster before whaling finally ended. A newspaper article from 1912 describes an attack by an infuriated sperm whale six hundred miles off Barbados, killing one of the men, injuring another, and destroying two of the whaleboats. The whale made a head-on run on the *Wanderer*, which is probably what killed it. The whale was found floating four miles away the next morning during the funeral of the crewman. Wasting not, Captain S. A. Mosher cut short the ceremony and brought in the whale, noting that its remains "made just 100 barrels."[7]

Legends of rogue whales date back to the fifth-century tale of Porphyrius, which terrorized Byzantium's shipping lanes. Mocha Dick was an albino seventy-foot sperm whale, one of the two (along with the one that sank the *Essex*) that inspired *Moby-Dick*. Its name came from Mocha Island off the coast of Chile, the gateway to the Pacific Ocean. The whale prowled those waters and was believed to have killed thirty men. During the one hundred attempts to capture it over the course of twenty-eight years, Mocha Dick destroyed about twenty of the ships that hunted it. Explorer and writer Jeremiah Reynolds wrote that Mocha Dick was finally killed but took a whaleboat with it. Ralph Waldo Emerson overheard a sailor talking about a white whale named Old Tom that "crushed the boats to small chips" in its jaws. Caldera Dick was a sperm whale that could snap boats "like twigs with one blast of its tail," even after it was harpooned. It too was killed eventually.

Herman Melville's fictional tale of the white whale is rooted in truth, and his portrayals are accurate. "Timor Jack" was the colorful name his character Ishmael used for a whale "scarred like an iceberg." "New Zealand Tom" was said to have destroyed nine boats and was "the terror of all cruisers in the vicinity of Tattoo Land," and "Don Miguel" was "marked like an old tortoise with mystic hieroglyphs upon the back."[8]

Whaling Captains Killed by Whales

At least forty-seven captains were killed by whales (see appendix E).[9] Whales were color-blind when it came to killing the whalers who hunted them. Severino Pierce and Joseph P. Benton, both black, were killed by whales. Master Peter Green was promoted to captain after his captain

(Seth Myrick, himself a replacement captain) was probably killed by a whale. We do not know what happened to other masters of color lost at sea, but the odds are that their deaths had more to do with whaling than the whales themselves.

SEVERINO D. PIERCE (PIRES) (OCTOBER 19, 1817–JUNE 29, 1871)

Racial identification in whaling days was not always obvious or properly recorded, and researching the topic today is difficult. A few generations of mixed-race sexual unions tended to make darker skin light, while extended time on sunny decks typically made light skin darker. Diarist Mary Chipman reflected on meeting Captain Severino D. Pierce in 1859: "Portuguese with . . . considerable black blood in his veins, but a very likely man for all that."[10]

Pierce's given name was Pires, and he was born on the island of Brava in Cape Verde in 1817. On his first known trip he served on the *Magnolia* as second mate from New Bedford to the Indian Ocean from 1845 to 1848. If that was really his first trip, it would have been fairly unusual for him to have been an officer, but he could have shipped as a seaman or in some lesser capacity and been promoted along the way on the three-year voyage. A month after he got back, in November 1848, Pierce was married in Stonington, Connecticut, to Harriet H. Nichols. They were married twenty-three years, during which Pierce was on land for fewer than thirty-two months.[11]

Pierce was first mate on the *America* for a three-year trip to the North Pacific from June 1851 to June 1854. Back on the *Magnolia* from October 1854 to May 1858, he served as first mate again; on the subsequent trip to the North Pacific beginning July 27, 1858, he was the master. The ship was condemned in Sydney, Australia, in 1862 but sent sperm oil and whale oil back to New Bedford worth $57,120 ($1,645,000 today). He was a replacement captain on the *Europa* during another successful five-year trip (1862–67) for Captain Anthony Milton, who was reported lost in 1865. Pierce then served as first mate and log keeper of the *Washington Freeman*, which sailed from Fairhaven in 1868 to 1870.

Pierce's luck ran out on June 29, 1871. While master of the *Thriver* on a trip from Boston to the Atlantic, he was killed, presumably by a whale.

He was responsible for more than $4.6 million in sperm oil and whale oil and whalebone during his career.

JOSEPH P. BENTON (BENTO)
(1861–JUNE 15, 1901)

All whale ship captains commanded respect. All of them were hardened men of the sea who brooked no disorder or disobedience. But even in that context Joe Bento stood out. He first appears at the age of twenty in records for the bark *Ohio*, which left New Bedford on November 1, 1881, under the command of his brother Anthony, headed for the Atlantic hunting grounds. Ten years later he earned his first master position on the *Clara L. Sparks*, and he later captained the *A. R. Tucker*. Benton was often the first in the whaleboats when a whale was sighted and harpooned the most whales. That eagerness got him killed.

Joe Benton was born in Maio, Cape Verde, in 1861 and was a successful captain on a few voyages, though not nearly so successful as his brother Anthony. On Joe's trip as master of the schooner *Clara L. Sparks* from July 2, 1891, to August 2, 1895, he and his crew killed 63 whales that produced 900 barrels of sperm oil and 200 barrels of whale oil, grossing today's equivalent of about $714,964. If his percentage was the 1/17th lay typical of most masters of the day, he would have earned about $42,000 per year (in today's dollars) on this voyage.

The *Clara L. Sparks* was a small schooner built in Salisbury, Massachusetts, in 1861 and listed at 130 tons. It shipped for whaling thirteen times between 1862 and 1898, always—except for Joseph Benton's trip from New Bedford—from Provincetown. It was reported condemned in the Seychelles in 1899.[12]

Ship's logs are not easy reading, but Benton's log for the *Clara L. Sparks* on the voyage lasting from July 2, 1891, to August 2, 1895, is a fascinating and detailed study of whaling life toward the end of the era.[13] Some of the actions it documents could have gotten him thrown in jail. His handwriting is neat, and the consistency of each entry reflects a true professional. He did not take insubordination lightly and ran a tight ship. That meant no fighting and no loud talk among the men.

On March 10, 1892, he intervened in a dispute between a crewman and a steward, pronouncing the steward to be correct without even interviewing the crewman. In his log entry for that night he wrote, "For I never speak with the men." He fought with his men and his officers (and won) and did not hesitate to use the whip and irons to adjust behavior to his liking. Though flogging was outlawed in 1850, Benton had no problem using it for punishment, including for the "crime" of reporting it.

There were times when he was sick for alarmingly long periods (and others wrote the log), and it is fairly easy to tell when he was bored or distracted because his handwriting got worse and his words less distinct. Handwriting aside, I was unable to guess at his emotions when reading the log. Regardless, though, there is no question who was in charge.

Sometimes listed as Joseph Bento, he identifies himself in his own handwriting as Joseph P. Benton. At times, he and other log keepers refer to him as Bento. The spelling is believed to be a phonetic type of short-hand rather than miscommunication or poor handwriting.

An entry in the log for January 7, 1892, offers a hint at how tough Captain Benton was. In the middle of a melee with a pod of whales:

> the starboard boat whale was killed by the iron, and the school brought too so snug and hit my line and I came to lose my whale [Benton had a harpoon gun powered by black powder that went off accidentally in the scrum] and hurt my hand so I could not work after the whale was pretty near dead. I asked my mate if he had the confidence enough to strike another whale as the second mate was coming close to us. He refused and said it was too late. So I told him if he did not have the confidence enough to strike one I would even if I was hurt.

It appears that the frenzied action continued—it is amazing that Benton's account is so devoid of emotion—and the mate was given other opportunities to strike a whale but did not. "I asked him the reason he did not come and make a chance, all he said was that the whales was all around him. So I told him never do any more whaling for me like that."

They killed whales until after sunset at 9 p.m. that day. The next day, January 8, Benton wrote that "at 4am we started the fire [signaling that they had begun butchering and trying the catch]—it was a calm, nice morning."

A total of fifty-nine men (including Benton) served on the 1891–95 voyage. On such a small ship, that number is a sure sign of many desertions (sixteen men signed on for the initial voyage; eleven were added on August 3, 1891). New names appear throughout the voyage, as was typical of the industry—green hands often decided one leg of a whaling voyage was enough, and on voyages such as this one tribulations and drama caused crew changes and dismissals. Fifteen of the men were black, including three of the four officers. Black master Valentine Rosa was on this trip as a mate and boat-steerer. Throughout the log there is little evidence that any crewmen were treated differently because of race (although one crew-member evidently disagreed).

Captain Benton's log indicates he had a modicum of education. Many whaling logs begin and end using almost identical words. They begin with the weather—the most important variable of a whaling trip. Benton, however, makes an effort to change his up, adding interesting facets of the day, activities, and his thoughts. For much of the log for this trip, his entries begin, "Remarks on board [day, date, and time]" or "[day, date] First part of this day commences . . ." He often ends with "So ended the day" or "So ends"—a ubiquitous expression in logs—and frequently lists the longitude and latitude of the ship's position.

Run-on sentences, poor spelling, and random capitalization abound, but his meaning and intentions are clear. He wrote with no apparent change in emotion—even on days when he was sick. His thirty-three-word log entry of December 25, 1891, does not mention Christmas—other holidays are also ignored.

Benton's log mostly details the pattern of life on board a relatively small ship: the frequent stops needed to resupply the boat with food and water and, of course, to remove the barrels of oil for shipment home. Necessary repairs were made while anchored; changing and maintenance of the sails and lines are mentioned frequently; and sometimes crewmen were replaced while in port. Some of the more difficult chores such as scraping the anchors or cleaning the cooking supplies were assigned to crewmen as punishment, and the log illustrates Captain Benton's and the crew's tempers shortening as the days wore on.

In the first sentence of that day's entry, Benton notes that he was a man short after one Charles H. Scott "diserted" and was replaced by Charles Williams, whose name comes up again later. Exiting New Bedford's harbor with "Cuttyhunk Island distant 2½ miles distant," he set the watches and appointed the crew to their responsibilities.

Within only a few days Benton reports a petty altercation: "[Black crewman] Frank Silva was threatening the man right before my very face that he would pay him when he got ashore so I stopped him and keep quiet and answer the question he was asked, so he allowed the man was a liar, very soon I was talking with Emile Cardoso . . . out comes this Frank [Silva] again and said he would fix him when he got ashore so he would not stop his threatening before me so I shut him in irons."

Irons were crudely fashioned handcuffs attached together with a short piece of chain. They could be hellish at sea, especially on a relatively small ship such as the *Clara L. Sparks* (130 tons). More so for acting up in front of the captain than the seemingly minor altercation itself, Frank Silva was placed belowdecks in irons from 7:20 a.m. until 3 p.m. that day, almost eight hours in darkness on a pitching, rolling ship.

On August 19, 1891, the *Sparks* was in the middle of the Atlantic Ocean, southeast of New Bedford and northwest of the Cape Verde Islands and just south the Western Ground, an area where thousands of whales were killed. The voyage's first whale was spotted, and although they got two boats into the water to give chase, the whale eluded them.

Captain Benton wrote, "So I lost 90 barrel whale for it was only 12 clock on day time was no time to try the whale." Notice that whaling captains describe a whale's size by the number of barrels it might produce rather than by its length or weight. An average size sperm whale was an 80-barrel whale, and a right whale, 150 barrels. Notice also the use of "I lost," which seems to indicate Benton took it personally.

On Friday, August 21, Frank Silva, who two days before had been in irons, killed the voyage's first whale—a seventy-barrel one that Benton described as small. A fifteen-barrel whale also caught was probably the larger one's offspring. Whales traveled in pods, and a baby rarely left its mother's side. Jim Murphy, author of *Gone a-Whaling*, notes that "whalemen were clever hunters. Knowing that whales were very protective parents, they often harpooned a calf first and then waited for the mother to return to help her injured baby."

Typical of many logs, Benton records other creatures seen on the trip, such as blackfish (pilot whales) and porpoises, which they sometimes killed for oil, food, or sport.

Benton diligently filled the log's margins with the provisions used, remaining, and added throughout the voyage. The description is not very appetizing. Food was one of the major causes of controversy on board ship. Fights were started and cooks were sometimes punished. Of 451 known mutinies in whaling, at least 3 were linked directly to poor food (*Globe* 1822, *Junior* 1857, and *Pedro Valera* 1876). The *Clara L. Sparks* had its share of food and water issues.

On March 10, 1892, Benton wrote: "A seaman Joseph Williams got a pot of water and carried it forward to wash his face or clothing after I had ordered my officers not to let anybody carry any water forward because I am short of water." A steward upbraided Williams—and unbeknownst to either, the captain heard the whole argument from below in his quarters. Williams got away without punishment that time, as did mate William D. Tolland the next day for opening a cask of "slops" (garbage) that he thought was bread but had been put in the wrong place. The mistake was highlighted by the laughter of the rest of the crew.

A few days later Benton had the first of several confrontations with a steward who evidently doubled as a cook. He seemed to like the man—or at least respected the challenges of the steward's job—since he was not punished like others who showed similar impudence. Benton castigated the steward for having just cleaned out his bread pan for the first time since they left New Bedford eight months earlier. He added: "If I only want to find a fault I could find enough of them, it ain't more than one hour ago since I hauled out one of your shirt sleeves in the pantry where you clean your dishes with it." As for the steward's bread, "Your pantry is dirty and I have questioned you all the time to keep the pantry clean, furthermore your bread is sour and no one can eat it."

Undaunted, the steward defended himself: "Captain when you came out from home you did not have no yeast provided so I could not make bread and I will give you 75 dollars if you can find any one that can make good bread without yeast." Benton backed down, writing, "You had best keep your 75 dollars for I do not want none of it."

Probably the most humorous episode recorded in the log occurred on August 24, 1892, about forty-five miles from St. Helena—a tiny, isolated British protectorate in the middle of the South Atlantic Ocean used by whalers as a stopping place for provisions and water, and also the site of

Napoleon's exile. Captain Benton was standing on his quarterdeck when an enraged Charles Williams approached him to complain: "Captain Benton, that makes 3 times that I would be sitting on my chest [in the forecastle] and this Antona Evero would come and fart right in my face. . . . Charlie called him a black nigger, and Antona cursed his mother." In an attempt to get to the bottom of the issue, Captain Benton interviewed both men, telling Williams that he should have come to him if he had a problem, and "in the first place I do not want any man to call another a bad name on board my vessel for I do not want any especially Nigger because I am a coloured man myself and all of my officers are coloured but one."

Perhaps overcome by anger, Williams apparently did not take the hint and continued talking. Benton shoved him around the deck, put him in irons, and "made him fast on the rigging." While Williams continued his tirade and threats, Benton had Antona put in irons, too, for about ten minutes, probably after Williams accused Benton of favoritism toward his presumed countryman.

"Oh you need not put Antone in irons," Williams said. Benton told Williams "not to tell him what to do and would punish him accordingly. . . . I have nothing to do with Portugal. I am Portuguese birth but American citizen. I told him if he did not stop I will stop his noise for him. I should gag him with a belaying pin in his mouth."

Benton went on to tell Williams he could complain to the American consul (presumably at St. Helena when they docked), and that he could stay there (tied to the rigging in irons) five minutes or two hours. Williams responded, "Oh American Consul you can buy them for a plug of tobaco [sic]." Williams finally calmed down and was let out of irons. Indicating the whole fracas lasted almost an hour and a half, Benton wrote that this was Charles Williams' "third offence"; no more is written about him.

The entry for Thursday, August 25, 1892, details the stop in St. Helena. While in port, Captain Benton had the crew wash the schooner and transfer casks of oil to the schooner *Lottie Beard* to be sent back to New Bedford, as well as taking on "14 tons of [fresh] water," which works out to about 94 barrels of water weighing 291 pounds each—all brought on board by hand.

On November 2 of that year, there is a Captain Winslow on board, and a note in the log (written by another hand) says that Captain Benton was sick. No reason or diagnosis is provided, but Benton remained ill until mid-December.

In early January 1894 the *Sparks* was near Argentina, and the tenor of the log had changed. Benton reported that the men were getting sick, although the log does not specify the illness or the cause. Henry Bibeiro was logged as sick January 20–31, for example. Several times the writing on the log changes hands, indicating Benton was not in the best of health either, although that is not mentioned.

On February 23, José B. Gomes, standing watch for the captain, noted that Antone Lopes refused lookout duty. His punishment was to scrape the deck. On March 18, several crewmembers found themselves locked in irons. This rates only a brief note in the log. They arrived back at St. Helena on March 23, where five men were fired five days later when they refused duty, and the second and third mates were discharged on March 29. The ship left St. Helena on April 10. On April 23, Antone Lewis' name comes up in the context of the phrase "strictly attended to," leaving to the imagination what happened to him.

By May 13, 1893, the log shows definite signs that someone other than Benton was writing it. The handwriting is relatively neat, and the entries are more detailed than Captain Benton's entries. May 13 featured still another controversy over food. In one incident, the port watch seemed satisfied with the dinner, but the starboard watch complained they had been shorted and refused to eat. "Charles Isaacs he refused his dinner and said it was not good and complained that he only got meat twice a week." This was the second time Isaacs had voiced issues about the food. Another crewman, Thomas Bennet, for whatever reason, "told a falsehood" to the captain when asked what the problem was, saying they had eaten dinner. The result was that "the Captain put him in irons [for ninety minutes] in order to prevent any more trouble." It seems Captain Benton's illness left him with far less patience.

On May 16 they captured a blackfish (pilot whale), and the next day "took the blubber off the black fish and minced it." On Friday, May 18, they "started the works to boil the black fish," finishing at 7 p.m. This notation is further proof that when they hunted whales, they were not too particular about the species.

On May 21 the crew noticed a leak in the boat after leaving St. Helena. After the ship anchored south of the intriguingly named Shark Point on May 23 for repairs, the harbormaster refused to allow the men ashore because the ship lacked a bill of health. The ship stayed at anchor for the leak to be attended to until May 31.

The June 9 entry indicates that Captain Benton had taken sick with a fever. Nonetheless on June 11, business continued and the *Clara L. Sparks* landed a large sperm whale—it took four days to boil and produced a substantial 83 barrels of oil, for a value in today's dollars in excess of $57,000. The whale may have been 75,000 pounds and 50 feet long—close to half the length of the *Clara L. Sparks* (about 106 feet).[14]

Prior to that it had been three months since they last captured a whale (other than the modestly sized blackfish), and behavior clearly suffered in the interim when the crew was not busy.

The days wore on, with several sightings of porpoises and an English "gun boat" but no whales. On June 25, George Liu, Robert Brooks, and Antone Lopes apparently decided to create their own entertainment by throwing some of the ship's precious firewood at porpoises. The cook reported it to the captain, who refused them water and had them scrub down the bricks of the try-pots before placing them in irons.

Meanwhile the ship continued to leak. The crew spent July 2–6 trying to fix it while the ship listed badly and was difficult to sail. Ingeniously, they brought "all our empty casks" up from below "and put them as far aft as we could get them and filled them with salt water"; they right the ship and pump out what water they could. They also put full casks of fresh water on the stern to balance the ship until they finally found the hole beneath the copper sheathing. The water was rough that day and they could not do anything else—but they did send a letter back to America with a passing schooner. Spotting whales at 11:30 that morning, they struck one, but after a chase the "iron parted" (the barb of the harpoon came out) and they lost it. The listing boat remained of concern.

On July 6 Charles Isaacs and Charles Bennet got into a fight and were "put in punishment to scrape iron works."

It is not clear whether Benton was still sick, but someone else was writing the log. On July 16 Captain Benton found beef and bread on the forecastle floor. Bringing it on deck, he learned from two of the men that

Henry Silvester had thrown it on the floor and called the captain a "son of a bitch" and "son of a whore." Silvester denied it but told the captain that Charles Isaacs had also called him names. Benton put them both in irons. They were released two days later on July 18 and put to work scraping the iron works (try-pots). On July 24 both were relieved from the scraping "with the understanding that they shall behave better and never make any more trouble."

On August 8, they caught five whales. As was the custom, they attached empty kegs to each whale killed so it would not be lost while the crew was getting the next one. One apparently did get away, and Benton, relentless, lowered a boat to go find it—at 10 p.m. in a pitch black night. The next day they commenced the cutting, and the boiling took two days. While the work was being done, they were served only "flour and hard bread."

On September 6, one whale came to the aid of another and damaged a whaleboat so badly that it had to be towed back to the ship. One officer was "hurt," but there is no note of his condition or any treatment he may have been given.

The next day's log entry notes that one of the whaleboats harpooned a cow and a calf and was lost to sight. The whaleboat reappeared the next morning towing the dead cow and calf. They left one of the whales in the water overnight and raised it the next morning to discover "a shark had eaten a lot of him."

The *Clara* dropped anchor in Barbados on December 6 for provisions and repairs. On December 23 boat-steerer Joe Gomes was accused of molesting a woman, who complained to the captain that Gomes "did not give a dam for nobody." Gomes was put in irons until they left port the next afternoon. They landed at Prince Rupert Bay in Dominica three days later, hired a man, and took on water and wood. Just before they left, boat-steerer Charles Isaacs, who had complained about the food and called Captain Benton names, deserted.

Benton had not written in the log for some time. The January 23, 1895, log entry notes again that "captain takes sick," still not saying what he had or whether he had recovered from his earlier ailment. More ominously, the February 2 entry says "Antone Lopes off duty sick with venereal disease, Captain still sick in bed"; several others were also sick.

On Sunday, April 14, a doctor from a nearby English warship who was called on board to see to Captain Benton's condition pronounced him unfit to continue. The American consul was called to the boat to speak with Benton, who evidently refused to leave the ship. The next day, First Mate Charles Brown was registered as master for the balance of the voyage.[15]

It may be that Brown was black—Benton had indicated in the dustup with Charles Williams that "I am a coloured man myself and all of my officers are coloured but one," but did not indicate which one that was. If so, Brown should have been included in this book as a replacement master. Unfortunately, there is no Charles Brown listed in the 109 iterations of the name Brown in the *Clara L. Sparks* crew lists. When the American consul checked to see whether all hands were willing to go to sea, six men—William Shay, Antone Ellis, William Herbert, James Smalls, William Samson, and Joseph Glennings—asked to be discharged. Captain Brown passed the log writing over to Lionel L. Brooks, and on Tuesday, April 16, the ship departed.

Lionel L. Brooks' handwriting is clear and easy to read. Like Brown, Brooks was one of Benton's officers and may thus have been black and a replacement captain. It is almost certain that one of them was black, but I have been unable to determine which.

Like Benton's, Brooks' observations also lean toward the factual—the weather, other ships sighted, the ship's location, and sailing conditions. After leaving Barbados, the *Clara L. Sparks* cruised to the Charleston whaling area northeast of Cuba, east of Florida, and due south of New Bedford. On April 20 Earnest Hassell pointed out an issue with the mast, so Brooks had the captain look at it. He in turn asked Brooks and the second mate for their opinions. They agreed the mast was no longer seaworthy, so the ship limped to Crooked Island (in the Bahamas) for repairs. Brooks signed his daily logs with "so attended" and "so ended" or "so ends."

That Tuesday, April 23, they anchored at Great Inagua (south of the Bahamas), where the log reports: "Captain Brown went ashore and reported his mast was gone carpenter came aboard and measure it so attended to so end." The next day, obviously in better health, Joe Benton regained command.

On April 27, Joe Gomes was once again in irons, this time for fifteen minutes "for wanting to fight." While Joe Gomes may have spent an inordinate amount of time in irons, he and Benton were the most productive men on the ship, each having killing eleven whales.

Whaling logs rarely report on the ship's return to port, the doing so perhaps anticlimactic.

Over the course of the voyage's three and a half years, Benton and his crew killed sixty-three whales, about one every twenty-one days.[16] Otherwise, as Lionel L. Brooks indicated in a log entry, there was "nothing to do."

The *A. R. Tucker*

Captain Martin Van Buren Millard sailed the bark *A. R. Tucker* (built by black ship designer John Mashow in 1851) out of New Bedford's harbor on June 6, 1899, on a whaling voyage but died of unknown causes early in the trip. Joe Benton, four years after docking the *Clara L. Sparks*, was on board the *A. R. Tucker* as first mate and took Millard's place as captain.

The whaling barks *Platina, Sunbeam, A. R. Tucker,* and *Daisy* docked at Retole's Wharf in New Bedford. The *Tucker* was Joseph Benton's last command. The barrels are surely filled with whale oil. *Courtesy of the New Bedford Whaling Museum*

Before this opportunity, his troubles on the *Clara* may have prevented another appointment as captain.

The log of the *A. R. Tucker*, written in several hands, does not report anything remarkably different from other logs of the time. The June 15, 1901, entry, written in English, reads that the "Captain and Mr. Barrez and Mr. Matthews" lowered three boats on four whales "raised" (spotted) by Miguel Rosa.

The *A. R. Tucker* returned to New Bedford September 9, 1901, under the command of replacement captain Joseph Avilla, his only command (Avilla was believed to be from the Azores). The balance of the log was written in Avilla's native Portuguese. He wrote that the three boats had taken off after the whale, with two becoming entangled so the lines had to be cut: "But it didn't turn out well, the Captain was taken away [killed] and we had to lose the five whales we had killed because it was very late and we arrived aboard around eight o'clock at night and thus ended the day with such bad luck."[17]

The same flat, unemotional language Joseph P. Benton had used in his own log details the day he met his demise in a conflict the whale won.

The gross production of both trips Joe Benton took as captain was $1,881,448 in today's dollars.

JOSEPH R. LEWIS (JOSÉ LUÍS) (1875–1918)

José Luís was born on Faial in the Azores. While there were certainly whalers of African heritage in the Azores, most of the islands' population was from Portugal. I have accepted Lewis as a man of color because he is so described in all of the sixty-eight iterations of "Joseph Lewis" on the crew lists at the New Bedford Public Library, which describe his skin variously as brown, black, and dark. His documented whaling career as Joseph Lewis began in 1887 as second mate on the *Eleanor B. Conwell*. He was master of six whaling trips on five different ships, several of which had other captains of color: the *Arthur S. Woodruff* (Joseph G. Belain, August P. Gomes, José M. Domingoes), the *Greyhound* (Benjamin Costa, August P. Gomes), the *John R. Manta* (Julio Fernandes, August P. Gomes), and the *Valkyria* (Louis M. Lopes, José Perry). Joseph Lewis also served on a ship that returned with an astonishing 125-pound piece of ambergris

The *Greyhound* was captained by Benjamin Costa. *Courtesy of the New Bedford Whaling Museum*

according to an undated and unidentified newspaper clipping stored at the New Bedford Whaling Museum Library. Lewis' luck ran out in 1918 when, as master of the *Viola* and with his wife and five-year-old daughter on board, the ship went missing in the North Atlantic. Donald Warrin speculates that the ship might have been a victim of "an Atlantic gale or even a German U-Boat."[18]

CHAPTER 7

·—·⟐◆⟐·—·

The Whale's Story

*[People] did not know that . . . a young calf would attempt to suck on
a vessel that contained nothing but the rendered scents of his parents.*

—Naturalist ANDREW NIKIFORUK[1]

*Since man will never change, only when [the whales] cease to exist
shall these enormous species cease to be the victims of his self-
interest. They flee before [man], but it is no use; man's resourcefulness
transports him to the ends of the earth. Death is their only refuge now.*

—Naturalist BERNARD-GERMAIN-ETIENNE LACÉPÈDE[2]

There are those who say that whales are the first animals mentioned in the Bible (Genesis 1:21, King James version: "and
God created great whales"), but I'm fairly certain it was that
pesky snake.[3] Nevertheless, whales have captured the imagination of
humans for millennia. In these enlightened times we sigh fondly when we
think of whales. The smiling pink sperm whale logo of Vineyard Vines, the
clothing retailer that began on Martha's Vineyard, exemplifies our attitude.
We love whales, admire them, want to save them. Those fortunate enough
to have seen a whale breach or even to have glimpsed a whale's tail slide
beneath the surface of the water offshore never forget it. Today, almost no
one thinks of whales as food, commerce, candles, or a lubricant. And even
in the heyday of whaling, few appreciated the sheer brutality of the trade.

A close friend of mine, Byron Marchant, graduated from the U.S.
Naval Academy and served his country as a naval officer on board submarines in both the Atlantic and the Pacific. From our discussions I learned

that the Navy categorizes whales as "biologicals." He recalls that when whales were present, they emitted sounds so loud they could disguise Russian submarines from ours, and vice versa. They can be so loud that they interfere with common aids to navigation. Submariners around the world have come to understand that whales "speak" various dialects.

Technically there are seventy-five species of whales (and dolphins) in nine families. The French naturalist Lacépède in his 1804 natural history of whales describes the whale as a unique, intelligent creature capable of feeling pain. Philip Hoare writes that "studies show cetaceans [whales] can solve problems and use tools; exhibit joy and grief; and live in complex societies." He goes on to say that whales, like elephants, have long memories.

In his book Philip Hoare discusses the work of Hal Whitehead, a whale expert at Dalhousie University in Nova Scotia. Dr. Whitehead posits that whale culture is passed down matrilineally and that the sperm whale's brain has the capacity for complex thought and self-awareness. They know how to hurt each other, have a moral code, and live in a complex social structure. He believes sperm whales may even have their own religion. In short, whales are smarter than most creatures in the animal kingdom.[4]

The skeleton of a forty-nine-foot fifteen-year-old North Atlantic right whale named Reyna (Spanish for "queen"), accidentally killed by a boat in 2004, hangs in the New Bedford Whaling Museum. Beneath her hangs the skeleton of a whale fetus. Reyna was ten months pregnant when she died, and both she and her baby have fins with five appendages that look remarkably like human hands.

Whale Facts

Whales range in weight from the 340-pound dwarf sperm—about the size of a large National Football League defensive tackle—to the 300,000-pound blue whale—about the size of the entire NFL.

—DAVIS, GALLMAN, and GLEITER, *In Pursuit of Leviathan*

There does not seem to be a reliable estimate of the total number of whales killed by the industry—but there were many. The bulk of American whalers' targets were gray, humpback, sperm, bowhead, and right whales. Right whales and sperm whales were whale hunters' preferred prey, the former because they were slower and did not sink when killed, making them easier to process shipside, and the latter because of their superior oil, particularly the spermaceti in the whale's head. Spermaceti is technically a wax, a product of the condensation of mono-alcohols and fatty acid. The rule was that right whales were found in cold water and sperm whales in warm water.[5]

BARRELS

While whale oil was priced on a per-gallon basis, the barrel was the measure used for reporting the catch. Many logs describe whales by their output (a hundred-barrel whale, for example). The size of a barrel varied but generally was thirty to forty gallons (I used the forty-gallon definition to compute the number of whales killed). Coopers made the barrels from lumber and metal hoops that were brought on board before the ship left port or obtained during the voyage.[6] New Bedford's *Whaling Shipping List and Merchants' Transcript*, a publication that listed all things whale from 1843 to 1914, priced and discussed whales in terms of barrels of "sperm" and "whale" oils and whalebone; Starbuck and Hegarty compiled lists of ships and the quantity of each product that was returned.

SPERM WHALES

The largest toothed creatures on the planet (blue whales are larger but have baleen rather than teeth), sperm whales dive down thousands of feet to capture and eat squid and fish. Because they spend most of their time below the surface they are hard to spot, even with their signature spout, which tilts forward and to the left instead of straight up. The name is derived from the spermaceti found in the whale's head. The waxy oil—first mistaken for the whale's semen—was an excellent lubricant and produced candles that burned with almost no smoke.[7]

While spermaceti was the most valuable oil product of whaling, we are still not certain how the whale itself uses it. One thought is that spermaceti controls the whale's buoyancy; another is that it is involved in sound generation. Another possibility is that the spermaceti cushions the whale's brain when ramming something—like a whale ship. There are countless descriptions and paintings of whales attacking the thirty-foot whaleboats launched to capture them, some showing the boats chopped in half and men flung asunder.

Sperm whales have been recorded at depths of 10,000 feet below the surface, with one study determining that a whale was able to descend at a rate of 550 feet per minute, or more than 6 miles per hour. Sperm whales' teeth are four to eight inches long, making them a good medium for scrimshaw (carved, inked artwork). In attacks on whale ships, the teeth were often incidental to the whale's true weapon, its head. The sperm whale's speed, deep diving ability, and evident ability to protect itself have aided in its survival. Today, it is the only whale species that is not endangered. Estimates are that more than a million remain.[8]

From 1835 to 1872, the high point of American whaling, about 147,000 sperm whales were killed, and another 15,000 were hunted but lost for one reason or another (missed, got away, lost after capture due to weather).[9]

The Whaling Industry

Whaling was the first American endeavor to achieve commercial viability. People used the oil for lamps, soap, and smokeless candles. Whale oil was also used for curing leather, carding wool, and lubricating the machines of the Industrial Revolution.[10] Indirectly the industry fueled commerce and jobs related to whaling. Shipbuilders, riggers, blacksmiths, metal forgers, carpenters, sailmakers, and chandlers (those supplying provisions and victuals) all benefited from whaling, as did towns collecting taxes on such transactions.

Whale parts were used for bristles of brushes and brooms, hoop skirts, corsets, and umbrella frames; and each of these products sparked industries, made lives easier, and resulted in increased consumption. Yankee ingenuity eventually developed other natural and man-made sources to replace whale products. But it was the oil that initially made men rich, built communities, and spurred the financial and industrial growth of America.

Whales produced other valuable products, too.

AMBERGRIS

Ambergris has always been the most valuable whale product, even though it is often found outside the whale, afloat or washed on shore. Ancient Egyptians used it for incense. In India it was believed to be an aphrodisiac—and it was used for that in the Middle Ages, as well as for medicinal purposes. Today, its trade is banned.

The origin of free-floating ambergris was initially a mystery; it was once thought to have come from tree roots, seabird droppings, or underwater volcanoes. Marco Polo was said to have realized it came from whales, but it was not until 1724 that Dr. Boylston of Boston was given credit for discovering that it came from sperm whales. A technical description from the U.S. Commission of Fish and Fisheries states:

> Ambergris is a wax-like substance found at rare intervals, but sometimes in relatively large quantities, in the intestines of the sperm whale. With the exception of choice pearls and coral it is the highest-priced product of the fisheries, selling upward of $40 per ounce. It is now generally conceded that ambergris is generated in either sex of the sperm whale, but far more frequently in the male, and is the result of a diseased state of the animal, caused possibly by a biliary irritation, as the individuals from which it is secured are almost invariably of a sickly appearance and sometimes greatly emaciated. It occurs in rough lumps varying in weight from less than one pound to 150 pounds or more. It generally contains fragments of the beak or mandible of squid or cuttle-fish which constitutes the principle food of the sperm whale. When first removed from the animal it is comparatively soft and emits a repugnant odor, but upon exposure to the air, it grows harder, lighter in color, and assumes the appearance it presents when found floating on the ocean. Its color ranges from black to whitish gray, and is often variegated with light stripes and spots resembling marble somewhat.[11]

Captain David Conwell Stull (b. 1844) of Provincetown, nicknamed the Ambergris King is said to have sold 2,000 pounds of ambergris for upward of $500 per pound.[12] Other ships that returned with ambergris valued at up to $2 million per ship were the *Montreal*, *Watchman*, *Pioneer*, *Splendid*, and the *Southern Harvester*. Ships with black captains that brought back ambergris included the *Bertha*, *A. E. Whyland*, *Bartholomew Gosnold*, and the *William A. Grozier*, *John R. Manta*, and *Viola*, the latter three based in Provincetown.[13]

Maecelino Debarro Costa

Maecelino Debarro Costa was the replacement master of the *Bartholomew Gosnold* (April 28, 1881–October 5, 1885), which returned with a three-hundred-pound piece of ambergris. Its value exceeded the worth of the

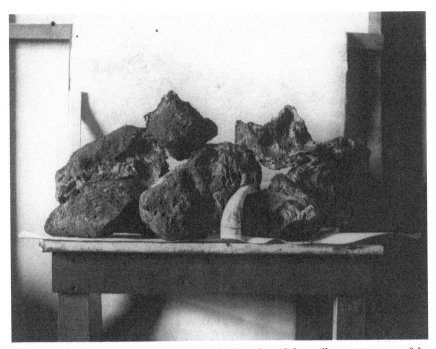

Ambergris and a scrimshaw tooth brought back on board the *Valkyria*. *Courtesy of the New Bedford Whaling Museum*

oil a typical whale trip might have brought back. The twenty-two-year-old Costa replaced James H. Hammond, who had in turn replaced William Henry Poole, the original captain of the trip to the Pacific. The *Bartholomew Gosnold*'s voyage, which lasted four years and six months, was one of the longest trips involving a captain of color. The ship's agent/owner, John F. Tucker, gave Captain Poole succinct instructions before the ship left port. He was to: "Write short logs: mark the whales seen. Keep a/c [account] of every man absent by desertion, until you know he is out of reach. Keep a/c of every change in boards by promotion in any way."

The ship's barely legible log achieved the owner's goal of brevity. Not counting the value of the ambergris, the *Bartholomew Gosnold* returned with 2,800 barrels of sperm oil worth $2.1 million in today's dollars.[14]

An undated New Bedford newspaper story reported that Captain Louis Lopes found a fifty-pound piece of ambergris on a voyage of the *A. E. Whyland*. The dates are unclear, but Lopes captained the *Whyland* on trips from 1912 to 1914, and again from March to September 1915.[15]

Louis M. Lopes. *Courtesy of Bill do Carmo*

LOUIS MANUEL LOPES
(OCTOBER 20, 1877–MARCH 7, 1929)

Over a twenty-eight-year whaling career beginning in 1893, Louis Lopes commanded eight whaling voyages on the *A. E. Whyland*, *Bertha*, *Margarett*, *Claudia*, and *Cameo*.[16] He sailed on at least fourteen voyages in total during his storied career, once each from Providence and Provincetown and the rest, from New Bedford. Lopes was the only whaling captain of color whom records show sailed from Providence.

Part of Lopes' valuable experience came from his time as boat-steerer on board the troubled brig *Sullivan*, where he kept the log for Captain William Hegarty. Excerpts from the log describe a smallpox outbreak on board that lasted from October 29, 1905 to December 27, 1905:

10-29-05   Picked up 10 men at St. Nicholas, Cape Verde Islands.

11-04-05   One man broke out with smallpox today.

11-16-05   We buried one man out of the 10 we got at St. Nicholas.

11-20-05   We saw . . . one sailing vessel our captain went alongside of him to try and get a little Sulphur for the sick men he would not let him have any because he had no money with to pay for it.

11-23-05   Another man has taken sick with the smallpox so the captain has started for land.

11-24-05   Another man is half sick today.

11-30-05   The second mate and another man has broke out with the smallpox.

12-01-05   So we put into another village and the doctor came aboard and he claims the disease is smallpox . . . all hands were vaccinated today at Benvente we are ordered away from here to rio janeiro we have a man on board looking out for the sick men.

12-04-05   One of the sick men can't take food.

12-05-05   One man died at 3 pm we buried him at 4 pm.

12-08-05   We got on the way at noon and arrived on the quarentine [*sic*] grounds at 5 pm the doctor came on board also the custom house officer to men were ordered to the hospital.

12-09-05   We were . . . burning some of the sick men's clothes.

12-12-05   Laying at rio the fumigator came alongside today and fumigated the ship no one is able to sleep below tonight. [The fumigating procedure consisted of placing pans of water with sulfur about the decks spaced twenty feet apart, lighting the sulfur, and sealing the ship completely for two days and a night.]

12-13-05   The doctor ordered the ship to be painted.

12-17-05   Three men are not feeling right.

12-18-05   2 men went to the hospital today with smallpox.

12-20-05   One more man went to the hospital today . . . fumigator has been alongside again today fumigating.

12-22-05   One of our men came out of the hospital today.

12-27-05   One man came out of the hospital today.[17]

The outbreak seems to have ended at that point, and the whaling continued. Things could have gotten much worse had not Captain Hegarty separated the sick men, probably saving many lives. The experience would have prepared Lopes for an outbreak under his own command.

Lopes was from St. Eustatius, a tiny Dutch island in the Caribbean, and although he became a naturalized U.S. citizen in 1905, his native island remained his home. It was where he met his wife and (she) raised their children. He married Alice Ann Elizabeth van Putten (Lopes) on

October 14, 1909, and they had nine children: Pansy, Gladys, Marjorie, Erica, Vincent, Arthur, Hugh, Cyril, and Clifton.[18]

Lopes killed about 112 whales. He whaled until 1928 and died of consumption the following year. The $2.5 million worth of whale oil that Lopes brought back as captain could not survive four generations, but the pride of accomplishment certainly influenced the richly fulfilled lives he produced.

BALEEN

This bone once in a sperm whale's jaw did rest,
Now 'tis intended for a woman's breast.
This my love I do intend
For you to wear and not to bend.[19]

Baleen was used as plastic and spring steel are used today. *Courtesy of the New Bedford Whaling Museum*

Whalebone, or baleen, consists of pliable, hairlike plates as much as fourteen feet long that hang from the roof of the mouth of certain types of whales. Some baleen whales have 460–720 of these plates. When baleen whales feed, they suck in huge amounts of seawater. The baleen strains the seawater for the small marine organisms (collectively called krill) the whales eat. Although sometimes called whalebone, baleen is not bone; it is keratin, a protein also found in human nails and hair and the hooves and claws of other mammals. When heated and molded, whalebone retains that shape when cooled. It was used when strong, flexible materials were needed. Harvesting baleen was about as gruesome a procedure as extracting whale oil, with hoists used to strip the baleen from the whale's head.[20]

Baleen was used in a variety of nineteenth-century products, including back supports, billiard cushions, brushes, buggy whips, combs, corsets, cushion springs, divining rods, fishing rods, flue brushes, hats, hoops, paper cutters, pen holders, police clubs, riding crops, shoe brushes, shoehorns, stays, suspenders, tongue scrapers, and umbrellas.

Whalebone extended the life of the whaling industry for almost seventy years beyond the discovery of shale oil in 1859. The market for whalebone coincided with the rise of San Francisco as the industry's main port after 1850. Whalebone, like whale oil, was eventually replaced by less costly materials. When spring steel was brought to market in 1906, whalebone was selling for five dollars per pound; by 1909 the price had dropped to twelve cents.

Fashion had a good deal to do with the demise of whaling. When the French decided the corset was no longer au courant, demand for whalebone dropped dramatically. Oil was more easily found in the ground than harvested from whales, and whales had not been harvested for food since the early 1700s.

CHAPTER 8

—•+ ☲✛☲ +•—

Whaling versus Slavery

Make me a grave where'er you will,
In a lovely plain, or a lofty hill;
Make it among earth's humblest graves,
But not in a land where men are slaves.

—"Bury Me in a Free Land," FRANCES ELLEN WATKINS HARPER[1]

lavery has been practiced at least throughout recorded history. The philosopher Aristotle (384–322 BC) emphasized the importance of nationality to the institution by proclaiming Greeks superior to all people who were not Greek. Labeling Africans, meaning Ethiopians, "burnt faces" was a way of dehumanizing them and justifying making slaves of conquered people. The Romans perpetuated the practice, as did the Christians. The Spanish enslaved the indigenous people of the New World immediately, calling them "*los negros de la tierra*" (blacks from the land), but by the early 1500s had started to replace them with African slaves who were deemed stronger workers. The Puritans, who believed in "bringing social order to the world," tried to mask the economic model of slavery as a loving family relationship. The British colonists thus landed in Virginia in 1607 with the concepts that would establish slavery in America.

Supporters of slavery intellectualized Africans as savages to justify the practice. In 1636 John Cotton drafted New England's first constitution legalizing slavery—and not just of Africans. During the Pequot War in New England in 1637, the British killed hundreds of Pequot women, children, and old men in the Mystic River Raid and spent months hunting

138

down and killing the adult men. The surviving women and children were enslaved by either the colonists or their Indian allies, and the surviving men were sold into slavery in the West Indies. In 1719, South Carolina's governor declared that all slaves "not entirely" Indian would be counted as black, and in New Jersey both Indians and Africans were listed as "negro" in official documents.[2]

Southerners tried to keep their slaves and the slaves' offspring in servitude through the concept of hypodescence—the idea that one drop of inherited black blood made a person black. In Virginia in 1642, black women (but not white women) were legally tithable (taxable). In 1662 the General Assembly of Virginia decided that any child born to an enslaved woman would also be a slave, and any person with mixed blood who resulted from such a pairing would be assigned the race of the *non*white parent. In 1705 all black, mulatto, and Indian slaves in Virginia were considered real property. The "blood-fraction" laws of 1705 ruled that anyone who was at least one-eighth black—that is, had one black great-grandparent —could not be labeled white. Well into the twentieth century, hypodescence was codified in some states' laws. A 1911 Arkansas law declared that citizens would be considered black if they had *any* Negro blood whatever. A 1970 Louisiana law defined as black anyone who had at least 1/32 African American blood—and a state court upheld that law in 1985.

The justifications for this racial control began for economic reasons. The colonists needed labor to build the New World, and slaves were essentially free labor. Allowing slaves to have children perpetuated the resource without cost. Less principled slave owners found that forcing slave women to bear their children accomplished that in addition to sexual entertainment because the "brood belongs to the owner of the dam [mother]."[3] By producing light-skinned women with the "appealing" attributes of white women, some slave owners found themselves with the best of both worlds.

The salient point, summed up by James Oliver and Lois E. Horton in their book *In Hopes of Liberty*, was this: "The liberty most white Americans spoke of was intended only for whites, yet [blacks] did not accept this limitation willingly."[4]

For more than two-thirds of the time whaling was a thriving industry, slavery of blacks was the law of the land. The industry was already in decline by the time President Lincoln issued the Emancipation Proclamation in 1863 and the Thirteenth Amendment to the Constitution was adopted in 1865.

—·— ≡◆≡ —·—

Geography and chronology had a great deal to do with the whaling industry and those involved in it. Almost all American whale ships operated out of about seventy-five principal ports in twelve coastal states (California, Hawaii, Maine, and North Carolina are not included; and, of course, California and Hawaii were not yet states). All of the whaling ports (except San Francisco and Honolulu) were in the eight states shown in the table below (see appendix J).

Slave Population of the North in 1775 and 1790

State	1775	1790	Number of Ports
Massachusetts	3,500	0	41
Connecticut	5,000	2,648	10
Rhode Island	4,373	958	8
New York	15,000	21,193	8
New Hampshire	629	157	1
Pennsylvania	10,000	3,707	1
Delaware	9,000	8,887	1
New Jersey	7,600	11,423	1

Sources: Horton and Horton, *In Hope of Liberty*; Starbuck, *History*; and Hegarty, *Returns of Whaling Vessels Sailing from American Ports*.

From 1775 to 1790, the slave population decreased in Massachusetts, Connecticut, and Rhode Island, where almost 80 percent of the country's whaling ports were located, although people in all three states continued to participate in the slave trade.

Slave Ships

Thanks in part to the Quakers, whose notions of abolitionism forbade slavery and who owned most of the whale ships in New England, few ships were converted from whaling to slaving, even though the oversized brigs and barks used for whaling were well suited for slave carriers. The wide-bodied, slow-moving, deep-decked ships had been designed to carry rows upon rows of barrels of oil (and provisions and water), ideal for stacking Africans for transport like any other commodity. In 1854, when whale ships were bringing in approximately $16,000 in annual income each, similar-sized slavers carrying 600–800 captured Africans could deliver their cargo for about $250 each, earning $150,000–$200,000 *per single trip*. A captain who earned $900 for a year of whaling could make $9,000 from one trip carrying "black ivory." The only shipping business more profitable than whaling, even as late as 1861, was slavery.[5]

There were isolated instances of whale ships carrying slaves, most occurring in Rhode Island, which for seventy-five years after the American Revolution led the slave trade. Jay Coughtry affirms Rhode Island as the leading state in the trade and cites 934 voyages from 1709 to 1807 that returned with 106,000 slaves. And it was not just whites who participated. "Although the slave trade might seem an unlikely occupation in which to find free black seamen," Coughtry writes, "they were represented in considerable numbers. . . . [W]hen blacks comprised 7 percent of Newport's population, black seamen made up 21 percent of all Newport crews engaged in the West Indian, European, and African trades."[6]

This participation in the slave trade continued after Nantucket had abolished slavery in 1773, and ships from Massachusetts, Rhode Island, Connecticut, New Hampshire, and Maine were known to pursue the practice even after 1807.

Because of Rhode Island's checkered record on slavery, it should come as no surprise that I could find only one captain of color who sailed from Providence—Louis Lopes—and his voyage on the *A. E. Whyland* did not come until 1902.

The Whaleman's Shipping List and Merchants Transcript reported on the slaving activities of the *Fame* in 1847, the *Brutus* in August 1861, and the *Margaret Scott* in 1862. Each, originally a whale ship, wound up in the slave business at a time when blacks composed substantial portions of whaling crews and thus found themselves involved in the trade.[7]

The *Fame* was bought in Boston in 1844 as a whaler but later used in the slave trade. The ship left New London on June 18, 1844, for Desolation Island under the command of Joseph B. Mitchell. Mitchell died in 1846, and his first mate was killed by a whale, so the ship came under the command of the second mate, Anthony Marks of the Azores. Marks took the ship to Rio de Janeiro and told the U.S. consul there, Gorham Parks, that he would continue the trip as captain. Instead of whaling, though, he sailed for the African coast, where he took 530 slaves on board. He returned the ship to Brazil and was paid $40,000 for the trip. There is no record of what happened to the *Fame* afterward.[8]

Edward S. Davoll was a whale ship captain from 1848 to 1862. He took a ship to Africa for a cargo of slaves in 1860. Caught and under threat of a federal indictment for slaving, he died of typhoid fever in 1863.[9]

Given the potential profits—and the ease with which whalers could be converted to slavers—it is remarkable that there are only a few documented cases of its occurrence. Many whale ships did not return from whaling voyages, however, so there might well have been others.

Henry Alexander Wise (December 3, 1806–September 12, 1876) served in Congress, was a governor of Virginia, and was the U.S. minister to Brazil when in 1845 he wrote to Secretary of State John C. Calhoun: "I beseech, I implore the President of the United States to take a decided stand on this subject. You have no conception of the bold effrontery and the flagrant outrages of the African slave trade . . . and every patriot in our land would blush for our country did he know and see, as I do, how our own citizens sail and sell our flag to the uses and abuses of that accursed traffic in almost open violation of our laws."[10]

Wise's letter was specifically motivated by slavers' use of the American flag while participating in the trade. Later, however, Wise became an advocate of Virginia's secession before the Civil War, and as governor would sign the death warrant of John Brown, the white abolitionist who espoused armed insurrection to end slavery in America.

In any event, despite Henry A. Wise's missive, slavers were allowed to use the American flag for another fifteen years. It is probably no coincidence that Calhoun, a South Carolinian, was a slave owner himself who once called slavery not merely a "necessary evil" but a "positive good." Calhoun was one of the more prominent U.S. officials supporting its continuation.

＊—＋—▰◆▰—＋—＊

Whalemen of color were well aware of slavery, of course, and many recognized that their profession did not protect them. They might be taken from ships and sold in any port that allowed slavery. By 1822 several southern

Known Whale Ships That Became Slave Ships

Name	Date	Port	Owner	Captain	Disposition
Laurens	1841	Sag Harbor	Tiffany & Halsey	Atkins Eldredge	Seized by U.S. Navy and sold in Bahia
Cynosure	1841	Stonington	J. F. Trumbull	Walter Simonds	Seized by U.S. Navy and Sold in Bahia
Fame	1844–47	New London	William Tate	Joseph Mitchell	Unknown
Herald[1]	1845	Stonington	Ch. Williams	Samuel Barker	Sold in Rio
Brutus[2]	1856	Warren, R.I.	R. B. Johnson	James S. Henry, unknown	Burned 1864
Margaret Scott[3]	1857	New Bedford	Rodney French, Oliver S. Cleaveland	Stone Fleet	
Augusta	1857	Sag Harbor	A. O. Smith[4]	James Madison Taber	Condemned (sold at auction in New York)

Notes:

1. The *Herald* was sold to Captain Barker, who used it for a slave ship; it subsequently disappeared.
2. The *Brutus* was sold in New York in 1860, then in New Bedford. Its captain after James Henry is unknown.
3. The Stone Fleet: during the Civil War, the North embarked upon a plan, proved foolish, to sink twenty-five ships, using stones for ballast, in front of Charleston Harbor on December 19, 1861. Twenty-four were whale ships: fourteen from New Bedford; five from Mystic; and three from Nantucket, Edgartown, and Sag Harbor. A second group of twenty was sunk January 25–26, 1862; neither activity had the desired effect.
4. Appleton Oakes Smith was a son of the poet Elizabeth Oakes Smith, a well-known suffragette. Appleton found himself on the opposite side of the North on two issues, in a controversy supporting rogue general William Walker in Nicaragua but mostly for siding with the Confederates in gun-running and allowing his ships to be used in the transport of slaves. In December 1861, Appleton was captured on Fire Island, New York, and indicted for equipping a slave ship.

Sources: Spears, *Story of the New England Whalers*, pp. 356–58; Starbuck, *History*; Lund et al., *American Offshore Whaling Voyages*; Malloy, *African Americans in the Maritime Trades*; Dolin, *Leviathan*, pp. 309–16.

states had passed "Negro Seaman Acts" ordering the arrest and/or detention of black seamen and passengers arriving in southern ports, principally to identify runaway slaves.[11] Prior to 1846, more than a thousand black seamen were essentially kidnapped because of racist, restrictive laws in New Orleans, Charleston, Savannah, and Mobile, according to the *National Anti-Slavery Standard* newspaper. Merchants from Massachusetts—who needed the labor black sailors provided—petitioned Congress to end the practice.

Most sailors took whatever steps were necessary to avoid enslavement. Some went to extremes. For example, two Africans recruited as members of the crew of the Rhode Island–based whale ship *Cassander*, believing that they *might* be sold into slavery, set the ship afire in the middle of the Pacific Ocean in 1848. Both of them jumped off the ship, and one refused the rope thrown to him and chose to drown. The *Cassander* was lost, but the crew took to the whaleboats and managed to make it to shore after ten days. The other African, rescued by one of the whaleboats, admitted he and his friend had set fire to the *Cassander* because they were worried they would be sold at the next port. Still concerned, he apparently stabbed himself and leaped off the boat to his death.[12]

White sailors with no knowledge of life in bondage could not resist comparing their lot to slavery, calling themselves "vassals" and "slaves of the lowest caste." Jeffrey Bolster recounts their lament: "And now I ask what slave at the South suffers more hardships or feels more keenly the bitterness of oppression than the poor care worne sailor."[13] Frank Thompson, captain of the *Pilgrim* (not listed as a whale ship by Lund), apparently agreed. In 1834, stringing two men to the rigging before whipping them, he screamed: "You see your condition! I'll flog you fore and aft, from the boy up! You've got a driver over you. Yes, a slave driver—a nigger driver! I'll see who'll tell me he isn't a nigger slave!"[14]

The *Anti-Slavery Standard* printed letters by prisoners and former prisoners:

> Several of our contemporaries of the political press have lately had the boldness to question whether, inasmuch and anybody may be made a slave of, at the North, to oblige the South. . . . Is it asking too much that free northerners who go South shall be permitted to remain so. . . . We should love the slaveholders better than ourselves,

the only wonder is that somebody, beside the Abolitionists, has not
before discovered that to imprison Northern seamen in Southern
ports if they are not of the pale tint, and sell them for slaves . . . we
must be thankful for things as they come, hoping to live long enough
to look at the Declaration of Independence and the Constitution
without laughing.[15]

The atrocious practice reached absurd extremes. For example, a colored
Portuguese (Cape Verdean) sailor on board a *British* brig sailing into the
port of Charleston was arrested and jailed because of the color of his skin.[16]

To contextualize the timing, by 1822 Paul Cuffe; Michael, Thomas,
and Paul Wainer; Alvan Phelps; John Masten; Peter Green; and Absalom
Boston were all free and whaling masters. Merely stopping at a southern
port, however, would have endangered their freedom and their lives. *The
Liberator* successfully argued that at a minimum, black sailors in South
Carolina should be allowed to stay on board the ship on which they arrived
rather than be placed in jail during the duration of the ship's visit.[17]

Life was much safer for such men in the North. Massachusetts, for
example, was heavily engaged in the African slave trade in 1700, but by
1783 the practice was largely abolished. On Nantucket in particular, site
of the Quakers' early settlement, the few remaining slaves were viewed
more as status symbols than workers— "refuse slaves" so old or sick it was
not worth the shipper's cost to transport them South to be sold.[18] Freeing
slaves by manumission became the rule rather than the exception. William
Rotch Jr. summarized the Quakers' belief when he wrote in 1791: "It is
looked upon that the struggle on the part of the Negroes and Mulattoes is
as just as was the American struggle for liberty."[19]

Nantucket Timeline

Nantucket played an important role in the abolition of slavery and as the
first major whaling port where black men became famous as whalers.
Paul Cuffe gained his navigational expertise learning to dodge the British
during the Revolutionary War to supply the ocean-bound island. His first
known whale trip of 1778 made Cuffe a contemporary of Prince Boston,
the slave signed on board a whale ship by his master in 1772 who sued to
receive his wages. Thus began an important time line that arguably led to
men of color becoming successful as whalers.

1600s   African slaves arrive on Nantucket.

1717   The island's African American community is first recorded in town meeting records. The first count of the black population records forty-four people.

1772   Nantucket whaleman Prince Boston is acknowledged as the first black man to have been freed from slavery on the island.

1773   Nantucket abolishes slavery.

1822   Absalom Boston takes his first voyage as captain of the *Industry*.

1823   Peter Green is named replacement captain of the *John Adams*.

1836   Edward Pompey commands the *Rising States* (with an all-black crew and black owner Richard Johnson, as well as Paul Cuffe's son William Cuffe as first mate).[20]

1840   Blacks account for 6 percent (571 persons) of Nantucket's population.

1842   Samuel W. Harris becomes captain of the *Phebe*.

1849   The California Gold Rush causes many sailors to abandon whaling and head west.

1850–   Whaling begins its decline in New Bedford. Nantucket's
1900   black population declines in direct proportion to the fall of fortunes derived from whaling.

1870   Only eighty-five black people remain on the island.

"Nigger"

The substantive reports of discrimination during the whaling era are hardly surprising. One of those manifestations, however, may have been less prevalent on board whale ships (not merchant vessels) than would be expected. The "troublesome word" "nigger," according to Harvard law professor Randall Kennedy's book on the subject, derives from the Latin word for black, *niger*. An early recorded use was by John Rolfe, who listed a shipment of Africans to Virginia as "negars" in 1619. A 1689 inventory of an estate in New York characterized a slave boy as "niggor."[21] While it is fair to presume the word was in wide use during whaling days, that was not the case, apparently, on board whale ships.

Historian Dennis D. Nelson's book *The Integration of the Negro into the United States Navy* relates acts of heroism by Negro sailors in the War of 1812 and their shipboard acceptance over the years. William Swift notes that despite the U.S. Navy's discriminatory policies, personnel records (like whaling logs) were essentially "colorless," evidence of a lack of racial prejudice on board ship. There is good reason for that. As Harold Langley notes: "The small size of Navy and merchant ships made segregation impractical. The nature of surviving evidence suggests that they [Negroes] lived and worked without difficulty alongside their white comrades. . . . Virtually all of the sailors who wrote about their non-white shipmates referred to them as Negroes, colored, or blacks. Almost without exception the term 'nigger' is used only when a sailor is quoting an officer."[22]

William P. Powell, writing in the *National Anti-Slavery Standard* in 1846, claimed: "There is no barrier, no dividing line, no complexional distinction, to hedge up the cabin gangway or the quarter-deck, to prevent

"Set to": a fight between the steward and the cook. *Courtesy of the New Bedford Whaling Museum*

the intrepid, enterprising, and skillful coloured sailor from filling the same station as the white sailor."[23]

Langley's point about the small size of naval ships making "segregation impractical" becomes an understatement when the forecastle of a whale ship is considered. The cramped quarters gave each man space equivalent to the backseat of an SUV. Men learned to get along.[24]

Of course, there were exceptions.

The *Sharon*, 1842

"The *Sharon* mutiny," notes Charles Batchelder, "was the direct result of the brutality of one man, a man whose mind was twisted by some severe derangement." Indeed, the story of the mutiny on the whale ship *Sharon* is one of the best examples of what can go wrong at sea. Departing Fairhaven on May 25, 1841, the *Sharon* was under the command of Captain Howes Norris of Martha's Vineyard, who inexplicably treated the "mulatto" steward, John (George) Babcock, like an animal. He summoned Babcock every morning with, "Where are you, you damned nigger you?" For nearly a year, from at least December 12, 1841, to September 1, 1842, Norris beat and flogged the eighteen-year-old Babcock with no justification. Babcock finally died after a two-and-a-half-hour flogging and kicking in front of the entire crew—because he had not managed to eat "a morsel of meat from the previous night's supper."

The type, number, and viciousness of the beatings Norris gave Babcock were outrageously cruel. Babcock was not the only black on board; Samuel Leods and Henry Mills (the cook) were also black. Babcock and Mills were thought to have been fugitive slaves. During a stop at Ascension Island in the South Atlantic on October 15, 1842, six weeks after Babcock's death, twelve men deserted, saying they would not sail with a murderer. Several Kanakas (Polynesians) replaced the deserters, but Norris beat and berated them too, as well as John Brown, a white crewman who was tied up, placed in a canoe, and set adrift, never to be seen again. When whales were sighted on November 5, there were only enough crewmembers left to launch two whaleboats. After they went out in pursuit of the whales, three of the Kanakas along with a steward beheaded Captain Norris. The steward apparently repented, because he helped Benjamin Clough, one of the officers left on board the ship, kill two of the mutineers and hold the ship until the whaleboat crews returned and took the last mutineer captive. Enough different stories were told by Benjamin Clough and two other officers to create some controversy—but the only denial of Howes Norris' cruelty and treachery came from his family, none of whom was present on board the *Sharon*.[25] Captain Howes Norris was a vicious racist, but fortunately, there seem to have been very few other men like him in whaling.

Even though the word "nigger" crops up far less often in whaling records than one would expect, there are indications that racism was present in some form. There were various code words and oblique references. For example, the master of the *Lucy Ann* out of Greenpoint, New York, described his crew, "All hands employed with myself & worked like a negro." Briton Cooper Busch cites several additional passages from logs and journals. From the captain of New Bedford's *Draco,* James V. Cox, believing a crewman was feigning sickness: "He has been with me nearly eleven years and this voyage he shows the negro." When a black crewman missed catching a whale, the log keeper's report on the *Charles Colgate* said he *"niggered"* the opportunity. Snide references aside, use of that word could start serious trouble. In 1866, on the *Atlantic*, James Brown from New Granada stabbed James Foster to death. Brown "sayed that Foster had called him a nigger was the reason he did it." There is no indication that Brown was punished.[26]

Calling someone a nigger directly—on a relatively small whale ship where men spent years together and harmony was enforced—might have been uncommon, but that did not mean there was no prejudice. Duncan McClellan, on board the *Triton* in 1840, said of a (white) crewmate: "Mr. Hansen was the most unpopular person on board, both with the officers and men, more so than the nigger cook."[27] Captain Henry J. Gonzales was regularly called nigger—although apparently not to his face.[28]

Respect for rank was crucial on board whale ships. Black officers insisted on being called "Sir" or "Mr." along with their last name—and never "boy."[29]

Frank T. Bullen told the story, mentioned often in books about whaling, that soon after boarding the *Cachelot* in 1875, he was upbraided by a black officer: "I said 'yes' very curtly, for I hardly liked his patronizing air; but he snapped me up short with 'yes, sir, when yew speak to me, ye blank limejuicer. I'se de fourf mate ob dis yar ship, en my name's Mistah jones, 'n yew jest freeze on to dat ar, ef yew want ter lib long 'n die happy. See sonny.'"[30]

Walter Noble Burns recorded a similar instance when as a crewman he was forced to take orders from a relatively cruel black officer (whom he refers to as a nigger behind his back), although Burns does not otherwise mention that his captain, William T. Shorey, was black.[31]

The notion that black officers could give lashes to white whalers at sea but dared not look them in the face once on land is attributed to Jeffrey Bolster.[32]

In *With Sails Whitening Every Sea*, Brian Rouleau describes the expansion of shipping from America and the concurrent decline in the number of men of color in the merchant marine business. Stories in the book include that of Silas Fitch of the whale ship *Charles Phelps*, who claimed to "have seen many negroes" in his day but complained that he had to go to sea to find "the proudest and the sassiest darkey that I ever saw." Other sailors repeatedly commented about "sass" from people of African descent. One man in Antigua noted, "I never saw so saucy a nigger before . . . if he'd talked in Virginia as he did on our vessel, he would certainly have had 9 and 30 lashes the next morning." George Thayer, when faced with an "impudent" black man, exploded: "You damned nigger, if I had you back in Georgia, I would sell you."[33]

One might get away with such talk on a merchant vessel. On board a whale ship, calling someone a nigger could get you killed.

CHAPTER 9

Identity

*A*n important part of black whaling masters' stories is how they identified themselves—what race they claimed as their own. When researching their stories I sifted through mountains of information that offered hints as to their race, but in fact there is no straightforward answer when it comes to race in America. Black people were involuntarily shipped to America, and the combination of rape and miscegenation dramatically altered how the descendants of these Africans looked. Generations of mixing produced legally black people with blond hair and blue eyes, and many other combinations. Intermarriage between blacks and indigenous people also complicated the racial background, particularly in Sag Harbor and on Martha's Vineyard, both sources of whalers—and harpooners in particular. Black and Indian intermarriage began there in the 1760s, and by 1790 three quarters of Gay Head's population of 440 claimed dual ancestry.

It was no secret that a person who did not appear to be black had better options in life than one who did. Those who appeared black always had to fear being kidnapped into (or returned to) slavery. Financial opportunity was also a powerful motivator. Nonblacks had far more opportunities both for employment and for advancement. Some people were lucky enough to have the choice to identify as either. Particularly in New England, children of mixed marriages could choose which race to identify with.

Paul Cuffe, Michael Wainer, and Absalom Boston each had one black parent and one Native American parent and seem to have identified as black. Cuffe went further and insisted that all of the captains of his ships and most of his crews be black. Cuffe's close family and business friend

Michael Wainer was mulatto, but his sons clearly identified as black. Half black and half Native American, Absalom Boston "identified himself wholeheartedly with the African American side of his heritage."[1] The Lee brothers, on the other hand—whose father was a runaway slave and mother a Shinnecock—seem to have identified as Native American. Similar observations can be made for Cape Verdeans whose ancestries reach into Spain or Portugal or the Azores. Because one is from Cape Verde does not necessarily mean one has African (black) heritage—although it is likely. The generalization is based on the view of the white majority, and these men of color were treated as if they were black.

In the northern whaling towns, where marriages among the black and Native American communities were common, "mulattoes constituted 20 percent to one-quarter of the black population in some locales. These percentages rose dramatically during the late eighteenth and into the nineteenth century," the heyday of the whaling industry.[2]

In 1796 the new American Congress passed the "Act for the Relief and Protection of American Seamen," largely to protect American sailors from British harassment on the high seas. The act called for customs officials to maintain a record of U.S. citizens serving on U.S. vessels, with each to be given a Seaman's Protection Certificate. These certificates vouched for the citizenship of the individual and included identifying information such as age, height, complexion, place of birth, and in some cases eye and hair color. It is thanks to these papers that we are able to identify—with some degree of accuracy—which whalers were men of color. The New Bedford Whaling Museum's relatively new spreadsheet database (the "crew list") is in part derived from the Seaman's Protection Certificates.[3]

It is ironic that it was often white customs officials who made the (sometimes mistaken) determinations as to skin, hair, and eye color on crew lists. It is also ironic that the Seaman's Protection Certificates helped some black people escape from slavery, including Frederick Douglass. In New Bedford alone, more than 50,000 individual men participated in whaling between 1809 and 1927, and many are listed on the certificates as "Negro," "mulatto," or "Indian," with skin color "black," "brown," "dark," "yellow," or "copper."[4]

Researchers today can also use archived ships' logs to determine the race and nationality of crews. Maritime law required the keeping of logs to detail the events of whaling trips.[5] Generally it was the captain or the first mate who kept the log. More often than not, first mates were former crewmen who were adept at harpooning whales and willing to learn navigation but had no formal education. It is thus not unusual to see words and names in logs spelled phonetically (Paul Cuffe's writing is a good example), particularly when the mate may have been from a foreign country such as Cape Verde.

It should be noted that while whaling took place between the early 1700s and the early 1900s, the New Bedford database (crew list) spans only 1809 to 1927. Further confusing the issue are the many duplicate entries for those who took several or many whaling trips. First and last names are spelled differently from one crew list to the next, and hair color, height, eye color, and skin color often differ from one entry to the next as well, but logical comparisons can be made when ships and ports match. Most but not all of the captains of color appear on lists as black because they had physical characteristics derived from the mixing of Africans, West Indian, African American, Cape Verdeans, and of course Native Americans.[6]

Men described as "dark," "yellow," or "copper" on crew lists were not necessarily black, of course. Skin color is affected by exposure to the sun, and many of the men were of Mediterranean, largely Portuguese, ancestry. While Cape Verdeans were considered black, there were dark-skinned people from Portugal and the Azores who identified themselves otherwise. A prime example is Joseph Gomes, born in the Azores. Gomes is listed as having "dark" skin, which could easily be construed as his having been black. And that was not necessarily a disadvantage. In his book *Captain Joe* he recounts the story of stowing away in 1910 to become a whaler: "The crews of the whalers at that time were mostly Cape Verdian [*sic*] fellows and West Indians, mostly blacks, but some were mulattoes. To get on board a whaler, I would have to fool the authorities. I would have to pass as a member of the crew. I had to be black. . . . Well, I was black all right—a good, shiny black. I had bought a can of shoe polish and covered every visible portion of my skin with it."[7]

In the latter years of the whaling industry, the workforce consisted largely of workers from Cape Verde who had the usual good reasons not to want to be identified as black. Whaling historian James Farr notes that the Cape Verdeans were considered as "nearly full-blooded negroes [*sic*] and black as ebony, but hardworking, industrious, and good whalers. . . . The Portuguese skippers are skillful whalers, good businessmen, strict disciplinarians and [they] secure catches which would make the old-time whalemen turn green with envy."[8] Cape Verdeans, with their ancestry so closely linked to Africa, are almost always treated as black in records regardless of their appearance.

Of 123,598 New Bedford crew list entries, 4,474 men held the rank of master and 350 had skin that was black, dark, Indian, or brown. Almost all the entries are duplicates—that is, the person made multiple voyages. Another complication is that of all whaling ports, only New Bedford kept and retained detailed records. Fires on Nantucket and in Sag Harbor destroyed a great deal of information; so again, it is almost a certainty that I have omitted several captains who were men of color. In determining who was "black," it ultimately came down to a simple reality: whites made the call.

Seaman's Protection Certificates and the Crew List

"The Act of 28 February 1803 contained the first legal mention and requirements for keeping a crew list as part of ship's papers. Before a vessel could depart from a port on a foreign voyage, the master had to deliver a list of the crew, verified by his oath, to the customs collector at that port. The collector then supplied the master with a certified copy of the list, copied in a uniform hand, along with a Clearance Certificate, at which time the master entered into a four-hundred-dollar bond to exhibit the crew list to the first boarding officer he encountered upon his return to a U.S. port. There he was required to produce the persons named and described in the crew list to give account for any crewmembers who were not present. Notes certifying sickness, discharge, or desertion, usually signed by a consular official, were often included with the original list in order to prove that individuals not present were legally accounted for. Crew lists of various kinds are commonly found in maritime collections. In addition to the formal document described here, a list of crew members usually appears on the articles of Agreement, and such lists are often written in ships' logbooks or journals."

Source: Stein, "American Maritime Documents 1776–1860."

Historian and researcher Mary Malloy points out that "there is no easy way or precise way reliably to identify all of the African Americans from among the tens of thousands of men involved in the whaling industry as sailors, officers and investors, but certain kinds of documents can provide helpful information."[9] In my research, I used the standard works by Starbuck, Hegarty, and Lund to identify these captains of color. I relied heavily as well on the databases of the New Bedford Whaling Museum in its library (and online) and the crew list card catalog of the New Bedford Free Public Library that drew on these compendiums. Author Nancy Shoemaker's databases (whalemen/Filepro and NARA crew lists/Word) were particularly helpful. Shoemaker's works *Native American Whalemen* and "Mr. Tashtego: Native American Whalemen in Antebellum New England," Mary Malloy's *African Americans in the Maritime Trades*, Martha Putney's *Black Sailors*, Harold O. Lewis' work and Donald Warrin's *So Ends This Day* were invaluable in determining who these men were and providing color on their backgrounds and lives. Any errors or misinterpretations are mine alone.

CHAPTER 10

◄━ ►━◆━◄ ━►

The Whaling Captain

*During the course of an average voyage . . . the master was almost
certain to act as a physician, surgeon, lawyer, diplomat, financial
agent, entrepreneur, taskmaster, judge and peacemaker.*

—ELMO P. HOHMAN, *The American Whaleman*

*I*n *The Provincetown Book,* Nancy Smith describes the qualities
that made a good whale ship captain:

The captain of a whaler must be unafraid. He steers his boat
within ten feet of the whale for the man with the harpoon must never
be able to say: "He did not put me near enough to the whale." He
must be undismayed, whether the whale runs or dives or fights, or
whether the line around the roller blazes up aflame. He must never
cut loose till the boat is pulled under. He must be a good marksman,
or he would not have become captain. "He missed a whale!" is said
as one speaks of a general who lost a battle. He must be something of
a doctor, a dentist, a surgeon; for men get sick with the scurvy in the
long cruising before they go into port for lemons, onions, potatoes,
yams, cocoanuts; men are often hurt in killing a whale; a broken leg,
a bad cut, a shoulder out of joint is for the captain's care. He must be
judge and father to the homesick boys. He must be a man of business if he goes into a foreign port and ships his oil home. The mates
have the rough work to do. They must keep order aboard ship. If the
weeks lengthen into months and the men never once hear: "There
she blows!" from the watch in the cross-trees they get restless and
hard to manage.[1]

156

We tend to think of whale ship masters in terms of their abilities as seamen, but a whaling enterprise was the financial equivalent of a private equity company or hedge fund in which a group of investors looked to profit from a risky investment. A good captain was thus also a good businessman. A whaling voyage, notes an industry case study, was "treated as a firm . . . since each voyage involved new planning, refitting the vessel, new provisioning, raising a new crew and, frequently, a turnover of owners, or captain, or agent, or all three."[2]

Performance counted heavily, and skill in the various aspects of whaling got people promoted regardless of race. Perhaps most important, to maintain the rank of master, captains had to manage often unskilled and at times unwilling men.

Management

Discipline was key. It was up to the captain to execute the business plan by maintaining order, motivating the crew, and taking whatever actions were necessary to accomplish the goal of a safe return with a full hull. Successful masters had to strike a balance between good discipline and harshness, because neither desertion nor mutiny resulted in success. And the men who selected whaling as a vocation were not easy to manage. In 1836 the *Nantucket Inquirer* lamented that "too many ungovernable lads, runaways from parental authority, or candidate for corrective treatment, too many vagabonds just from the clutches of the police of European and American cities . . . too many convicts . . . are suffered to enlist in this service." No surprise, then, "that revolts, mutinies, and murders, conflagrations and immense destruction of property so frequently arise. . . . The whale-fishery shall not be converted into a mere engine for the repair of cracked reputations and the chastisement of those against the reception of whom even the jail doors revolt."[3]

Frank Thomas Bullen witnessed firsthand how one whale ship captain maintained discipline when no whales were about to keep the crew busy. "We were worked as hard as if the success of the voyage depended upon our ceaseless toil of scrubbing, scraping, and polishing. Discipline was indeed maintained at a high pitch of perfection, no man daring to look awry, much less complain of any hardship, however great. Even this humble submissiveness did not satisfy our tyrant, and at last his cruelty took a more active shape." Perhaps to make an example of one crewman who had the temerity to steal six potatoes to make beer, the captain used fishing line to string him by his thumbs to the rigging. When the boat was still, his toes touched the deck. When the boat rolled, he was supported only by his thumbs. In addition, he received two dozen lashes with an improvised cat-o'-nine-tails.[4]

Bullen's introduction notes that he purposefully did not use any real names of people or boats, but it is possible to deduce some details. Bullen is eighteen when he begins his story. Finding that he had been born in 1857, I deduced that the trip took place in 1875. Even though flogging had been outlawed in 1850, the captain evidently used it to maintain discipline. Later in the book Bullen describes how the captain had a dozen crewmembers flogged who, drunk at the end of shore leave, attempted to assault a black officer who was large and powerful enough to subdue them all—so violently that more than half were rendered insensible. Bullen admits the punishment was deserved, affirming that the maintenance of order and discipline was necessary on a whale ship where rank had its privilege.[5] Black or white, a captain could easily lose his command without discipline.

Edward S. Davoll (1822–63), who began his whaling career at age eighteen and became a captain on his fourth ship at age twenty-five, made his expectations clear in a comprehensive nine-page document for his officers and crew titled "The Captain's Specific Orders on the Commencement of a Whale Voyage." Among his "specific orders" were the following:

> To the crew; the goal of the trip is to get oil; discipline is of most import, obey your officers. Don't fool around or complain, sing out when whales are spotted, stay in your quarters and assigned places aboard ship (in front of the try pots), man your watch and don't pretend to be sick. To the cook: Keep the galley, your area and utensils clean, cook everything, waste nothing. To the Steward: Remain aft, stay away from the foremast crew, watch after all the stores, clean the cabin every day except Sunday, keep the pantry clean and do not let me find a dirty dish, knife, fork or spoon. To the Boatsteerers: Stay away from the crew, stay awake on watch, decide if you are for me or against me and keep aft or forward [apparently the boat-steerers could choose whether to be officers or crew]. To Officers: I'm in charge of you and you are of the men[,] who will come immediately

when called . . . and if they don't you will cause them to obey. Not by brutality or by being tyrants but make them obey. Keep things ship shape, maintain order and discipline. To the Mate: Make the boat and crew ready to catch whales; see that the ship is kept clean, keep good account of ships supplies, maintain the log, manage the processing of the whale, hit the crew only when you have to but exercise restraint. To the Second Mate: Keep your distance from the crew; obey the first mate and me. Keep your distance from the men; you are responsible for the aft rigging [sails] and keep things ship shape.[6]

Davoll's promising career ended when he attempted to use his whale ship as a slaver. Ironically, his first whaling trip in 1841 was on board the *Elizabeth* of Westport—captained by black master Pardon Cook.[7]

There is no evidence that Paul Cuffe ever had crew problems on board ship (although his subordinate masters sometimes did). Having adapted his whale ships to merchant service when that proved more practical or profitable, in 1807 Cuffe captained his newest (at the time) and largest ship, the *Alpha,* with an all-black crew that included Thomas Wainer as first mate and his fourteen-year-old namesake son, Paul Jr. They sailed from Westport to Wilmington and Savannah, and then on to Russia and Sweden to avoid threats of a blockade by Napoleon's navy. A young Swede named Abraham Rodin signed on board after agreeing to Cuffe's terms: "Always obey the master, protect his goods, and indicate your own whereabouts at all times; you must 'avoid fornication, marriage, cards, dice, haunted houses, taverns, and playhouses.' In return, you are guaranteed food, lodging, clothes, health care, and instruction in reading, writing, seamanship and other industry. You will be given new clothes and a Bible at the end of your six-year apprenticeship."[8]

Owners' Expectations

Captain Samuel Harris commanded the ship *Phebe* when it left Nantucket on September 19, 1842; it was condemned in Australia on December 24, 1846. According to a Nantucket newspaper article, before Harris departed he received the following illuminating (and extensive) "letter of instructions" from the ship's owners. There is nothing in the letter to indicate that they felt such instructions were necessary because Harris was black; they simply wanted to spell out what was expected of him.

Captain Samuel W. Harris

Sir:

Having put you in command of the ship *Phebe*, we wish you to proceed to sea with all convenient dispatch and to make the best of your way to the Western Islands, where you will take on board a good recruit of fresh vegetables, and also look over the ground a little after sperm whales, and should you be so successful as to obtain any oil, you can put it in care of the American consul at Fayal, to be shipped home. Our consignees are Joseph Bradley & Co., Boston, and Josiah Macy & Son, New York.

After leaving the Western Islands, the prospect is generally good for sperm whales until you have passed the Cape Verde Islands, and again along the eastern edge of the Abrolhos Bank and off the River Platte also, and wherever you find sperm whales you are at liberty to cruise. On your arrival in the Pacific Ocean you will consider yourself at liberty to cruise wherever you may think the prospect best for a cargo of sperm oil, steering by your own compass and following no man's lead because he is going to this place or that place.

You will go into port as often as it is necessary to refresh the crew and refit the ship, taking care not to go into any port that is not a port of entry; and you must not prolong your stay in port beyond the time necessary to procure your recruits; social purposes or company must not detain you anywhere. We have had so much cause to complain of what the sailor calls "gamming," or keeping company with other ships for the purpose of visiting, that we hope you will avoid this error. When in port you will allow no smuggling or contraband trade to be carried on from the ship, but if you have anything on board which you wish to sell for the purpose of buying recruits, you must first obtain permission from the proper authority.

You will not permit your men to sell their clothes to buy liquor with, and this article you will not allow to be brought on board the ship at any time, except in a very small quantity, for medical purposes only. When fruit is plenty, you may give it to the men freely, at the ship's expense.

Serious losses have occurred, both to lives and property, by suffering the officers to neglect a part of their duty, which you will not allow; we mean the practice of leaving the deck in charge of boat-steerers, who are not paid for that service; but we recommend to you to require the mates to take their regular watch in the nighttime, while at sea, through the whole voyage; it will be no justification for them to omit that part of their duty because it is not practiced aboard some other ship.

We wish you to maintain perfect order on board the ship; suffer no quarreling among the officers, and do not allow them to abuse the men; but if the men are impudent to the officers, require them to report to you, that you may be the judge of the case, and when punishment is required, cause the whole case to be written out in the log book—both offense and punishment; but punishment should not be inflicted when it can be avoided, as the success of the voyage depends very much on harmony and united exertion.

It is well understood by you that in making a contract with you to take charge of this ship, you are to head your own boat, as well as to head the voyage, and we have every confidence in your obtaining a voyage, by proper perseverance.

If you require more money for the ship's expense, you are at liberty to draw on us for the deficiency, and we would recommend to you to take a right whale or humpback, and sell the oil to assist you in obtaining recruits.

This is a very essential subject to be attended to, as the health of the crew depends on having plenty of fresh vegetables and fruit. When your voyage is drawing to a close and it is near time for you to leave for home, you need not consider you are under any obligation to keep your present men good, provided there are any vacancies by desertion or otherwise, or that you have men on board on monthly wages. If you have enough to man three boats it is all that is required or necessary to navigate the ship home. We mention this to guard you against hiring men on monthly wages, merely to assist in navigating the ship; the law requires no such thing while you have enough, in your own judgment, to take care of the ship.

On the passage home we wish you to have an inventory of everything on board the ship, which belongs to her, made out; and have the tools put up in good order and secure from being pilfered. Please write to us by every opportunity and keep us informed of the state of the ship and progress of the voyage; and when you go into port and no direct opportunity occurs of sending letters home, leave them in care of some consul or other person who will take the trouble to forward them by first conveyance. Wishing you a happy and prosperous voyage, we are very respectfully,

Your assured friends,
C. Mitchell & Co.[9]

The instructions were clear: find whales, kill and process them, maintain order without abuse, leave little room and time for desertion, send the oil home, and take care of the ship.

SAMUEL W. HARRIS (1813–1904)

Samuel W. Harris was the first mate and navigator of the *Loper* when it departed Nantucket on June 21, 1829, and returned with 2,280 barrels of sperm whale oil on September 7, 1830—fourteen months and fourteen days later. The *Loper's* victorious return was celebrated by a parade and dinner in honor of the nearly all-black crew hosted by Obed Starbuck, the ship's white captain. The parade was led by Absalom Boston and Harris— "two Negro navigators of note"—mounted on horseback in front of a procession of the crew carrying harpoons, lances, and other whaling tools. They sang their way down Nantucket's Main Street, making the "cobbles reverberate." Boston and Harris were also investors in the highly successful venture.

The 2,280 barrels of oil, worth more than $50,000 in 1830, would be worth more than $1.3 million today. The *Nantucket Inquirer* crowed that it was the "Greatest Voyage Ever Made." Obed Starbuck retired a rich man at age thirty-three. No one, black or white, wanted to go whaling more often than necessary.[10]

Nantucket's reign as the premier whaling port was coming to an end in 1842, largely due to the sandbar at the entrance to its harbor. Longer voyages to the Pacific required larger ships with deeper hulls, but the shallow sandbar denied such ships entry to the harbor. One Peter Folger Ewer came up with an ingenious solution. Borrowing from earlier Dutch designs, he designed two hollow wooden pontoons, connected by chains, that were to be used to raise whale ships—reducing their draft—and float them across the bar and into the harbor. He called them "camels," like the animals that carried heavy loads and held a lot of water. The 135-foot-long, 29-foot-wide, 19-foot-deep camel would be filled with water and sunk so a whale ship could sail onto it, after which its built-in steam engines would pump out the water, raising the pontoons and allowing the whale ship to be towed over the sandbar. The first test was with the 379-ton *Phebe* on September 4, 1842. The ship's weight proved too great, and the chains connecting the pontoons broke. The *Phebe* sank back into the water and required extensive repairs after the chains damaged its copper-sheathed hull. Ewer identified the cause of the breakage—general ship chains were used instead of those expressly designed for the purpose—and fixed the problem. Thereafter the system performed as contemplated.[11]

After repairs, the *Phebe* with Captain Harris commanding—the largest of all the ships commanded by a black master—left Nantucket on September 19, 1842, for the Pacific whaling grounds. One cannot help but wonder if the camel mishap had anything to do with the *Phebe* being condemned in Australia four years later on Christmas Eve 1846. The ship was "leaking 290 strokes per hour," indicating a severely damaged hull. Up to that point the ship and Harris had performed admirably. Its 500 barrels of whale oil were sold in Sydney, and its 1,175 barrels of sperm oil were shipped home on board the *Carolina* of Boston. Harris returned to Nantucket on board the *Eagle* from Salem with the log that exists today detailing the facts and adventures of the voyage. The proceeds of the oil would have been worth $1,175,000 today. The voyage was Samuel Harris' only recorded voyage as captain.[12]

Upon his return to Nantucket Harris learned that his father had died during his absence, and he took over the family farm at Polpis (a village on Nantucket). Captain Harris died in March 1904 at the age of ninety-one.

Captains as Doctors

Captains were charged with managing the health and well-being of their crews. Arthur Lipman notes that generally, a captain's "medical knowledge was limited to what he might have learned by observation and experience"; nevertheless, the captain was the doctor who made the diagnosis, effected various cures, and all too often performed surgery, which tended to involve amputation.[13] At times the captain himself was the victim and someone else had to provide medical care. In 1822, for example, George Clark of the *Parnasso* had just been promoted to replacement captain when, attempting to kill a "50 barrel whale" that fought back, Clark was struck by the whale's tail and hurt so badly that a crewman said of the damage, "The extent of the injury done him cannot be ascertained as it is so much swelled as to scarcely retain the appearance of anything human." Captain Clark was eventually put ashore and recovered.

It was not uncommon for limbs to be lost when arms or legs became fouled in lines attached to fleeing whales, and injuries caused by slipping on oil and entrails were even more common. Captains dealt with shipborne ailments ranging from scurvy to fever using crude instruments, Stone Age treatments, and placebos. Ships carried medicine chests with suggested remedies numbered for ease of use. In one oft-told story, a cure for a sailor's ailment called for use of drug number 11; to the captain's dismay the container was empty, so he mixed number 5 with number 6 to administer to the ailing crewmember. The crewman apparently regained his health.

When Dr. John B. King joined the crew of the *Aurora*, which left Edgartown on Martha's Vineyard Island on November 5, 1837, he carried with him a medicine chest that included:

1. Alum, for bleeding from the bowels
2. Antimonial wine, for coughs
3. Basilicon ointment, for blistering
4. Blister plaster
5. Blue vitriol, for removing warts and chancres
6. Burgundy pitch, for blisters
7. Calomel and jalap, purgatives
8. Calomel pills, ditto
9. Camomile, ditto
10. Castor oil, ditto
11. Camphor gum, for fever and nervousness
12. Salts of lemon, given with opium for fevers
13. Cream of tartar, for scurvy and fevers
14. Dover's powder, for boils, dysentery, dropsy, and insomnia
15. Balsam copaiba, for venereal disease, piles, and dysentery
16. Elixir vitriol, ditto
17. Emetic tartar, taken with camomile for fever
18. Ether, for seasickness
19. Flax seed, drunk as a tea for "clap" (gonorrhea)
20. Flowers of sulphur, for skin eruptions and itch
21. Glauber salts, a cooling purge and for swollen testicles
22. Ipecac, an emetic
23. Kino, for diarrhea
24. Laudanum, for pain and seasickness
25. Mercurial ointment, for syphilis and chancres
26. Nitre, for stoppage of the urine
27. Olive oil, a purgative for cholera
28. Opium, for dysentery and vomiting
29. Paregoric, for indigestion

30. Peppermint, for colic
31. Rhubarb, for loose bowels
32. Simple ointment, for blisters and chafing
33. Hartshorn, for faintness
34. Spirits of nitre, for dropsy
35. Syrup of squills, for coughs
36. Myrrh, for ulcerated gums (as in scurvy)
37. White vitriol, for "clap" (and sore eyes!)
38. Quinine, for intermittent fever (malaria)
39. Gum arabic, for indigestion
40. Chloride of lime, for destroying infection[14]

Several of the items on this list are used in holistic medicine today. Others such as laudanum (no. 24) and opium (no. 28) are clearly outside modern-day treatments. Several were evidently used for sexually transmitted diseases the men picked up on shore leave.[15]

Master Joseph P. Benton assumed command of the *A. R. Tucker* after Martin Van Buren Millard fell sick in 1899. Benton's log makes several references to treating Millard's illness; for example, giving the captain "a doce of spirit-Of Nitre and 20 drops of Lowdnam" (laudanum). Before Millard died a week later, Benton suggested that he write a note to his family: "he Sais bento thise is my last—So I sais Captain why you not write you family few lines he sais yes I like to write my wife but I cand now."

Benton neglected to say what killed Millard, but according to the list in Dr. King's medical chest, no. 24 laudanum was used for pain and seasickness and no. 33 nitre was for dropsy. Millard was sixty-two when he died, relatively old for a whaling captain.

CHAPTER 11

━━ ◄◆► ━━

Innovators

*B*lack men made contributions to the whaling industry other than finding, catching, and processing whales. They owned ships and established successful retail stores onshore. One was a ship designer whose vessels were sailed by captains of color. And one was a blacksmith who invented a vital piece of whaling technology.

Richard Johnson, Whale Ship Owner

Richard Johnson owned whale ships in the early 1800s, an astonishing accomplishment for a black man at that time. He owned the *Industry*, on which Absalom Boston served as master with an all-black crew, as well as the *Rising States*, which Edward J. Pompey and William Cuffe commanded. The latter had an all-black crew on the 1837 voyage that claimed William Cuffe's life, after which it was condemned in the Cape Verde Islands.

In *Black Sailors*, Richard Johnson is described as the supercargo, the individual in charge of the vessel's cargo. This is no doubt how he gained the expertise that allowed him to manage and own whale ships. Johnson's role was to buy and sell the goods and merchandise used on board the ship and keep records of the business transactions. He was not a part of the ship's command team, but the captain clearly recognized his value. When his ship stopped in Charleston, South Carolina, in 1824, local officials tried to place all the black men on board in jail during the ship's time in port, in accordance with state law. The ship's captain was expected to pay a bribe covering the cost of the imprisonment. The white officers refused to allow Johnson to be taken and willingly posted a bond to keep him free. Few other black seamen were so fortunate. The ship was the *Rodman*—a trader financed by Johnson himself and a white merchant, Peleg Crowell; and Johnson was effectively one of the owners.[1]

William C. Nell, a black activist, documented Johnson's early history in *The Colored Patriots of the American Revolution* (1855). Johnson was born in 1776 in Pennsylvania or Virginia and had a long career at sea. Like Paul Cuffe he was caught and confined by the British during the War of 1812. "Manifests and newspaper advertisements" show him to have been active in trading from April 1812 to November 1813, February to mid-April 1814, and in January 1815.

In 1815 he became Ruth Howard's second husband—and thus a relative by marriage of Paul Cuffe. Ruth was the widow of Paul Cuffe's son-in-law Peter, who, with Cuffe's other son-in-law, Alexander, had owned the family retail store, P. & A. Howard, later renamed Howard & Johnson. "In early life," Nell wrote, Johnson "was engaged as a mariner, and filled every capacity, from a cabin boy to a captain." There are no records of Johnson captaining any whaling ships, so he must have been a merchant mariner—something that would have been useful in acquiring Peter and Alexander Howard's business. Nell continued: "He was distinguished for prudence and sagacity in his business operations, and, despite the obstacles that prejudice against color so constantly strewed in his path, he succeeded in his mercantile affairs, accumulated a competency, and retired from business several years since. Mr. Johnson was always ready to extend the hand of relief to his enslaved countrymen, and no one was more ready to assist, according to his ability, in the elevation of his people."[2]

Ships Owned by Richard Johnson

Ship	Year	Master
Industry	1822	Absalom Boston (Samuel Harris and Edward Pompey, part owners)
Rising States	1836	Edward J. Pompey (part owner)
Rising States	1837	William Cuffe (ten black owners) (Each of the voyages above had all-black crews)
Francis	1835–42	owned one-eighth share
Washington	Unknown	n/a

After his death, Johnson's share of the *Washington* went to his sons, Richard C. and Ezra R. Johnson. They were part owners of the *Wade*, and Richard C. was an owner of the *Pleiades*. Richard Sr.'s brother Nathan was part owner of the *Draper*.

Richard Johnson was no dilettante when it came to protecting the rights of black people and the whaling community. He was the New Bedford agent for the *Liberator*, the publication that fought for the end of slavery, sharing that role with Nathaniel A. Borden, a co-owner of the *Rising States*. Whaling masters Absalom Boston and Edward J. Pompey were his counterparts for the *Liberator* on Nantucket. Johnson and publisher William Lloyd Garrison were said to have been close friends. He served with the New Bedford Union Society (an affiliate of the American Union for the Relief and Improvement of the Colored Race) and the annual West Indies Emancipation Day.

Johnson lived a life of success and respect, dying at age seventy-seven on February 15, 1853, after seeing his wife, Ruth, die a day earlier. His funeral was well attended by the citizens of New Bedford.[3]

John Mashow, Ship Builder and Designer, 1805–December 20, 1893

A Mashow Ship Considered One of the Very Best

—New Bedford newspaper headline

John Mashow was a builder of whale ships between 1830 and 1860. Born into slavery in South Carolina, at age twenty-five he made his way to freedom in Dartmouth, near New Bedford, in 1815. Three years later he became an apprentice to a shipbuilder named Laban Thatcher. In about 1845 he, Alonzo Mathew, James Madison Babbitt, and Frederick Smally built the Mathew, Mashow & Co. shipyard in Padanarum (the Mashow Shipyards), today an affluent seaside village south of New Bedford. Mathew, Mashow & Co. went out of business in 1858 after having designed more than one hundred ships and built about sixty—fourteen of which were whale ships (see appendix H).

As part payment, shipbuilders usually retained a share of the boats they built—another reason Mashow became financially successful—and he is believed to have held shares in seven ships. For thirty years it was said his ships were among the best afloat.[4]

Mashow married Hope Amos from Mashpee, probably a Native American of the Wampanoag tribe (she was listed as a person of color), July 17, 1830. They had eight children, five of them sons who became whalers and sailed in their father's ships.[5]

The adjacent towns of Mattapoisett, Dartmouth, and Westport were home ports to several black masters, including the Cook family, the Cuffe family, Amos Haskins, Henry Lewis, Alvan Phelps, and the Wainer family, many of whom may have sailed in Mashow's boats. Six different Mashow-designed vessels, in fact, had black captains (see appendix H); the *Morning Star* had three and sank on a trip led by Valentine Rosa.

Mashow may have been the only black man of his time to have a ship named after him. It is an interesting footnote that three of the whale ships he designed were burned to the waterline (along with more than sixty others) by the Confederate warships *Alabama* and *Shenandoah*.[6]

After building the schooner *J. W. Flanders*, Mathews and Mashow declared bankruptcy in 1858 as a result of the financial downturn of 1857. When their shipyard closed, John Mashow was recognized as "a thorough, practical master shipbuilder and a most worthy and respected citizen." He was listed as a "ship carpenter" in New Bedford city directories until his death in 1893. To his last days he was principally a carpenter and shipwright.

His obituary read: "John Mashow, a well-known shipbuilder in the

palmy days of New Bedford's whaling interests, died at his home in Dartmouth today in his 88th year. He has built some of the finest and stanchest of the vessels which comprised the whaling fleet. . . . He was honorable and upright in his dealings, and commanded the respect of all who knew him."[7]

This drawing of John Mashow is from a newspaper clipping printed after his death in 1893. *Courtesy of the New Bedford Whaling Museum*

Lewis Temple, Inventor, 1800–March 18, 1854

It is safe to say that the Temple Toggle was the most important single invention in the whole history of whaling.

—CLIFFORD W. ASHLEY, maritime historian

The Temple Toggle was named after Lewis Temple, a black man who in 1845 invented an indispensable piece of whaling technology. Born into slavery in Richmond, Virginia, around 1800, Temple, a blacksmith, made his way to New Bedford in 1829. It is unknown whether he escaped or was bought out of slavery. Surrounded by the whaling industry, Temple thought to improve the harpoon—basically a stick with an iron point—by adding a barb, or "toggle," that opened when stuck into a whale and held it in place. The value of harpoons to whale ships was immeasurable: a four-year whaling voyage often required 150–200 harpoons. One calculation indicates that more than a million were used in all.[8]

Temple married Mary Clark from Maryland in 1829 and had a son, Lewis Jr., in 1830. They had two daughters, Nancy in 1832 and Mary, who died at age six. By 1836 Temple was an established citizen, and by 1845 the former slave had become a prosperous shop owner on Coffin's Wharf, where he invented whaling's major innovation.

Toggle harpoons were in use as early as 1654, as evidenced by a portrait in the National Museum in Copenhagen of a west Greenland Inuit whale hunter holding one, but the technology seems to have been ignored for almost two hundred years. After Temple began producing and selling his toggle harpoons, James Durfree, a New Bedford whalecraft maker, jumped on the bandwagon and copied and produced close to 13,000 of Temple's harpoons between 1848 and 1868 in his shop, one of 10 such

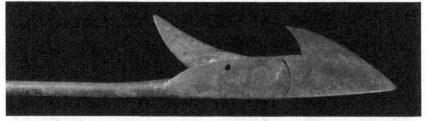

An original "Temple's Toggle" made by the inventor himself. *Courtesy of the New Bedford Whaling Museum*

shops in New Bedford. The value of the toggle is clear in a report on the voyage of the *Ohio* in the *Whalemen's Shipping List*. The ship reached port in May 1853 with 2,350 barrels of oil from 21 bowhead whales—and used *only* 8 harpoons. Temple never secured a patent for his invention, although it was known to all as "Temple's Toggle," "Temple's Gig," and "Temple's Toggle-Iron." There was apparently little effort to disguise whose invention was being reproduced with such alacrity—and without compensation. Little is known about Temple's early life or how he developed his blacksmithing skills, but he never learned to write his name.[9]

During the fall of 1853 Temple tripped over a plank and injured himself so badly that he could no longer work. He petitioned the city of New Bedford for two thousand dollars in compensation. It wasn't until ten days after his death in March 1854 that the Common Council ordered it paid—but it never was. His shop and home were sold off to pay his debts, leaving nothing for his widow and children.

Today a life-size bronze statue (created by a black sculptor) of Lewis Temple stands outside the New Bedford Public Library in a small, well-kept park, and the Temple Toggle is known as "one Negro's contribution to the prosperity of the country."[10]

Ship Owners

Well before the Civil War, John Mashow's son Isaac H. Mashow was a boat-steerer on the *Benjamin Cummings* (designed by his father). His ownership during the *Cummings'* 1854–59 trip earned him $152. Others who invested in whaling included George Belain (Joseph G. Belain's brother) on the *Massasoit*, captained by Amos Haskins in 1852, and Asa Wainer (Paul and Thomas Wainer's brother) on the *Elizabeth*, captained by Pardon Cook in 1841.[11]

When whaling declined, Cape Verdean masters acquired the whale ships to use in the more profitable packet trade. Among them were José Domingues, John Z. Silva, James Franklin Brown, Antonio Joside (José) Senna, Joseph Gaspar, A. J. Senna, and Luiz D. Oliveira.

Master Antone L. Sylvia owned or partly owned whale ships, including several used by other captains of color: the *Tekoa* (Jasper Ears); *Crowninshield, Lydia, Peru* (Anthony Benton); *Minerva II, Greyhound*

(Benjamin Costa); *Mary E. Simmons*, *Adelia Chase* (Ayres J. Senna, Joseph H. Senna); *Pedro Varela* (Frank Lopes, Anthony P. Benton, Theophilus M. Freitas); and the *Carleton Bell*.

These enterprising captains learned from Paul Cuffe that whale ships were still just boats that could be placed into service for other profitable pursuits.

CHAPTER 12

━ ✦ ━

The Cape Verdeans

We're the only Africans who came to America by choice.

—AL VICENTE[1]

Ship Ahoy . . . Ship Ahoy
Americans are arriving
Midst the hubbub of the quay
There are tears of joy
Fugitive crystals
Lighting up, the women's eyes.
All have passed by
—Chinese, negroes, Americans, Dutchmen—All have passed by
and casually left
their race
in the bellies of the harlots
of the port.

—JORGE BARBOSA, "Islands"[2]

he Cape Verde archipelago is about 350 miles from Africa's
west coast. It consists of 10 islands with a combined landmass
of about 1,500 square miles (about the size of Rhode Island)
in an area of the sea roughly 350 miles by 200 miles (about the size of
Washington State). Colonized by the Portuguese in the fifteenth century,
the archipelago is now an independent country, Cabo Verde, and a member of the United Nations. The population today is about 512,000. Most of
the Cape Verdean whaling masters hailed from the islands of Brava, Maio,
or Fogo.

The arid volcanic islands were uninhabited until the Italians and Portuguese arrived in 1456. In the sixteenth century, Cape Verde was important to the slave trade because it was conveniently located in the Atlantic near Africa and on the shipping lanes to the New World. The resulting polyglot population is aptly described by the Cape Verdean poet Jorge Barbosa in his poem "Islands." Until 1836, when Portugal outlawed slavery, the islands' proximity to Africa made it practical for the Portuguese to bring slaves to work on their plantations there. Italian and Spanish explorers and seafarers were granted land by the Portuguese, and settlers also arrived from South America, other European countries, and even Asia. Over the years, the racial admixture left the country with a Creole (black and white mixed) population. The Portuguese encouraged miscegenation between the colonists and Africans (soldiers and officials were rewarded with monetary or land benefits if they married slaves who had been left behind on the islands). A 2010 genetic study conducted in Portugal concludes that the Cape Verdean population is significantly blended with other races.[3]

The Cape Verdeans developed a language called Crioulo or Caboverdeano. Their mixed-race background and odd language and accent made the "Bravas" vulnerable to discrimination when they came to America. Even in Cape Verde, this complicated society used skin tone, slave heritage, and wealth as a means of social stratification. Terms such as "black" and "Negro" were viewed as racial slurs; "persons of color" was the acceptable description.[4]

Cape Verdeans began immigrating to the United States in the early nineteenth century when New England whale ships replaced deserting crewmen with islanders. A drought-caused famine killed 12,000–30,000 Cape Verdeans during the period 1831–33, and another 30,000 died between 1863 and 1865. Each of these human catastrophes accounted for 10–20 percent of the population. The people suffered further from out-breaks of cholera and smallpox. In 1864, half the population of the island of São Tiago (25,000 people) died when the crops failed. When "famine is often the reigning monarch," as historian Briton Cooper Busch observes, Cape Verdeans had a life-sustaining interest in leaving their homeland.[5]

Yankee captains valued Cape Verdeans as crewmembers because they "worked hard to save what they could while on board vessel [and] they could be hired for much less money than American seamen. Furthermore, they made a disciplined crew."[6] This was at the tail end of the once-thriving whaling industry, when owners were looking to cut costs as the price of oil declined. Cape Verdeans would ship on for as little as a 1/200th lay while American cooks, green hands, and cabin boys shipped for lays that rarely dipped below 1/140th according to most historical sources.[7]

The Portuguese in America were not particularly helpful to their island cousins, wishing to distance themselves from the darker-skinned Cape Verdeans of African descent. The immigrants were treated much like the Irish and Italians had been in the early 1800s who likewise were not classified as "white." The distancing process continued when the Cape Verdeans worked with black whalers and saw how skin color reduced options and encouraged discrimination. Cape Verdean writer Lucy Ramos explained in the 1980s, "Do you know the ridicule that a black man faces when he says, 'I'm white, I'm Portuguese.'" By the time Cape Verdeans were joining the industry, most white men were fleeing, and anyone "who displayed energy and talent aboard ship was virtually assured of rapid promotion."

The 2010 U.S. Census counted 355,329 persons of Cape Verdean ancestry throughout the United States, including the 35,000 born outside the United States. Described as "Africa's largest voluntary immigration to the United States," 350,000 Cape Verdeans live in New England.[8]

New Bedford and Providence, Rhode Island, are home to the oldest and largest Cape Verdean communities, which are marked by close ties and interdependence among families, a practice passed down through the generations. When whaling died, Cape Verdean captains bought the old ships for a fraction of their initial worth and converted them to packet ships used to transport goods to the islands and return with families who wanted American lives. This immigration grew as Cape Verde suffered further drought, starvation, and economic decline. The burgeoning packet trade allowed them to send home money and news of other family and friends already in "the land of opportunity." From 1860 to 1965 Cape Verdeans owned more than 41 percent of the packet business, and most of the owners were former whaling captains.

While the Cape Verdeans suffered discrimination because they looked black, it is important to note that they initially did not think of themselves as black. They retained a unique culture apart from that of the African

Acculturation and Assimilation

Cape Verdean Americans carry with them a history of hardship and devastation. The strength they developed in the islands fortified them as they faced obstacles in their new country. Cape Verdean immigrants continue to work for the betterment and survival of their fellow Cape Verdeans who remain in the islands. The distinction between "black" and "white" in the America to which the Cape Verdeans arrived subjected them to immediate prejudice. Dwayne Williams, the executive director of the Rhode Island Black Heritage Society, explained that even when Americans attempted to classify Cape Verdeans as black, and often dismissed them because of that, "Cape Verdeans [still] refused to fit within this framework." They did not think of themselves as "African Americans" in the same way that the descendants of America's slaves did. For them, their European blood was as much a part of their ancestry as was their African blood. That was true especially for those who settled in the Midwest, away from the concentrated Cape Verdean environments of New England. Because a majority of them were Roman Catholics in a country where few African Americans shared that faith, Cape Verdean Americans more often found themselves in the company of other white Catholics. Many of these white Catholics were immigrants from Eastern Europe who were also struggling to blend in to their new country. Although many of them were forced into black neighborhoods because of their skin color, earlier generations of Cape Verdean Americans maintained a society separate from other African Americans surrounding them. Their customs, their language, and their religion kept them together in close-knit extended families. When the children and grandchildren of the first immigrant waves became involved in the civil rights movement of the 1960s, a new sense of solidarity with other African Americans emerged. As Cape Verdean Americans intermarried with African Americans of a different background, many of whom were descendants of African slaves and American slave-holders, the cultures began to share traditions and find common sympathies.

Source: Jane E. Spear, http://www.everyculture.com/multi/Bu-Dr/Cape-Verdean-Americans.html #ixzz57Nzem3Gp.

Americans who were descendants of slaves in the United States. They continued to live in separate communities well into the civil rights struggles of the 1960s, when it became clear that it was "them" (whites) against "us" (those whom whites viewed as black). When Cape Verdeans saw similarities between their own struggle and that of African Americans, a sense of solidarity emerged.

In portraying themselves as Portuguese, Cape Verdeans believed they could distance themselves from the extreme prejudice that whites practiced on black Americans. William W. Crapo (founder of the Old Dartmouth Historical Society, forerunner of the New Bedford Whaling Museum) pointed out in 1916 that this was another reason for their "cultural separatism." Crapo was the man who insisted that the whale-man statue outside the New Bedford Public Library depict a fair-skinned Yankee harpooner instead of a Gay Head Indian, a black man, or a Cape Verdean, even though they performed overwhelmingly in that role before and after—and even in—*Moby-Dick*.[9]

Walter Noble Burns was intrigued by the Cape Verdeans he met on the *Alexander* in 1890 (captained by William Shorey), particularly some of the officers:

> Gabriel, the second mate, was a negro from the Cape Verde Islands. His native language was Portuguese and he talked funny, broken English. He was about forty-five years old, and though he was almost as dark-skinned as any Ethiopian, he had hair and a full beard as finely spun and free from kinkiness as a Caucasian's. The sailors used to say Gabriel was a white man born black by accident. . . . Mendez, the third mate and Long John, one of the boat-steerers, were also Cape Verde islanders. Long John was a giant, standing six feet, four inches; an ungainly, powerful fellow, with a black face as big as a ham and not much more expressive.[10]

Historian A. Hyatt Verrill described New Bedford whalers in 1923 as "mainly men of a different sort, Portuguese from the Azores or the Cape Verde islands, many of them nearly full-blooded negroes and black as ebony, but hardworking, industrious and good whalers."[11]

While the Portuguese became "whiter" in Provincetown, "African Americans and black Cape Verdeans remained targets of racial tension and prejudice" there.[12] The Cape Verdeans, often including the darker-skinned ones, refused to associate with blacks, claiming to be both white and Portuguese. It didn't take Cape Verdeans long to figure things out in America, but the lessons came hard. On the Cape Verde Islands, wealth rather than race stratified society. But in the United States in 1852, Manuel Pereira, a "coloured Portuguese" sailor on board a British brig driven into Charleston by a storm, was arrested and jailed.[13]

In New Bedford, younger generations of Cape Verdeans are reclaiming their unique ethnic identity along with their African roots. The New Bedford Historical Society is an example of that and celebrates the sameness of our differences—and Cape Verdeans' substantial contributions to whaling.

JOHN (JOÃO) DA LOMBA (1885–1968)

John da Lomba was born on Brava in the Cape Verde Islands in 1885 and was fourteen when he made his first whaling voyage, on board the *Antarctica*. He served later on the *Swallow* with Captain Benjamin D. Cleveland, and the two developed an almost lifelong business partnership. They sailed the southern oceans in Antarctica hunting elephant seals and together owned the *A. E. Whyland* and *A. M. Nicholson*. Da Lomba

The *William A. Graber* with a man believed to be John (João) da Lomba, perhaps with his daughters, at the wheel. *Courtesy of the New Bedford Whaling Museum*

JOHN da LOMBA.

João da Lomba, from a newspaper picture. *Courtesy of the New Bedford Whaling Museum*

also owned shares in Cleveland's *Daisy*, another whaler. While first mate on the *Daisy*, he met the ornithologist Robert Cushman Murphy from the American Museum of Natural History, who joined the ship in 1912 to collect birds. Murphy praised da Lomba's seamanship and whalecraft, pronouncing him "as competent as any man could possibly be."[14]

The *Daisy* was built in Brookhaven on Long Island in 1872, and Murphy was on its last successful trip (1911–13) when it returned with 1,700 barrels of sperm oil and 1,200 barrels of whale oil. Writing in Portuguese, da Lomba kept the *Daisy*'s log from November 1, 1911, to June 28, 1913. All but three of the *Daisy*'s crew of twenty-seven, including da Lomba and most of the ship's officers (except Captain Benjamin Cleveland), were black, according to Murphy, who published an account of the voyage in the form of letters to his wife, Grace, titled *Logbook for Grace*. The photographs he took on the trip were published in *A Dead Whale or a Stove Boat*. Murphy was with the right crew for a "stove boat."[15]

An undated newspaper article headlined "Whale Stove Boat" details the story of two crewmen badly injured by a whale when Second Mate Antone Martin threw a harpoon that did not stick in its target. The whale retaliated, badly damaging the whaleboat. Da Lomba was first mate of the *A. E. Whyland* at the time, and the story mentions Da Lomba's plans to join Benjamin Cleveland as first mate of the *Daisy*. Coincidentally, an article on the same page titled "Mate Enos Killed by Whale" was about the *Daisy*'s second mate, a Cape Verdean who left a wife and child behind.

Da Lomba served as boat-steerer, second mate, and first mate before becoming master of the *William A. Graber* in 1920. He was described

João da Lomba (*right*) sharpening a blade on the *William A. Graber*. Da Lomba was owner and master of the *Graber*. *Courtesy of the New Bedford Whaling Museum*

as "well over six feet in height" and may have honed his whaling skills to get promoted out of the cramped forecastle with its notoriously low overhead. Da Lomba sailed with several captains who found him an exceptional crewman and mate; but lacking education he could not comprehend navigation, and so his captaining experience was sorely limited. He succeeded his friend and mentor Benjamin D. Cleveland, captain of the *William A. Graber*, as the ship's managing owner/agent in 1922 for its last years (it was sold into the packet trade to Louis Lopes and lost in the Cape Verde Islands in 1928). At the end of whaling, da Lomba went into the packet ship business, owning his own ships in addition to the *William A. Graber*; he was a partner with José Andrade in the schooner *Blossom*, a former whaler, in the mid-1920s. He commanded the *Blossom* until it was wrecked at Cape Verde in 1930.

John da Lomba was also a talented scrimshaw artist. A 2015 exhibit dedicated to Cape Verdeans at the New Bedford Whaling Museum featured a sea elephant (elephant seal) tooth da Lomba had carved. On a voyage on the *Daisy* in 1906 he carved a self-portrait that depicted his African ancestry.[16]

MANUEL J. DOMINGUES (DOMINGOS)
(JULY 2, 1902–SEPTEMBER 11, 1989)

Manuel Domingues is the subject of a remarkable sepia-toned DVD of probably the last living whale captain. The correct spelling of the last name is Domingues, according to his cousin Bill do Carmo, who provided the video, and Domingues himself, who spells out his name in the video. On the DVD, eighty-five-year-old Manuel speaks lucidly and enthusiastically about his whaling career, which began in 1919 on his father's ship, the *Cameo*, when he was seventeen. He had come over from Brava when he turned fifteen in 1917. On this trip from New Bedford to the Atlantic whaling grounds, which lasted from February 18 to September 11, 1919, the *Cameo* was caught in "rough" weather, and even with all sails stowed the ship was traveling at ten knots (almost twelve miles) per hour. Manuel was instructed to take the wheel while the more experienced deckhands manned the pumps. This was the same storm that sank the *Ellen A. Swift* and *Pedro Varela* (captained

(Cat. No. 517.)

Bill of Sale
OF
REGISTERED VESSEL

Benjamin D. Cleveland
TO

Louis Lopes
CALLED THE

A. E. Whyland

Custom House

May 16, 1912

Received for record,

Recorded, Book

Clerk.

Bill of sale transferring the schooner *A. E. Whyland* from Benjamin D. Cleveland to Louis M. Lopes. *Courtesy of the New Bedford Whaling Museum*

Manuel Domingues on board a Gulf Oil ship, where he worked after retiring from whaling. *Courtesy of Bill do Carmo and Diane Hazleton*

by Frank Lopes) with all hands. It was quite a baptism into whaling. The *Cameo* returned with 525 barrels of sperm oil.[17]

Domingues tells how he enjoyed the harpooning— the "catching" part of whale trips—and how sperm whales spout in a slanted stream. This was how the spotter, even from a distance, knew that it was a sperm whale. He recalled the Nantucket sleigh rides, especially on calm water with no wind, after which the crew had to row back to the mother ship towing their catch. On this trip he caught two whales, one at sunset when the setting sun prevented those on the mother ship from seeing his whaleboat. He did not say how long it took to tow the whale back but did say the ship was "very far away."

Domingues was clearly proud of the "wooden ships and men of steel," as he called them, who went whaling. But by 1920 he had had enough. In 1918 he had earned just $70 in seven months. The crew list reports Domingues as master of the schooner *William A. Graber*, which departed New Bedford in March 1920 and returned in September 1920, the year Domingues says he retired from whaling. Even though black captain John da Lomba is listed as master (the *Graber* and the *Cameo* were acquired by Benjamin D. Cleveland), absent any better information it is believed that the two shared the voyage, with Domingues as replacement captain for at least part of the short trip.

Diane Hazleton, Captain Domingues' daughter, supplied more details about his life. Because her father spent most of his life at sea she did not spend much time with him, but she collected articles, information, and stories about him, including crew lists of ships he and his father, José M. Domingues, served on. Manuel Domingues was one of an unknown number of the whaling captains of color to acquire a master's license qualifying him to captain ships of not more than 100 gross registered tons on any waterway. After whaling, Domingues worked on board Gulf Oil ships for thirty-five to forty years. Mrs. Hazleton had no evidence that his whaling career was more financially rewarding than his work for Gulf Oil—as a cook.[18]

Domingues died at age eighty-five on September 11, 1989, at his home on Bonney Street in New Bedford. He was probably the last living

The *Morning Star* with staves for making barrels in the foreground. *Courtesy of the New Bedford Whaling Museum*

black whaling captain, and his daughter Diane Hazleton may be the last living immediate family member of a whaling captain of color.

Domingues was not the only Cape Verdean who distinguished himself in a difficult business in which promotion came as a result of merit. There were others.

JASPER MANUEL EARS

Jasper Manuel Ears was second mate on the *Morning Star*'s first voyage in 1853. According to the ship's log, Ears was born and resided in New Bedford, was thirty-two years old, five feet six inches tall, and was black with "curley" hair. Ears served as a master on three voyages (*George J. Jones, Peru,* and *Ellen Rodman*) and as a replacement master twice on board the *E. H. Hatfield* on back-to-back trips in 1880. From 1849 to 1884 he also served on the *John A. Robb, Tekoa, Star Castle, Eunice H. Adams, Sea Queen,* and *Elliot C. Cowden.* As a captain his trips returned with whale oil that would be valued at about $973,000 today.[19]

JOSÉ PERRY

José Perry was a frequent replacement captain, serving on the *Bertha D. Nickerson* (1908–9; Manuel F. Santos, captain), the *A. M. Nicholson* (1911; Horace Perry Smith, captain), and the *Valkyria* (1918–19; Joseph A. Viera, captain). The whale oil returned from his three trips had a value of about $897,000.[20]

CARLO COSTA

Carlo Costa was the replacement master on board the *Milton* (1880–84; Sylvanus B. Potter, captain). The crew list indicates he was five-feet-five, twenty-three years old, and had black skin. The trip's results were impressive: the *Milton* returned with oil worth $1.8 million dollars in today's dollars.

ANTONIO JOSIDE (JOSÉ) SENNA, ALSO
ANTONE JOSÉ SENNA OR ALBERTINO DE SENNA

Antonio Joside Senna was master of the *Pedro Varela* (1891–94) and returned with oil valued at $883,000 in today's dollars. Well past the glory days of whaling, he bought the *John R. Manta* in 1929, the last of the whale ships to be placed in the packet trade.[21]

The three men on the *John R. Manta* are unidentified. In 1925 the *Manta* became the last whaling ship to return with a cargo of whale oil. It was also one of five ships used by black captains to return with ambergris. *Courtesy of the New Bedford Whaling Museum*

AYRES J. SENNA

By the time Ayres J. Senna became a captain, the days of long voyages to unexplored whaling grounds had ended. On three trips commanding the *Adelia Chase* between 1901 and 1905, for example, the schooner rarely cruised farther than Faial, Brava, and Dominica.[22]

Ships Captained by Ayres J. Senna

Ship	Departure	Return
Golden City	1897	1899
Adelia Chase	1899	1901 (replacement captain)
Adelia Chase	1901	1902 (owned by Antone Sylvia)
Adelia Chase	1902	1904 (owned by Antone Sylvia and Senna)
Adelia Chase	1904	1905 (owned by Antone Sylvia and Senna)

Joseph H. Senna on his ship the *Carleton Bell*, which was also captained by master Antone Sylvia. Ayres J. Senna was Joseph H. Senna's father. *Courtesy of the New Bedford Whaling Museum*

Senna was on board a whale ship almost continuously for seven years from November 13, 1897, to September 1, 1905. His ships returned with oil that would be valued at $1.6 million today.

JOSEPH H. SENNA

Joseph H. Senna served with his father, Ayres J. Senna, on the *Adelia Chase* in 1901, 1902, and 1904, beginning when he was twenty, and captained the *Adelia Chase* himself from May 30 to August 21, 1906. The Cape Verdean display at the New Bedford Whaling Museum shows Senna as captain of the *Carleton Bell*, which he, his father, and Antone Sylvia owned together. During Senna's career as captain, from 1906 to 1922, he was responsible for capturing about 122 whales with a value today of about $3 million.[23]

JOSEPH GASPAR (DE CONCEIÇAO)
(1867–1931)

Joseph Gaspar de Coneiçao sailed as Joseph Gaspar when he captained the schooner *Pilgrim*—which he also owned—on trips to the Atlantic in 1902 and 1903, when it was lost at Cape Verde. The 69-ton schooner was built in 1884 in Essex, Massachusetts, and appears to have made just the two whaling voyages. Gaspar was able to return on the first trip with oil valued at $32,000 late in the whaling game, when sperm oil was selling for only 56 cents per gallon and whale oil for 38 cents per gallon.[24]

The *Claudia* with sails drying. Julio Fernandes, Louis M. Lopes, and Joseph H. Senna are thought to have sailed together on the *Claudia* in 1919 with Fernandes as a replacement captain. *Courtesy of the New Bedford Whaling Museum*

JULIO FERNANDES

Julio Fernandes was twenty-two on his first voyage on board the schooner *Ellen A. Swift* from Provincetown in 1909. Fernandes was a frequent replacement captain and evidently well trusted by some of the leading New Bedford captains of the day. He served on the *Bertha*, the *Bertha D. Nickerson*, and the *John R. Manta* (each commanded by another captain of color). Fernandes sailed on the *Claudia* with both Louis M. Lopes

(October 28, 1919) and Joseph H. Senna earlier the same year (February 4, 1919), when he is believed to have served as Senna's replacement for a time.[25]

JOHN ZURICK SILVA

The picture of John Z. Silva in the New Bedford Whaling Museum was taken in 1911. Silva, born 1853 in Brava, was a pioneer in the packet trade, buying his first schooner, the *William E. Terry*, in 1886. He was in the whaling and merchant trade business for more than thirty-six years, culminating in the final voyage of the bark *Sunbeam*, which he bought to use as a packet ship in 1916. The *Sunbeam* was used as a whaler for twenty-six trips between 1856 and 1909—its last trip with Silva as master. The New Bedford Whaling Museum Library has a section devoted to whaling scrapbooks, and a newspaper clipping in one of them has another photo of Captain J. Z. Silva with the story about the wreck and loss of the uninsured *William A. Grozier* (all hands were saved), which he owned. The undated newspaper account, titled "Old Time Whaling Schooner Wrecked at Sea," reports that the ship was lost in the packet trade while shuttling Cape

Verdeans to New Bedford. The *William A. Grozier* had been heralded under its prior owner (George L. Dunham) as having had the shortest successful whaling trip on record when, after two and a half months in 1906, it returned full of whale oil, including in its drained water barrels, casks, kettles, try-pots, and coolers.[26]

John Z. Silva, captain of the *Sunbeam. Courtesy of the New Bedford Whaling Museum*

ANTONE L. SYLVIA

Antone L. Sylvia, born on São Jorge Island in Cape Verde in 1840, operated a clothing and outfitting store in New Bedford similar to the one Paul Cuffe and his partners owned.[27] Also like Cuffe, Sylvia owned or partly owned whale ships, including several used by other captains of color: the *Tekoa* (Jasper Ears); *Crowninshield, Lydia, Peru* (Anthony Benton); *Minerva II, Greyhound* (Benjamin Costa); *Mary E. Simmons, Adelia Chase* (Ayres J. Senna, Joseph H. Senna); *Pedro Varela* (Frank Lopes, Anthony P. Benton, Theophilus M. Freitas); and the *Carleton Bell* (Joseph H. Senna). By century's end he was a director of the Bennett Manufacturing Corp. (cotton yarn) and the New Bedford Board of Trade. Sylvia captained the *Fannie Byrnes* from 1879 to 1884, when it was condemned in St. Thomas but managed to send back oil worth $211,000 today, which may have provided for his subsequent investments. He was a captain of color evidently more successful on land than at sea.

LUIZ D'OLIVEIRA (LUIS D. OLIVEIRA)

A 1910 photo of Captain Luiz d'Oliveira shows him on board the *Charles G. Rice* wearing a jacket, tie, and what appears to be a vest. The caption describes him as an owner of packet ships that included the *Eugenia Emilia* and the whaler *Bertha*, a 168-ton bark that was built in 1877 and had its last whale trip in 1917 with d'Oliveira as master. Louis M. Lopes once served on board the *Bertha* as first mate to Captain John T. Gonsalves in 1907.[28]

Luiz d'Oliveira. *Courtesy of the New Bedford Whaling Museum*

JOSÉ (JOSEPH) M. DOMINGUES (DOMINGOS)

Listed on the crew list as "Joseph (José) Domingos," José Domingues gained experience on the *Sunbeam* when he was eighteen, the *Canton II*, the *Ellen A. Swift*, twice on the *Arthur V. S. Woodruff*, the *A. M. Nicholson*, and the *Cameo*, which he ultimately bought and captained. The 200-ton schooner *Cameo* was built in Bath, Maine, in 1878, the same year José M. Domingues is believed to have been born. He bought it from John Thomas Edwards in 1915 and sailed it as owner and captain on four trips until 1920, when it was sold to Benjamin D.

Joseph Domingues. *Courtesy of Bill do Carmo and Diane Hazleton*

Cleveland (partner with João da Lomba). On its last reported trip (1920), it sailed from Provincetown under the command of Louis Lopes. The *Cameo* returned from a March 1912–August 1915 voyage with an astonishing 5,300 barrels of sperm oil with an unfortunately low value of 15 cents a gallon (about $740,000 today).

José M. Domingues served on board several whale ships with others who were or would become captains of color: 1912, *Arthur V. S. Woodruff* with August P. Gomes (both were crewmen); 1917, *A. M. Nicholson* with John T. Gonsalves (master); 1919, *Cameo* with his son Manuel among the crew for his first trip.[29]

BENJAMIN COSTA

Benjamin Costa sailed the *Greyhound* on its final whaling voyage when it foundered off the Cape Verde Islands on March 8, 1922. It was his only trip as a master. He commanded the *Valkyria* after its conversion to a packet ship by Henry Rose, who claimed he once made the trip to the

Cape Verde Islands in ten days. With the estimated maximum speed of an empty whale ship being eight knots (nine miles per hour), this feat had to have been accomplished by sailing fifteen hours for each of those ten days. In 1924 Costa captained the *Yukon* and Captain John Sousa the *William A. Graber* (a former whaler), and both ships arrived at Brava the same day (May 13, 1924). The two made a $1,500 bet over who could make the return trip faster. Costa and Sousa were both upstaged when the *Valkyria* beat them both. She was called "Queen of the Cape Verde Packets" until 1926.[30]

The *Valkyria* at full sail. *Courtesy of the New Bedford Whaling Museum*

Changing Times

As whale oil prices plunged, ship owners and investors had to factor Cape Verdeans working for less into their business plans. The Quakers had withdrawn from whaling by then and had invested their profits in the new textile mills in southern New England. In 1846 New Bedford had two cotton mills, the New Bedford Steam Company and the Wamsutta Mills. The Potomska Mills started in 1871, and seven more mills were founded by 1880. The owner/investors' family names were Grinnell, Rodman, Howland, Knowles, Bourne—and Rotch, specifically William Rotch Jr., Paul Cuffe's friend and fellow Quaker.

Cape Verdeans could not get the better-paying jobs in the new mills, but they were talented, smart, and industrious. They found a way to profit by buying former whale ships and repurposing them as packet ships, merchant vessels that took supplies to a suffering Cape Verde—and brought families back to America.[31]

CHAPTER 13

⊶ ⊰⊹⊱ ⊷

Whaling Moves to San Francisco

*A*s shale oil began to fill the market and the price of whale oil dropped, whalers had to look elsewhere for profits. Some looked to baleen (whalebone). The whalebone market was not appreciable until 1835, when a million pounds of it, valued for the tensile strength it gave to corsets and other products, went to market. Seventy-five million pounds of whalebone were harvested from 1804 to 1876, with a monetary value that was only 23 percent of the whale industry's total

The *Andrew Hicks* (often captained by William T. Shorey), the *Platina* with sails drying, and the *Bertha D. Nickerson* docked in San Francisco. *Courtesy of the New Bedford Whaling Museum*

(including sperm oil and whale oil). William T. Shorey, Henry J. Gonzales, Joseph G. Belain, Ferdinand Lee, William Garrison Lee, and Peter Lopez were among the captains of color who sailed the Arctic waters of the Pacific Northwest to hunt baleen whales. San Francisco was the closest major port to their prey.

The call of the 1849 Gold Rush in California was enticing to whalers, whose profession required no aptitude for sowing a harvest, just collecting it. Digging for gold had that in common with whaling—without the danger. Several whale captains and crews tried their hands at mining gold with mixed results. But most did some whaling while they were in San Francisco. Unfortunately, the whales were found in the waters of the North Pacific, where the weather was even worse than in the North Atlantic and ice added to an already difficult business.

PETER LOPEZ (1869–1938)

A Cape Verdean, Peter Lopez whaled in the Arctic on the *Charles W. Morgan* in the 1890s (the *Morgan* berthed in San Francisco from 1887 to 1906); on the *Rosie* in 1914, where he served as a replacement captain; and on the *Northstar* and *Polar Bear* with the notorious Henry J. Gonzalez, who hijacked the *Polar Bear* and left a crew of explorers behind.

Stories abound about Peter Lopez's colorful life, although little is known about his early background. He is believed to have arrived in the North Pacific on board the *Alexander*, which wrecked on Diamond Rock near Cape Parry, off the Canadian coast, in 1906. The steamer had left San Francisco on May 2, 1905, and the "crew lived on blubber 13 days before rescue on August 12, 1906," according to Hegarty.[1] The rescue was well known to the local Inuits. Lopez remained in the area for the rest of his life and married an Inuit woman named Uttaktuak.

Described as a "Portuguese Negro," Lopez was esteemed both for his shipboard skills and as a trapper and hunter. One season Lopez caught three hundred foxes whose skins were worth $75–$95 each. He joined the Canadian Arctic Expedition in 1915 and took Uttaktuak along to help with the sewing. At the conclusion of the expedition—after Gonzalez was discharged—Lopez and Uttaktuak stayed at Cape Bathurst off the Northwest Territories, where Lopez pursued trapping. Their daughter, Lucy Adams, was born in 1931 at Tom's Bay. When Uttaktuak died in 1934, Lopez put

Lucy into a mission and saw her infrequently while he went about trapping, fishing, and supplying the mission with wood. Lopez died in 1938 when Lucy was eight years old, so she knew little about her parents. He remains alive in local legend, though. In a 2002 interview, Frank Carpenter from the town of Inuvik related the story of Lopez having jumped onto the back of a whale during a hunt.

Peter Lopez is buried in an old graveyard in Aklavik, on the other side of the world from his birth home.[2]

WILLIAM THOMAS SHOREY
(JANUARY 25, 1859–APRIL 15, 1919)

My whaling voyage was over. It was an adventure out of the ordinary, an experience informing, interesting, health-giving and perhaps worthwhile. I have never regretted it. But I wouldn't do it again for ten thousand dollars.

—WALTER NOBLE BURNS about his trip on board the *Alexander* captained by William T. Shorey (for which he was paid one dollar)

William T. Shorey was another tough black whaling captain; indeed, several escapades during his well-documented career might have earned Shorey the sobriquet "Black Ahab." The nickname was probably first coined by E. Berkeley Tompkins, historian and lecturer in history and senior fellow at the Hoover Institution on War, Revolution, and Peace at Stanford University, in a paper he wrote about Shorey.[3]

Colorful and committed to his craft, Shorey was a professional. At times he was impassioned, and

William T. Shorey. *Courtesy Oakland Public Library, Oakland History Room* he was relentless in his pursuit of whales, but it is difficult to see him as a damaged and obsessive man like Melville's Captain Ahab. Even Tomkins, whose work on Shorey is the most extensive, acknowledged that Shorey did not exhibit the monomania of an Ahab.

He did, however, have some close calls with whales. On an early voyage from Provincetown, Shorey almost lost his life to a whale. As he recounted it, "Evidently enraged, the whale attacked first one boat, smashing it, and then a second one, and then attacked the one I was in. By good fortune we were able to fire a bomb into him, which, exploding, killed him and saved us."

Shorey may not be as widely recognized as Paul Cuffe, but more is actually known about him. Born in 1859, one hundred years after Cuffe, Storey benefited from more press coverage documenting his exploits. Based on longevity and number of voyages, Shorey was one of the more successful black whaling masters. Only John T. Gonsalves' twenty-four voyages exceed Shorey's twenty. While all of his voyages as master were from San Francisco, Shorey initially sailed as a whaler from Provincetown. His career lasted thirty-two years, and he served as a captain for seventeen of those.

Shorey was the oldest of eight children born in Barbados to Scottish sugar planter William Shorey and West Indian Rosa Frazier, a "beautiful creole lady."[4] As a youngster Shorey apprenticed with a plumber, but finding few opportunities for a black man, Shorey joined a Boston-bound ship as cabin boy in 1875. He impressed the English captain, who began teaching him navigation and introduced him to Captain Whipple A. Leach, a successful whaler from Provincetown. Leach was also impressed with the young Shorey, and it is likely (but difficult to determine conclusively) that the seventeen-year-old shipped on the *Charles Thompson* as a green hand on its trip to the Atlantic from January 24, 1876, to September 17, 1877. Leach tutored Shorey in whaling and navigation and promoted him to boat-steerer on the trip. Rapidly promoted on the basis of his skills and aptitude, Shorey became third mate of the *Emma F. Herriman* at age twenty-one when it left Boston on November 8, 1880, for a three-year trip. And what a trip it was!

The *Herriman* crossed the Atlantic to the coast of Africa, rounded the treacherous Cape of Good Hope into the Indian Ocean, sailed on to Australia and the Tasman Sea, and then to Cape Horn in the southern Pacific. After several South American stops, the trip ended in San Francisco. By then Shorey had been promoted to first mate and never looked back.

Shorey's first captaincy came on the *Herriman* in 1885 when he replaced Henry Bronke for a time on a trip to the North Pacific. When he then replaced J. A. Hamilton on the *Herriman's* trip across the Pacific to Japan from 1886 to 1887 at age twenty-seven, he officially became a master. He returned with 150 barrels of sperm oil worth $3,960 (66 cents per gallon), 420 barrels of whale oil worth $5,376 (32 cents per gallon), and 5,000 pounds of whalebone worth $15,600 ($3.12 per pound), for a total of $24,936, a value today of almost $624,000. He had come a long way from Provincetown and Barbados.

Captain and Mrs. William T. Shorey and family in Oakland, California, after 1886. The younger child is Victoria, whose mother said of her, "Victoria is a remarkable sailor. She knows all the ropes, and has perfect command of her father." *Courtesy of San Francisco Maritime National Historic Park*

A Year with a Whaler

Walter Noble Burns signed on the *Alexander* on a whim and wrote a vivid and realistic book about his experiences. Although he never mentions that Captain William T. Shorey, his boss, is black, he has quite a bit to say about the other black crewmembers. Little Johnny, for example, was a mulatto from Barbados, "a strapping, intelligent young man . . . with all a plantation darky's love of fun." Five others serving in the forecastle included a tough American respected by the others for his skill and aggressiveness, a German, two Swedes, and a Norwegian. There were six other white green hands on board: a mule skinner, a cowboy, a country boy farmer, a man thought to have been running from the police, a thief, an old whaler seemingly a product of city slums—and Slim, an Irishman who had served with the English army. Rounding out the crew were three "Kanakas," or Hawaiians, one of whom was the cabin boy.

Burns took an immediate dislike to Third Mate Mendes, nicknamed the "Night King" by the crew. Describing him as "black as a bowhead's skin . . . imperious [with] thin and cruel lips . . . this little blackamoor [had] no glimmer of education [to] relieve his mental darkness. It was as though his outside color went all the way through." Mendes could neither read nor write, but Burns reluctantly acknowledges that he was a good sailor and the best harpooner on the ship. Of course the two men clashed. Burns, who lost every skirmish, found himself stunned that any but white men would be in charge. Mendes, sensing Burns' "smoldering resentment," took every opportunity to assign him the dirtiest and most menial tasks. Mendes earns the respect of Burns with his last act—cutting the line still attached to the diving whale that would have killed everyone else on board. "The qualities that had made him hated when he was indeed the Night King flooded back upon me, but I did not forget the courage of my enemy that had redeemed them all and made him a hero in the hour of death."

That single sentence sums up why black men went whaling—if you could perform, you were treated as a man—even if you weren't liked. Burns gives an excellent portrayal of whaling and of Shorey's fourth trip as captain. Published in 1913, the book is well worth reading to get a true sense of life on board.

By 1886 the whaling industry had shifted west. Eighty-nine whale ships left from eight ports: one each from Hartford (inexplicably) and Stonington, two each from Boston and Edgartown, three from New London, fourteen from Shorey's "home" port of Provincetown, seventeen from New Bedford—and a whopping forty-nine from San Francisco. During that year William T. Shorey, on the *E. F. Herriman,* was the only working captain of color. The next year, 1887, there were two—Shorey and Edgartown's William A. Martin on the *Eunice H. Adams.*[5]

Shorey commanded five different ships that brought back $2.3 million worth of oil (in today's dollars) during his career. The whalebone he brought back was valued at $5.5 million, far more valuable than the oil in his whaling years. In all, Shorey returned with more than $7 million of whale-based cargo.

Masters were tough—they had to be—and Master William T. Shorey was no exception. Given that the captain—and sometimes the first mate—recorded the daily activities in the log, it is rare to read in one that the boss was less than a gentleman. A few nonofficers, though, did write about events on their whaling trips. In Walter Burns' *A Year with a Whaler,* for example, we learn that Captain Shorey once pistol-whipped a man named Slim for insubordination.

A Year with a Whaler reads like a novel. In the following passage Slim describes what happened after he refused to work.

> The blood spurts all over me and I jumps up and yells, but the captain points his pistol at me and orders me to sit down again. He storms up and down the cabin floor. "I'll teach you who's master aboard this ship," he shouts and for a minute he was so purple in the face with rage, I thought he was going to murder me for sure. By and by he cools down. "Well, Slim," he says, "I guess I hit you a little harder than I meant to, but I'm a bad man when I get started. You need tending to now, sure enough." So he has the cabin boy fetch a pan of warm water and he washes the blood out of my hair with his own hands and then shaves around the cut and pastes sticking plaster on. That's all. But say, will I have the law on him when we get back to Frisco? Will I?

Encouraged by the crew to report Shorey, on the return trip to San Francisco Slim hailed the passing *Corwin,* a revenue cutter (forerunner of the U.S. Coast Guard). When two officers boarded the *Alexander,* Slim told his story and asked to be removed from the ship. An hour later the two officers emerged from the meeting with Shorey, puffing the captain's cigars in good humor, and left. While Captain Shorey and his officers spoke to Slim with "as much civility as they showed the rest" of the crew for the rest of the trip, he was assigned "any one of a hundred and one little jobs that didn't need doing." Three months later, at journey's end, "he was a pale, haggard shadow of his former self. It almost killed him."[6]

In 1884, shortly before Shorey's trip on the *Emma F. Herriman,* he married Julia Ann Shelton, a minister's daughter from a leading black San Francisco family. Good looking and genteel, Shorey rose to master because of his talent as "an experienced and skilled sailor, an excellent navigator, shrewd trader, an intelligent and forceful leader . . . able to assume all kinds of responsibilities."[7]

On their honeymoon the couple sailed on the *Herriman* to Mexico and then Hawaii. When they reached the islands Mount Pele erupted, sending lava racing to the sea, heating the water and killing fish for miles around. Interested in ecology, Julia Shorey wrote a letter describing the incident that was published in the *San Francisco Elevator.* In November 1886 Julia remained behind to accompany other wives for the return trip to San Francisco.

Shorey took over the *Alexander* in 1889, the year before Walter Noble Burns' eventful trip. At 87 feet and 136 tons, the *Alexander,* built in 1886, was somewhat smaller than the average whale ship, most of which were typically 100–110 feet long and 300–350 tons. The young black captain's skill would be tested in 1891 when the *Alexander* was crushed in the Arctic ice pack and sank, but Shorey was able to save the entire crew. The *Alexander's* owner kept faith with Shorey and assigned him to the *Andrew Hicks.* Built in 1867, the *Hicks* had seen better days. A previous captain wrote to part owner David B. Adams in 1889: "The old Hicks is about the same old sixpence only getting mighty shaky; her rigging is in terrible shape about ready to fall off her. I shouldn't be surprised to see the mainmast go over the side any day. She has the same old leaks only worse than last year, twenty minutes a day steady; it's forward somewhere; you can hear it running in but can't tell where."[8]

As captain of the *Hicks* in 1901, Shorey encountered storms so extreme that they nearly took his life: two typhoons, the first lasting more than thirty hours and a second, more violent one that lasted more than forty-eight hours and carried away the sails along with six of the whaleboats and their davits. When the skies cleared at storm's end, they found themselves a mere twenty feet from rocks that would have wrecked the ship. Shorey's seamanship saved the day—and he still returned to San Francisco with the equivalent of close to $74,000 in cargo. He led the *Andrew Hicks* on nine voyages until 1902. (The fifty-year-old *Hicks* sailed eight more times after Shorey left it, finally sinking in 1917 off Virginia as a merchant ship.)

Like all captains of color Shorey faced racial issues. In 1895, while he was captain of the *Gay Head* and berthed in Hawaii, three crewmen were arrested after attempting to set fire to the ship. After Ellis Mills, the U.S. consul in Hawaii, had them released, Shorey wrote a letter to the Honolulu newspaper citing Mills' indifference. Shorey took the three white sailors—Walter Ekerenkutter, William Bresling, and William Gehrmann—to court again in San Francisco, but the only other witness was another black man, and Shorey lost the case, unable to prove his accusations.

Shorey certainly had his share of press coverage. A colorful story in the *San Francisco Call* about Shorey's trip on the *John and Winthrop* recounted a whale diving under the ice in Dutch Harbor, Alaska, and shattering the whaleboat attached to it by a harpoon. In a separate encounter, another whale with a "whisk of his fluke" sent a whaleboat flying, dumped the crew for a cold bath, and smashed the boat. A front-page story detailed Shorey's return on the *John and Winthrop* in 1905 with 3,000 pounds of whalebone and 230 barrels of whale oil after a 10-month trip that included 11 days of gale-force winds. The result was a profit for the owners, "fair pay for the skipper and some of the officers and $1 for the green hands." The story recounted a duel between crewmen Harry Shelton and Joseph Ready during which Shelton "cut a strip of flesh from Ready's jaw" and was saved from Ready's harpoon by Captain Shorey, who put them both in irons.[9]

In a February 1908 interview Shorey spoke eloquently about whaling:

> For a vessel the size of the *John and Winthrop* a catch worth $40,000 is considered a fairly successful one. How many whales do we have to catch to amount to that? Well it depends on the size and species of whale. Four of the right kind will do it; three might. It might take five or six or even more. A cruise lasts ordinarily from eight to ten months.

There used to be fifty-four vessels go whaling from San Francisco every year. Now there are fourteen. I have been told that in the old days there were as many as three hundred whalers in this port at once.[10]

After retiring from whaling, Shorey worked as a policeman on the docks of San Francisco for the Pacific Coast Steamship Company from 1912 to 1919. At age fifty-three, on November 27, 1912, this son of Barbados became a U.S. citizen. Shorey was one of only a few captains of color to acquire a master's license, which permitted him to pilot any size ship, sail or steamship, anywhere in the world. Shorey maintained it until his death.

Shorey and Julia had five children: Zenobia Pearl (1888), Elvira J. (1891), Hazel E. (1893), Victoria Grace (1898), and William Thomas Jr. (1902). Elvira and Hazel died in infancy, and Zenobia succumbed to tuberculosis at age twenty.[11]

In 1912 Shorey was registered as a Republican. Active in politics, he hosted a dinner for Booker T. Washington in 1903 to help raise money for Washington's Tuskegee Institute. In 1916 Shorey was listed as a member of the Afro-American Cooperative Association of San Francisco. Julia was also civic minded. She was the treasurer of the board of directors of the Home for the Aged and Infirm Colored People in 1898, and was its president from 1901 to 1911. Julia died in 1944 of arteriosclerotic heart disease.

Victoria Shorey attended public and private schools and received a diploma from the Underwood Company as a typist. In 1917 she became Mrs. (Willie) Victoria Francis. She worked as a stenographer at Larche & Maurice and lived in Berkeley until her death in 1971. Her son, William T. Shorey Jr., worked as a waiter and died in 1969.

Captain Shorey died on April 15, 1919, during the Spanish flu pandemic at the age of fifty-nine. He is buried in the Mountain View Cemetery in Oakland with Julia and their daughters Zenobia, Elvira, and Hazel. Good evidence has it that Oakland's original Short Street was renamed Shorey Street in the captain's honor in 1907. In April 2013 the Shorey House was designated a historic landmark in Oakland.[12]

CHAPTER 14

So Ends

*T*he decline of the whaling industry was gradual but inevitable. Each of America's wars had a negative impact on whaling. Impressment and hostility from the British in the Revolutionary War and the War of 1812 hampered business. During the American Revolution the British captured or killed 1,200 American seamen and took 134 ships, many of them whale ships. That practice continued through the War of 1812. Confederate raiders and German submarines in World War I likewise took a toll.[1]

The cargo of a whale ship returning home was a valuable prize, but its bulk made it difficult to transship, and since there was no practical way to tow a fully loaded whale ship, captured vessels were generally destroyed. The pitch used to seal the ships' timbers and the highly flammable nature of their cargo made them tinderboxes. Among the largest ships at sea from the 1700s through the 1800s, whale ships were also among the slowest. With wide, blunt bows and deep hulls these heavy, seaworthy vehicles were the world's first factory ships; they delivered the manpower necessary to locate the largest creatures in the world, dissected them on board the ship, and contained and returned the harvest of oil and whalebone to land. While they carried a full complement of sails—some so large they would cover a third of a football field—whale ships could travel only about nine miles an hour (eight knots) on the way to whaling grounds and about three miles an hour (two to three knots) laden on the return trip. Whale ships were thus relatively easy to spot and catch.[2]

During the Civil War the Confederacy had two fast schooners built in Britain specifically to destroy whale ships to hurt the North's economy.

The two warships, the *Alabama* and the *Shenandoah*, were remarkably successful. The *Shenandoah*, in a four-day raid in 1865 on the fleet in the Bering Strait, destroyed twenty-five whalers and captured four others that were converted into Confederate transports. The *Alabama* destroyed more than a dozen whalers in the Atlantic, and the *Shenandoah* took another forty in the Pacific.[3]

When the Civil War ended, black and African whalers, known for working long years in the business for low pay, suddenly had other opportunities—and took them. Census statistics show a dramatic drop in New Bedford's black population after the Civil War. The new textile factories in the Northeast paid better and were substantially less dangerous than whaling, and so the skilled, experienced whaling workforce went elsewhere. By 1866 only about half of any whale ship's crew had real whaling skills, and one-third was illiterate. Only the Cape Verdeans, escaping from poverty and famine and lacking an entrenched community to support them, were left for whaling companies to exploit.[4]

The price of whale oil dropped as alternative oil sources were discovered. The business moved west in the hunt for whales whose baleen could be used for other products, but whalebone, known for its strength and flexibility, was soon replaced with better alternatives as well. Even its use, once *in* fashion, grew *out* of fashion. The business based on its unsustainable product was doomed.

Whaling's Legacy

Although whaling made many wealthy over its lifespan, posterity can only view whaling as an industry defying common sense and often lacking business judgment—an enterprise unlikely ever to be sustainable even as it endured. Whaling technology stagnated, and ship owners had to rely on unskilled laborers. Except for the rich and honored history retained in institutions such as the New Bedford Whaling Museum, the Nantucket Whaling Museum, and others on Martha's Vineyard, in Mystic, and in Southampton on Long Island, the industry that lasted so long left little in the way of a concrete legacy. Personal bravery was not a transferable skill, and that was the minimum requirement needed for success in whaling. Those who pursued whaling as an occupation—men such as Cuffe,

Wainer, Cook, Domingues, and Senna—were not able to get one more generation of children involved.

For captains of color in the industry's heyday, whaling was better than slavery or starvation. Only the clarity of hindsight illustrates their talent and skill in managing difficult people, overcoming dystopian situations, and wresting profits from the largest creatures on the planet. Their achievements were heroic.

Some captains' names are better remembered than others. Today, in addition to the literature and museum exhibits, there are a number of descendants who honor Paul Cuffe's memory. (A reported forty descendants of Paul and Alice Pequit Cuffe ranging in age from two to ninety-one gathered in July 2005 at the Friends Meeting House in Westport.) There is a Boston-based Descendants of Captain Paul Cuffe organization whose members have been gathering biannually since 1972, often at his memorial at the Westport Meeting House. There is a Paul Cuffe School in Providence, Rhode Island. A park adjacent to the New Bedford Whaling Museum was dedicated to Cuffe and the Wainer family in 2018.[5] And there are a few whaling "lasts," including the following.[6]

Last Remaining Whale Ship

The *Charles W. Morgan*, America's last whale ship was restored and is now docked at Mystic Seaport. It was launched in New Bedford in 1841 as a 251-ton ship and evolved into a 351-ton bark. The *Morgan* left on the first of its thirty-seven whaling trips—twenty from New Bedford and the rest from San Francisco—on September 2, 1841. At the conclusion of its last whaling voyage (a nine-month trip from New Bedford to the Atlantic), the *Morgan* returned in May 1921 with 2,702 barrels of whale oil valued at $37,828 ($469,000 today). Master John T. Gonsalves was its captain.[7]

Last Successful Whaling Trip

The *John R. Manta* left New Bedford on May 2, 1925, with a predominantly black crew and an Azorean master. It returned with 300 barrels of sperm oil worth $4,920 at 41 cents a gallon, or approximately $66,000 today. This was noted as the last successful American whaling voyage (although several left from Hawaii after this).

Last Whaling Voyage with a Whaling Captain of Color

Henry J. Gonzales sailed the *Charles Brower* from San Francisco for the North Pacific on June 15, 1927, returning with no catch.

Last Whaling Voyage

The *Patterson* left May 17, 1928, from San Francisco for the North Pacific. It returned October 2 with no catch.

Last Living Whaling Captain of Color

Manuel J. Domingues is believed to have been the last living black whaling captain—he died in 1989.

Epilogue

Whaling captains of color were just "colored" when they returned to land. Few found investment opportunities that allowed them to grow whatever profits they retained. These men led whaling voyages to every part of the globe; indeed, several contributed to the mapping of the world's oceans. They were adventurous, tenacious, fearless, and ruthless; their skills were honed before the mast in the second most dangerous enterprise (after mining) the world had seen.

Unlike their white counterparts they left no glistening white waterfront homes behind as testaments to their courage; to their families they left only pride. Little remains today of their accomplishments—tales of valor and a few monuments are all. It would be a tragedy to forget them.

Further Study

Using lists at the New Bedford Whaling Museum and New Bedford Public Library, I was unable to prove to my satisfaction that the following were either men of color or captains, but they deserve further study.

Robert Brown (1809–43)

Of his ten known whaling voyages, Brown took five as master (*Hope*, 6/10/1833–5/7/1834; *Hope*, 6/27/1834–3/13/1836; *Roscoe*, 5/26/1836–4/9/1837; *Roscoe*, 6/4/1837–6/21/1839; and *Emerald*, 5/2/1840–2/26/1843). Crew lists consistently list him as five-feet-eight and dark-skinned. There is little known about his death, other than it occurred during his last trip on the *Emerald*.[8]

ANTONE (BURDO) BURDICK (1846–?)

Described as black, Burdick took one trip as whaling captain, at age twenty-one. He was a replacement on the *Annawan II* during its voyage to the Atlantic from 1867 to 1870 when Edward K. Russell was master. This was Russell's last voyage as captain, and no other information is available about Burdick.[9]

ONE CONSIPAION (1873–?)

One Consipaion at age twenty-seven is believed to have been a replacement captain for Henry Mandly Sr. on the *Mary E. Simmons* (5/28/1900–8/6/1902). Listed as five-feet-seven and residing in Manila, Consipaion is difficult to cross-reference; nothing else is known about him.[10]

JOSEPH A. H. EARTHORP

A Joseph Earthorp is described as dark and age twenty-two on the crew list for the *Ellen Rodman*'s trip of October 20, 1869, and mulatto but age nineteen on the trip of the *Progress* from October 17, 1870 to May 10, 1875. The New Bedford crew list includes Earthorp as a master of the *Progress* during its voyage. Earthrop served on the *Marengo* with its then–replacement captain Henry Eldridge from 1859 to 1863, and again on the *Progress* in 1870 when Eldridge replaced Master James Dowden, who left the ship.[11]

JAMES FRANKLIN BROWN

The New Bedford crew list records Brown as "mulatto" on the *Atlantic* and lists his home as Granada. Brown's handwriting in the log of the *Atlantic* (6/24/1872–6/8/1876) is neat and easy to read. Brown served on the *Abraham Barker, Atlantic, Milton, Nantucket, Sunbeam, Wanderer,* and as master of the *Sea Ranger* on a trip of September 15, 1856.[12]

JAMES H. FISHER (1838–?)

Fisher served as a green hand on the *Nimrod* in 1851 and worked his way up to boat-steerer by time the trip ended in 1854. He served on the *Altamaha* as foremost hand in May 1856 and became a replacement captain. With the *Altamaha* on four sequential trips from 1855 to 1858, he shared the captaincy with two others. On the *Alto*, leaving in 1857, the nineteen-year-old Fisher was described as "mate." On this voyage Fisher and Captain Thomas H. Lawrence twice replaced each other due to illness. Fisher was described as having "light skin" (light skin for a black person?) and listed as five feet eight and one-half inches tall when he shipped on the *Nassau* in 1863 as third mate. He led the *Oliver Crocker* as master from 1868 to 1871, the *Java II* in 1871, and the *Lancer* in 1877.[13]

Hezikiah B. Gardener
(Hezchial B. Gardner) (1792–?)

Martha Putney includes Hezekiah *Gardener* as the probable captain of the *Abigail* that sailed from New Bedford in March 1825 to the Pacific. Except for being listed as master of the *Benezet* in 1822 as a replacement for Dennis Covell, there is no prior information on Hezchial B. Gardner (spelled "Hezikiah B. Gardner" by Lund). In fact, I could find no confirmation that the *Benezet* whaled in 1822; both Lund and Starbuck have the ship leaving New Bedford in December 1823.[14]

William B. Hazell

William Hazell, born in the West Indies, lived on Nantucket in 1850. Hazell had been a seaman on the *Russell* from 1845 to 1847, joining the crew in the Fiji Islands on February 17, 1846. He left New Bedford on May 26, 1849, as master of the *Persia* and was sick when it returned two months later. There is no information on the nature of his illness, and he again sailed on the *Persia* on August 4.[15]

Ezra Susex

Ezra Susex is listed on the crew list as black and master of the *Ann Alexander* on its voyage from New Bedford to Brazil on June 7, 1825, with a crew of eighteen (nine of whom were black and one Indian). Starbuck lists Walter Hillman from Martha's Vineyard as master. The crew list has the *Ann Alexander* departing again for Brazil under the command of Hillman on August 1, 1825, with a completely different crew of seventeen (three of whom were black, two Indian).[16]

WILLIAM H. WOOD

Born in the West Indies in 1810, Master William Wood lived on Nantucket in 1860. He was married to Eliza Ann Edwards and had three children born in Massachusetts and a fourth, son Alexander, born in Peru in 1852. Alexander followed his father into whaling and died at sea when he was seventeen. His birth in Peru suggests Wood's family may have traveled with him. The *Barney Genealogical Record* has Wood being "from New Bedford." Wood served as master of the *Science* in 1844, of the *Sarah Frances* in 1847, and as replacement captain (the second of three replacements on this voyage) on the *Richmond II* from 1851 to 1853, when the trip was reported as "broken up by desertion of the crew" but returned with its cargo. Henry M. Bonney took the ship from New Bedford, James Pickens took over from him (due to illness), then William H. Wood (who also left due to illness); and finally someone named "Martin" returned the ship home.[17]

Other possibilities for further study include Nathaniel Green, listed as having sailed on the *Atlas*, and Pardon Howland of the *Hepsa*.[18]

Malloy includes three names that deserve further study:

Manuel F. Gomes, *Eleanor B. Conwell*, *Bertha*, *Cameo*. Donald Warrin (*So Ends This Day*), indicates Gomes was from the Azores.

Gideon Randall, *Barclay*.

Henry Clay (Acquilla Rodrigues) (1836–1901). Clay was a whaling captain and whale ship owner. Warrin lists Clay as being born in the Azores, which is why I have not included him. But the crew list of the *Frances* records him as black with woolly hair at age twenty in 1852. On board both the *Elizabeth* in 1865 and the *Ellen Rodman* in 1866, he is listed as dark and as the master. Clay was replaced as master of the *Golden City* (12/9/1875–9/29/1876), one of the whale ships he owned, by James F. Avery and again (6/19/1877–9/21/1878) by William A. Martin. Of all the men reserved for further study, the whaler Henry Clay seems the most interesting subject.[19]

ACKNOWLEDGMENTS

*T*hanks come most easily to the special folks who went out of their way to help with my passion, especially Carole Sargent, Georgetown University's director of Scholarly Publications; Carole introduced me to Laura Davulis, then of the Naval Institute Press, who decided my book was worthy of publishing; and Mindy Conner, the Naval Institute Press copy editor who made it much more readable.

Several others provided incredible information and support.

Joan Barney was the genealogist at the New Bedford Free Public Library where the New Bedford crew list lives on in a 131-drawer card catalog. With her encouragement I read each of the cards and scanned many. In addition to being extraordinarily patient, she was persistent in helping me track down further information on captains.

W. Jeffrey Bolster is the author of *Black Jacks*. His book *The Mortal Sea* was reviewed in the *Vineyard Gazette* by Mark Alan Lovewell, a singer of sea shanties who was kind enough to put me in touch with Mr. Bolster, who shared his sources with me. *Black Jacks* led me to the work of Harold O. Lewis.

Sandi Brewster-Walker is a historian, genealogist, and freelance writer who has taught American history and African American and Native American genealogy and lectured on her research. She was of great assistance with the genealogy of the Long Island whalers in this book.

Carlene Cordwell, a friend and member of the New Bedford Historical Society, introduced me to people in the Cape Verdean Crioulo community knowledgeable about whaling. My wife and I attended the NBHS annual fundraiser, *Steppin' Out*, as Carlene's guests on May 17, 2015, where I met Carl Cruz, William do Carmo, and Edith Andrews, whose great-great-grandfather was Captain Amos Haskins.

Carl Cruz, a local historian and descendant of whalers, is heavily involved with the New Bedford Whaling Museum and New Bedford Free Public Library and was gracious in helping me navigate the heritage of the New Bedford whaling community.

William do Carmo was the first descendant of a whaling captain I had the honor to meet. He gave me a tour of the New Bedford Whaling Museum (where he served on the board of directors), provided me with copies of information on several Cape Verdean masters, showed me the grave of Captain Louis M. Lopes (his uncle), and allowed me to interview him about Captain Lopes and his brother Captain Frank M. Lopes. He provided me with a video of Manuel Domingues, the last living black whale captain, and introduced me to Domingues' daughter, Diane Hazleton, and Luis Lopes Rosita Silverman, Louis Lopes' granddaughter.

Eric Jay Dolin is the author of *Leviathan: The History of Whaling in America*. Anyone who desires a knowledge of whaling should read this book; it is digestible, authentic, and easy to read in a literate, nontechnical style. We met in June 2014 when he spoke at the Martha's Vineyard Museum, and his was one of the first books I read on whaling. In taking the time to discuss my book, he offered me the best kind of encouragement: "I'd like to read that book." Mr. Dolin was incredibly generous in recommending several constructive changes in my manuscript for which I am grateful.

Milton Alexander "Spike" Harris (1908–77) was an author, historian, and assembler of literature, artifacts, and pictures of African American history. He founded the Negro History Associates in 1964, an organization that had black history as its mission. It is thanks to his collection that I was able to access the work of Harold O. Lewis.

Philip Hoare is brilliant. I had the distinct honor of meeting him at a talk he gave at the New Bedford Whaling Museum on May 18, 2018. His book *The Whale: In Search of the Giants of the Sea* is educational, laugh-out-loud funny at times, scatological, and easy to read. Nathaniel Philbrick, an estimable writer himself, called it "genius . . . rhapsodic meditation on all things cetacean" in his *New York Times* book review. It's the bible of whales and, dare I say it, more interesting than *Moby-Dick*.

Frances Ruley Karttunen is a researcher, historian, and the author of several history-based tomes about Nantucket. Through her work I was able to identify and include a substantial amount of information on Nantucket and its heritage of whalemen of color.

John Kennedy, author of *A Course of Their Own: A History of African American Golfers* (2000), convinced me I would write. When he asked what I had written before, I told him business and strategic plans, loan documents, and business-deal based material—all of which I was tired of. He gave me a small book about writing that convinced me: writers write. More important, in agreeing to edit this book he brought it to a literary level I would have been unable to reach.

Maurice Klapwald, librarian, Interlibrary and Document Services, New York Public Library, provided me with material from the Middleton A. Spike Harris Collection, Schomburg Center for Research in Black Culture, Research Libraries, New York Public Library.

Harold O. Lewis (April 24, 1908–April 6, 1993) was professor emeritus of Howard University whose works are referenced by Martha S. Putney (*Black Sailors*) and Jeffrey Bolster (*Black Jacks*). I was fortunate to obtain copies of his "New Bedford/Westport, etc., Negro Ships Captains prior to Civil War" from the Schomburg Center. Lewis identified eleven of the masters, including John Masten, who otherwise would have been lost to history. Lewis wrote a profile of Paul Cuffe for the *Dictionary of American Negro Biography*.

Judith Navas Lund, an author, researcher, and historian, is responsible for the identification of 15,213 whale trips (as of this writing). *American Offshore Whaling Voyages, 1667–1927*, compiled by Lund and her associates, is based on Alexander Starbuck's work and is the basis of the New Bedford Whaling Museum Library's crew list. I had the pleasure of being introduced to her on March 10, 2017, and she was very supportive of my work.

Mary Malloy is the author of *African Americans in the Maritime Trades: A Guide to Resources in New England*, the first scholarly work I read about black whaling captains. Dr. Malloy is an associate at the Peabody Museum of Archaeology and Ethnology and a professor at Harvard University for maritime studies.

Nantucket Historical Association Library staff members Elizabeth Oldham (1927–2018) and Betsy Tyler (now retired) were incredibly helpful in assembling an astounding amount of material on African Americans and whalers of Nantucket.

New Bedford Historical Society Inc., founded in 1996 and led by president Lee Blake, is dedicated to documenting and celebrating the history, legacy, and presence of African Americans, Cape Verdeans, Native Americans, West Indians, and other people of color in New Bedford, Massachusetts. Thanks to the society I met several descendants of whaling captains of color.

Mark Procknik, New Bedford Whaling Museum librarian; the first time I went to the NBWML in 2014 to do research, it was Mark who was able to locate things I didn't know existed using descriptions I gave but knew nothing about. Had he not thought to share the New Bedford crew list spreadsheet, this book could not have been written. Mark is responsible for locating and allowing me to use most of the images in the book.

Martha Settle Putney (1916–2008) began writing her book *Black Sailors* as a 1972 study for the *Journal of Negro History*. One of the first black members of the Women's Army Corps during World War II, she worked for the War Manpower Commission and devoted her life to researching and documenting military achievements of black Americans. She earned a PhD at the University of Pennsylvania and taught at Bowie State University (chairing the History and Geography Departments) and at Howard University, her alma mater.

Paul Schneider, the editor of *Martha's Vineyard* magazine, allowed me to write the 2014 article on William A. Martin, a Martha's Vineyard–based whaling captain whose career inspired me to write this book.

Jane Seagrave, who I adore, is the publisher of the Vineyard Gazette Media Group. She let me write the weekly *Oak Bluffs Town* column, my first paid writing job. It is thanks to her that I discovered a whole new career. Without her this book would have been impossible.

Nancy Shoemaker is the author of *Native American Whalemen and the World: Indigenous Encounters and the Contingency of Race*. A professor of history at the University of Connecticut, she compiled a database from more than 2,100 logs to identify more than six hundred indigenous people who served as whalemen. She shared her research of the New Bedford crew lists at the National Archives in Waltham, Massachusetts (348 pages). Professor Shoemaker also generously shared her Indian whalemen database and "Mr. Tashtego, Native American Whalemen in Antebellum New England," a study that includes a substantial amount of information on Amos Haskins that is otherwise unavailable. I am particularly indebted to her for the research she shared on the Lee and Belain families.

Matt Stackpole was born on Nantucket. He is the son of Edouard Stackpole, author of *The Sea Hunters* and *The* Charles W. Morgan: *The Last Wooden Whaleship*. A maritime historian and former Martha's Vineyard Museum director, Matt is the Mystic Seaport Museum's historian for the *Charles W. Morgan*. Along with letting me board the *Morgan*, Matt spent hours with me discussing whaling.

A. Bowdoin Van Riper, Martha's Vineyard Museum librarian, identified several valuable documents and other information and provided several images for the book.

Hilary Wall, librarian of the Vineyard Gazette Media Group, provided inestimable assistance in locating articles from the *Vineyard Gazette*'s microfilm collection dating to its founding in May 1846.

APPENDIX A
Captains of Color, in Chronological Order

Confirmed as Captains of Color

Name	Date Became Captain
Cuffe Sr., Paul	1784
Wainer, Michael	1792
Wainer, Thomas	1803
Phelps, Alvan	1805
Wainer, Paul	1810
Masten, John	1812
Green, Peter	1821
Boston, Absalom F.	1822
Lewis, Henry A.	1833
Pompey, Edward J.	1836
Cuffe, William	1837
Cook, Pardon	1839
Harris, Samuel W.	1842
Jeffers, Amos, Jr.	1847
Haskins, Amos	1849
Hussey, Frederick	1854
Pierce, Severino	1858
Haskins, William	1859
Lee, Ferdinand	1864
Ears, Jasper M.	1870
Silva, John Z.	1878
Martin, William A.	1878
Benton, Anthony P.	1878
Sylvia, Antone	1879
Costa, Carlo	1880
Lee, William Garrison	1880
Costa, Maecelino DeBarro	1881
Shorey, William T.	1885
Stevenson, Collins A.	1889
Belain, Joseph G.	1889

Cont'd on next page

Name	Date
Gonsalves, John T.	1890
Benton, Joseph P.	1891
Senna, Antonio José	1891
Senna, Ayres J.	1891
Lopes, Louis M.	1902
Gaspar, Joseph	1902
Rosa, Valentine	1905
Senna, Joseph H.	1906
Lewis, Joseph R.	1907
Perry, José	1908
Freitas, Theophilus M.	1908
Fernandes, Julio	1909
Roderick, Joseph	1909
Lopez, Peter	1914
d'Oliveira, Luiz	1917
Lopes, Frank M.	1917
Gomes, August P.	1919
Domingues, José M.	1919
Da Lomba, João	1920
Domingues, Manuel J.	1920
Costa, Benjamin	1921
Gonzales, Henry J.	1926

Unconfirmed as Captains of Color

Name	Date
Gardener, Hezikiah	1823
Susex, Ezra	1825
Brown, Robert	1833
Wood, William H.	1844
Hazell, William	1849
Fisher, James H.	1857
Earthorp, Joseph A. H.	1859
Burdick, Antone	1867
Brown, James Franklin	1872
Consipaion, One	1900

APPENDIX B
William Haskins' Whaling Trips

Ship	Port	Destina-tion	Departed	Returned	Rank
Iris	New Bedford	Indian Ocean	1847	1850	Third Mate
Ansel Gibbs	Fairhaven	North Pacific	1854	1859	Boat-steerer
Hesper*	Fairhaven	Pacific	1859	1859 (condemned)	Master
Hudson	Fairhaven	Pacific	7/1859	3/1863	First Mate
Louisiana	New Bedford	Indian	1864	1865 (lost)	Master
John Hathaway	Fairhaven	Atlantic	1866	1866 (condemned)	Master

* The *Hesper* made three trips that left in 1859: January–February (returned leaking 300 strokes), April, and June 1859–63; all began with Captain Joseph Hamblin Jr. in command. It appears Haskins' trip as master was the April leg. The *Hesper* was condemned at Paita in 1864.

APPENDIX C
Theophilus M. Freitas' Whaling Trips

Ship	Port	Destination	Departed	Returned	Rank	Pay
Canton II	New Bedford	Atlantic	1899	1900	Boat-steerer	
Sunbeam	New Bedford	Atlantic	1901	1902	Boat-steerer	$593.85
Sunbeam	New Bedford	Atlantic	1902	1904	Fourth Boat-header	$1,047.42
Sunbeam	New Bedford	Atlantic	1901	1902	Second Mate	$1,781.79
Platina	New Bedford	Atlantic	1906	1908		$125.42
Sullivan	Norwich, Conn.	Atlantic	1908°	1911	Replacement Master°	
Andrew Hicks	New Bedford	Atlantic	1908	1910	First Mate	$3,063.38
Andrew Hicks	New Bedford	Atlantic	1911	1914	First Mate	$367.62
Sullivan°	Norwich, Conn.	Atlantic	1912°	1913	Replacement Master°	$593.85

Pedro Valera	New Bedford	Atlantic	1916	1916	First Mate
Pedro Valera	New Bedford	Atlantic	1917	1917	Master
Charles W. Morgan	New Bedford	Atlantic	1918	1919	First Mate
Athlete	New Bedford	Atlantic	1921	1921	Third Mate

* It is unknown why Freitas was listed as being on the *Sullivan* 1908–11 and the *Andrew Hicks* 1908–10, and on the *Andrew Hicks* from 1911 to 1914 and the *Sullivan* 1912–13. It is likely that the dates indicate the length of the trip and that Freitas disembarked from one ship to join the other.

Data collected from the New Bedford Public Library Whaling Card Catalogue.

Source for port, destination, and where marked by asterisk is Lund et al., *American Offshore Whaling Voyages 1667–1927*, vol. 1.

APPENDIX D
Amos Haskins' Whaling Trips

Ship	Port	Destination	Departed	Returned	Rank
Dryade	Rochester	Atlantic	1834	1835	—
Mattapoisett	Rochester	Atlantic	1839	1840	—
Chase	Mattapoisett		1841	1841	Second Mate
Annawan II	Mattapoisett	Atlantic	1842	1842	First Mate
Annawan II	Mattapoisett	Atlantic	1843	1844	First Mate
Cachalot	Mattapoisett	Atlantic	1845	1847	—
Willis	Mattapoisett	Atlantic	1847	1849[1]	—
Triton	New Bedford	NW Coast	1849	1850[*1]	—
Elizabeth	Mattapoisett	Atlantic	1849	1850	First Mate, Replacement Master[2]
Massasoit	Mattapoisett	Atlantic	1851	1852	Master
Massasoit	Mattapoisett	Atlantic	1852	1853	Master
Oscar	Mattapoisett	N Pacific	1857	1861	First Mate
March	Mattapoisett	Atlantic	1860	1861	First Mate

[*] Lund does not list these dates for the *Triton*.

1. From Pierce and Segal, *Wampanoag Families*, p. 342.
2. From Lund et al., *American Offshore Whaling Voyages, 1667–1927*, vol. 1.

Based on Nancy Shoemaker's NARA database and confirmed by Shoemaker, *Native American Whalemen*; Lund, *Whaling Masters and Whaling Voyages*; Starbuck, *History; New Bedford crew list*; and other sources.

APPENDIX E
Whaling Captains Known to Have Been Killed by Whales

Name	Source
Almy, William	1
Ames, Edwin	1
Benton, Joseph P.°	1
Brock, Peleg	1
Brock, Priam	1
Brown, Roswell	2
Browne, John	2
Burgess, Paul Cook	1
Burrows	2
Churchill, Ansel	1
Clasby, Meteor	2
Cook, Daniel Cross	1
Cook, Samuel E.	1
Cottle, Silas	2
Dexter, Ebeneezer	1
Eddy, Abraham T.	1
Ellis, Albert	1
Ewer, Alvan	1
Gloum, Alfred C.	1
Glover	2
Harlow, Stratton H.	1
Harris, William P.	1
Hiller, Edwin W.	1
Homer	2
House	2

Cont'd on next page

Name	Source
Howell, John Egbert	1
Howes, Edward	1
Howland, Isaac C.	2
Hussey, Isaac B.	2
Luce, Jesse	2
Munroe, John	1
Myrick	2
Needham, S. R. Soper	1
Norton, Abner P.	3
Nye, James L.	1
Paddack, Aaron	1
Pierce, Severino D.*	1
Pierson, William H.	1
Shearman, Prince	1
Smith, Robert B.	1
Southworth, Thomas J.	1
Sowle	2
Swain, Silas	1
Topping, Richard	1
Unk, Industry (1799–1800)	1
Winslow, Bradford W.	1
Wood, Elihu	1

*Men of color.

1. Lund et al., *American Offshore Whaling Voyages 1667–1927*, vol. 1; Lund, *Whaling Masters and Whaling Voyages Sailing from American Ports*.
2. Federal Writers Project, Whaling Masters.
3. Shoemaker, database compiled from more than 2,100 logs in the National Archives in Waltham, Mass.

APPENDIX F
William A. Martin's Whaling Trips

Ship	Port	Departed	Returned	Rank/Age
Benjamin Tucker	New Bedford	1846	1849	Green hand/16
Waverly	New Bedford	1851	1854	Boat-steerer/21
Europa	Edgartown	1853[1]	1857*	—
Corinthian	New Bedford	1854	1858	Boat-steerer/24
Europa	Edgartown	1857[1]	1862	First Mate, Log Keeper/27
Rebecca Sims	Fairhaven	1857	1861*	27
Gratitude	New Bedford	1858[2]	1862*	Boat-steerer/28
Almira	Edgartown	1864	1868	?/34
Clarice	Edgartown	1871[1]	1875	First Mate
Golden City	New Bedford	1877	1878	Master/47
Golden City	New Bedford	1878	1880	Master/48
Emma Jane	Edgartown	1881	1881	?/51
Emma Jane	Edgartown	1883	1884	Master/53**
Eunice H. Adams	Edgartown	1887	1890*	Master/57***

* The years 1857, 1862, 1861, and 1890 are when the ship returned to port; Martin evidently left earlier than that based on the dates of subsequent trips, something not unusual.

** Martin was replaced by James F. Avery.

*** Martin was replaced by Thomas E. Fordham.

Sources:

Hegerty, *Returns of Whaling Vessels Sailing from American Ports.*

1. Railton, *The History of Martha's Vineyard.*
2. Lewis, "New Bedford/Westport, etc., Negro Ships Captains prior to the Civil War: List of Black Captains, Mates and Harpooners."

APPENDIX G
Crew of the *Eunice H. Adams*, 1887

Original Crew

Name	Rank	Lay	Age	Residence	Disposition
William A. Martin°	Captain		57	Edgartown	Replaced 2/20/1890
Arthur O. Gibbons°	First Mate	1/18	28		
Philip Sylaveiro°	Second Mate	1/24	31		
Joseph Gomez°	Boat-steerer	1/25	28		Deserted
Benjamin Hazzard	Boat-steerer	1/75	55	Hawaii	
Thomas Taylor	Steward	1/120	28	Boston	
Domingo Fleming°	Boat-steerer	1/75	24	Fogo, CVI	
Joseph Lopes°	Cook (also listed as Boat-steerer)	1/140	40	Sao Taigo, CVI	
Manuel J. Pera°°	Ordinary	1/130			
Antone Roderique°	Seaman	1/125			
John Lopez°	Seaman	1/140	25	Sao Taigo, CVI	
Albert E. Vaughan	Greenhand	1/150	21	New Bedford	
S.F. McArther	Ordinary	1/150	21	Portland	Deserted
CC Briggs	Greenhand	1/150	26	Philadelphia	Deserted
James McNally	Greenhand	1/150	18	Marblehead	
CC Hamilton	Greenhand	1/150	21	Nantucket	Deserted
John McNamara	Greenhand	1/150	31	Boston	Deserted
Fred Ridson°°°					Deserted
George Ridson	Carpenter	1/140	21	London	
Abram L. Josh	Greenhand	1/150	23	Edgartown	

°Black.

°°Manuel Pera and Antone Roderique are not listed on the crew list.

°°°Fred Ridson is not listed in ship's log (but is listed on the crew list).

Replacements/Additions

Name	Rank	Lay	Age	Residence	Disposition
Thomas E. Fordham	Replacement Captain			Edgartown	
Theophilus S. Almeida	First Mate	1/18			
Frank Perry	Second Mate	1/28			
Henry Allen	Boat-steerer	1/75			
Isaac Simmons	Boat-steerer	1/80			
Girard (?) Solomon	Green Hand	1/125			
José Antonio Duarte	Green Hand	1/140			
Charles Thompson		1/140			
Edgar La Bruce (August?)		1/140			
John Alves	Third Mate	1/40			
Fred D. West	Second Mate				
John Domingo Lopes****	Green Hand				
Antoine Joseph****	Boat-steerer				
Cesar Brava****	Green Hand				
Segeo Marrier (?) Farrar					Deserted
Benjamin Dice					Deserted
John A. Chapman					
Ernest Kennedy					
Manuel D. Bourgo					
Joseph Queltho (?)		1/140			
John Le Canto (?)		1/140			

**** Lopes, Joseph, and Brava were hired "before the mast" in the Cape Verde Islands (CVI) (log entry).

Cont'd on next page

Replacements/Additions *(cont'd)*

Name	Rank	Lay	Age	Residence	Disposition
John Rodrick (?)					
Rufino Gonzales					
Lobario Farues (?)					
Mr. Perez					
Alan (?)					
Otten (?)					

Source: Data gathered from New Bedford crew list. Some spellings are uncertain.

APPENDIX H
Ships Built and/or Designed by John Mashow

Year	Type and Name	Master of Color	Disposition/ Comment
1831	Schooner *Gazelle*	—	Mashow drew model
1832	Schooner *Mogul*	—	Mashow drew model
1833	Schooner *William*	—	Mashow drew model
1833	Ship *Dartmouth*	—	Whaler
1835	Sloop *Mary*	—	Mashow drew model
1837	Schooner *William Brown*	—	Mashow drew model
1837	Ship *Elizabeth*	—	Whaler
1839	Schooner *Benjamin Tucker*	—	Burned by CS *Alabama* 1862
1841	Schooner *Nimrod*	—	Burned by CS *Shenandoah* 1865
1842	Schooner *Richard*	—	Fisherman
1844	Schooner *Angenetta*	—	—
1844	Schooner *Wasp*	—	Pilot
1845	Schooner *Mosell*	—	Not Whale Ship
1846	Schooner *Pearl*	—	Coaster
1846	Schooner *John Mashow*	—	Fisherman
1847	Schooner *Henry Baker*	—	Fisherman
1847	Schooner *Henry Payson*	—	Not Whale Ship
1847	Schooner *General Worth*	—	Fisherman
1847	Sloop *Abby Gould*	—	Fisherman
1847	Schooner *Sophie Wiley*	—	Fisherman

Cont'd on next page

Year	Type and Name	Master of Color	Disposition/ Comment
1848	Brig *China*	—	Merchantman
1848	Schooner *Luther Childs*	—	Fisherman
1848	Bark *Norma*	—	Merchantman
1848	Schooner *Mariah Theresa*	—	Fisherman
1848	Schooner *Ocean Queen*	—	Fisherman
1848	Schooner *Empire State*	—	Fisherman
1848	Ship *Lalia Rook*	—	Whaler
1849	Schooner *Bay State*	—	Not Whale Ship
1849	Schooner *J. S. Hopkins*	—	Not Whale Ship
1849	Schooner *Lucy Baker*	—	Not Whale Ship
1849	Schooner *Ella Frances*	—	Not Whale Ship
1850	Schooner *Fanny Bourne*	—	Fisherman
1850	Schooner *Allen Dale*	—	Not Whale Ship
1850	Schooner *Lizzie M. Stacy*	—	—
1851	Bark *Tropic Bird*	—	Condemned/Sold 1885
1851	Bark *A. R. Tucker*	Joseph P. Benton	Broken up 1908
1851	Bark *Sea Queen*	Jasper M. Ears	Condemned/Sold 1888
1851	Schooner *William H. DeWitt*	—	Packet
1852	Bark *George and Mary*	—	Burned 1896
1852	Bark *Henry H. Crapo*	—	Lost Indian Ocean 1857
1853	Bark *Jireh Swift*	—	Burned by CS *Shenandoah* 1865

Cont'd on next page

Year	Type and Name	Master of Color	Disposition/ Comment
1852	Schooner *Charles and Edward*	—	Sold 1865
1853	Bark *Morning Star*	Jasper M. Ears, John T. Gonsalves, Valentine Rosa (last master)	Sold 1914
1854	Bark *Cape Horn Pigeon*	Frederick Hussey	Lost 1897
1854	Bark *Benjamin Cummings*	Frederick Hussey	Lost 1875
1855	Bark *Eliot C. Cowdin*	Jasper M. Ears	Sold 1864
1856	Bark *Morning Light*	—	Sold 1862
1855	Schooner *Bouquet*	—	Pilot
1856	Bark *Aurora*	—	Whaler
1856	Bark *Matilda Sears*	—	Sold 1882
1858	Schooner *J. W. Flanders*	—	Whaler
1858	Bark *William Clifford*	—	Whaler
1861	Schooner *Thomas Borden*	—	Whaler

Source: "Old Time Shipbuilding," undated newspaper article in New Bedford Whaling Museum Library scrapbooks, July 15, 2016.

APPENDIX I

Whales Killed by Whaling Captains of Color, by Number and Dollar Value

Rank by Dollar Value	Captain	Number of Whales Killed	Dollar Value
1	William T. Shorey	82	$7,784,721
2	Henry Lewis	79	$7,043,367
3	Severino Pierce	75	$4,606,933
4	Valentine Rosa	134	$4,526,659
5	John T. Gonsalves	189	$4,374,779
6	Carlo Costa	89	$3,505,623
7	Collins A. Stevenson	95	$3,345,633
8	Joseph H. Senna	122	$3,019,983
9	Theophilus Freitas	29	$2,979,535
10	Amos Haskins	70	$2,824,266
11	Anthony P. Benton	60	$2,672,487
12	Louis Lopes	112	$2,553,844
13	Joseph P. Lewis	120	$2,507,350
14	Pardon Cook	42	$2,487,077
15	Macelino Costa	47	$2,186,744
16	Joseph P. Benton	82	$1,881,448
17	Ayers J. Senna	50	$1,624,336
18	William Haskins	18	$1,571,791
19	Frederick Hussey	20	$1,213,887
20	Sam Harris	26	$1,202,468
21	Jasper Ears	23	$1,172,594
22	William A. Martin	22	$973,424

Cont'd on next page

Rank by Dollar Value	Captain	Number of Whales Killed	Dollar Value
23	Ferdinand Lee	16	$933,002
24	Joseph Belain	6	$911,850
25	Antonio J. Senna	24	$827,962
	Total by Top 25 (48.1 percent)	1,632	$68,731,763
	Total by Captains	1,810	$73,857,976
	Top 25	90.2%	93.1%

Rank by Whales Killed*

Rank	Captain	Number of Whales Killed
1	John T. Gonsalves	189
2	Valentine Rosa	134
3	Joseph H. Senna	122
4	Joseph P. Lewis	120
5	Louis Lopes	112
6	Collins A. Stevenson	95
7	Carlo Costa	89
8	William T. Shorey	82
9	Joseph P. Benton	82
10	Henry Lewis	79
11	Severino Pierce	75
12	Amos Haskins	70

Cont'd on next page

Rank by Whales Killed* *(cont'd)*

Rank	Captain	Number of Whales Killed
13	Anthony P. Benton	60
14	Ayers J. Senna	50
15	Macelino Costa	47
16	Pardon Cook	42
17	Theophilus Freitas	29
18	Sam Harris	26
19	Antonio J. Senna	24
20	Jasper Ears	23
21	William A. Martin	22
22	Frederick Hussey	20
23	William Haskins	18
24	Ferdinand Lee	16
25	Joseph Belain	6

Notes:

Whaling captains killed all types of whales, from the large, violent sperm whales to smaller pilot whales (blackfish) and belugas, so it is difficult to determine the number of barrels from each. Estimates are the author's.

Sperm whale oil was kept separate from the oil from other whales. The more valuable sperm oil was placed into casks by itself, and other containers were mixed. I relied on Starbuck's and Hegarty's estimates of barrels returned, and "whales" are presumed to mean right whales. See Starbuck, *History* and Hegarty, *Returns of Whaling Vessels Sailing from American Ports.*

I used Hohman's estimate to establish a basis for comparison, according to which a sperm whale produced about sixty barrels of oil and other whales produced eighty. Note, however, that many of the whales counted as contributing to the catch produced substantially less than eighty barrels. See Hohman, *The American Whaleman.*

*There is no doubt these twenty-five individuals were responsible for (about) 90 percent of the 1,810 whales that masters of color are estimated to have killed. Note also that the dollar amounts include the value of whalebone.

APPENDIX J
American Whaling Ports, 1784–1928

Rank	First Year	Port	Last Year	Whaling Years
1	1791	New Bedford, Mass.	1928	137
2	1784	Boston, Mass.	1901	117
3	1800	Norwich, Conn.	1909	109
4	1821	Provincetown, Mass.	1920	99
5	1785	Dartmouth, Mass.	1877	92
6	1802	New London, Conn.	1892	90
7	1784	Sag Harbor, N.Y.	1871	87
8	1792	New York, N.Y.	1877	85
9	1785	Newburyport, Mass.	1868	83
10	1785	Wellfleet, Mass.	1867	82
11	1788	Nantucket, Mass.	1868	80
12	1816	Edgartown, Mass.	1894	78
13	1853	San Francisco, Calif.	1928	75
14	1839	Somerset, Mass.	1912	73
15	1811	Westport, Mass.	1879	68
16	1821	Stonington, Conn.	1889	68
17	1793	Providence, R.I.	1854	61
18	1815	Fairhaven, Mass.	1876	61
19	1785	Plymouth, Mass.	1845	60
20	1794	Wareham, Mass.	1853	59
21	1788	Gloucester, Mass.	1841	53
22	1788	Hudson, N.Y.	1841	53
23	1816	Holmes Hole/Tisbury/ Vineyard Haven, Mass.	1868	52

Cont'd on next page

Rank	First Year	Port	Last Year	Whaling Years
24	1818	Salem, Mass.	1868	50
25	1832	Honolulu, HI.	1880	48
26	1794	East Haddam, Conn.	1838	44
27	1786	Bristol, Mass.	1827	41
28	1821	Warren, R.I.	1861	40
29	1816	Newport, R.I.	1855	39
30	1820	Falmouth, Mass.	1859	39
31	1820	New Haven, Conn.	1858	38
32	1832	Fall River, Mass.	1860	28
33	1832	Mystic, Conn.	1860	28
34	1832	Greenport, N.Y.	1857	25
35	1840	Sippican, Mass.	1865	25
36	1816	Rochester, Mass.	1840	24
37	1849	Beverly, Mass.	1873	24
38	1830	Lynn, Mass.	1853	23
39	1841	Mattapoisett, Mass.	1864	23
40	1827	Bristol, R.I.	1846	19
41	1827	Bristol, R.I.	1846	19
42	1839	Cold Spring, N.Y.	1857	18
43	1867	Marion, Mass.	1885	18
44	1822	Marblehead, Mass.	1833	11
45	1851	Orleans, Mass.	1861	10
46	1833	Bridgeport, R.I.	1842	9
47	1841	New Suffolk, Mass.	1850	9
48	1832	Poughkeepsie, N.Y.	1840	8
49	1851	Sandwich, Mass.	1859	8
50	1834	Wilmington, Del.	1841	7

Cont'd on next page

Rank	First Year	Port	Last Year	Whaling Years
51	1832	Portsmouth, N.H.	1838	6
52	1833	Dorchester, Mass.	1837	4
54	1833	Newburgh, N.Y.	1837	4
53	1834	Wiscasset, Maine	1838	4
55	1837	Newark, N.J.	1841	4
56	1841	Freetown, Mass.	1844	3
57	1910	Stamford, Conn.	1913	3
58	1808	Greenwich, R.I.	1810	2
59	1847	Yarmouth, Mass.	1849	2
60	1785	Hingham, Mass.	1785	1
61	1786	Braintree, Mass.	1786	1
62	1789	Cape Cod, Mass.	1789	1
63	1789	Rhode Island	1789	1
64	1818	Philadelphia, Pa.	1818	1
65	1822	Tiverton, R.I.	1822	1
66	1824	Perth Amboy, N.Y.	1824	1
67	1831	Edenton, N.C.	1831	1
68	1841	Bucksport, Mass.	1841	1
69	1841	Duxbury, Mass.	1841	1
70	1846	Barnstable, Mass.	1846	1
71	1848	Chilmark, Mass.	1848	1
72	1849	Quincy, Mass.	1849	1
73	1850	Truro, Mass.	1851	1
74	1868	Groton, Conn.	1868	1
75	1886	Hartford, Conn.	1886	1

Sources: Starbuck, *History of the American Whale Fishery*; Hegerty, *Returns of Whaling Vessels Sailing from American Ports*; Lund et al., *American Offshore Whaling Voyages, 1667–1927*, vol. 1, p. 4.

Note: Over the life of the industry 130 different ports were used.

APPENDIX K
(Known) All-Black Whaling Voyages

Captain	Ship	Depart	Return	Sperm Bbl.	Est. Value Today
Absalom Boston	Industry[1]	5/8/1822	11/1822	78	$37,000
Alvan Phelps	Traveller	8/5/1822	1822	70	$24,500
Obed Starbuck[2]	Loper[3]	6/21/1829	9/7/1830	2,280	$1,750,000
Edward J. Pompey	Rising States[4]	11/6/1836	6/29/1837	78	$65,800
William Cuffe	Rising States[4]	7/29/1837	12/1837	143	$235,000
Amos Haskins[5]	Massasoit[3]	11/20/1852	7/24/1853	60	$92,300
Valentine Rosa[6]	Morning Star[6]	10/10/1912	9/17/1914	2,650	$1,190,000
Total=7				5,359	$3,320,000

1. From Putney, *Black Sailors*, p. 54.
2. Obed Starbuck, the captain, was the only nonblack man on board.
3. From Starbuck, *History*.
4. From Hegarty, *Returns of Sailing Vessels Returning from American Ports*.
5. Haskins, his officers, and twelve of the twenty-two crewmembers were black (Putney, *Black Sailors*, p. 65).
6. Rosa's "all-black" trip is credible but apocryphal.

NOTES

Preface

1. Frank, foreword to Malloy, *African Americans in the Maritime Trades*.
2. "Edwin Drake: American Oil Driller," *Encyclopedia Britannica*, http://www
   .britannica.com/EBchecked/topic/170909/Edwin-Laurentine-Drake;
   Starbuck, *History*; Hegarty, *Returns of Whaling Vessels Sailing from American
   Ports*.
3. *Martha's Vineyard* magazine, May–June 2014, p. 40; Lund et al., *American
   Offshore Whaling Voyages*; Lund, *Whaling Masters and Whaling Voyages
   Sailing from American Ports*, p. 3.
4. George Dvorsky, "1846: The Year We Hit Peak Sperm Whale Oil," *Gizmodo*,
   http://io9.com/5930414/1846-the-year-we-hit-peak-sperm-whale-oil.
5. Norling, *Captain Ahab Had a Wife*, chart, "Major 19th-Century Whaling
   Grounds," pp. 124–25.
6. Sherman, *The Voice of the Whaleman*, pp. 8, 24.
7. Putney: Joseph G. Belain, Absalom Boston, Pardon Cook, Paul Cuffe Sr.,
   William Cuffe (son), Hezikiah Gardner, Peter Green, Samuel W. Harris,
   Amos Haskins, Alvan Phelps, Edward J. Pompey, Paul Wainer, Thomas
   Wainer; Malloy: Joseph P. Benton, Paul Cuffe Jr., João da Lomba, John T.
   Gonsalves, Louis M. Lopes, Severino Pierce, Joseph H. Senna, William T.
   Shorey; Lewis: Absalom F. Boston, Pardon Cook, William Cuffe, Samuel
   Harris, Amos Haskins, John Masten, Alvan Phelps, Edward C. Pompey,
   Paul Wainer, Thomas Wainer; Lewis, "New Bedford/Westport, Etc., Negro
   Ships Captains Prior to Civil War": Warrin: Anthony P. Benton, Joseph P.
   Benton, Benjamin Costa, John da Lomba, José M. Domingues, Jasper M.
   Ears, Theophilus M. Freitas, John T. Gonsalves, Henry J. Gonzales, Frank M.
   Lopes, Louis M. Lopes, Peter Lopez, Valentine Roza, Antonio José Senna,
   Ayers J. Senna, Joseph H. Senna; Shoemaker: Joseph P. Belain, Ferdinand
   Lee, William Garrison Lee; New Bedford Whaling Museum crew list.
8. Shoemaker, *Native American Whalemen*, pp. 4–5, 199.
9. Murphy, *Gone a-Whaling*, p. 60.

10. Starbuck, *History*; Federal Writers Project, *Whaling Masters*; Hegarty, *Returns of Whaling Vessels Sailing from American Ports*; Sherman, Downey, and Adams, *Whaling Logbooks & Journals 1613–1927*; Lund, *Whaling Masters and Whaling Voyages Sailing from American Ports*, 2001 and 2010.

Introduction

1. Malloy, *African Americans in the Maritime Trades*, p. 4; Bolster, "To Feel Like a Man."
2. Cohn and Platzer, *Black Men of the Sea*, p. 61.
3. Lund et al., *American Offshore Whaling Voyages*, vol. 1.
4. Sherman, *The Voice of the Whaleman*, p. 77.
5. Almeida, "Cape Verdeans in the Whaling Industry," www.umass.edu/specialpro grams/caboverde/whale.html; unidentified newspaper article, August 8, 1910, scrapbook collection of the New Bedford Whaling Museum Library; Hoare, *The Whale*, p. 146; Mawer, *Ahab's Trade*, p. 245.
6. Hoare, p. 150.
7. Stackpole, *The Sea Hunters*, p. 413; Busch, *Whaling Will Never Do for Me*, p. 5.
8. Foner and Lewis, *Black Workers*, pp. 101–10; Karttunen, *The Other Islanders*, pp. 78–79.
9. Hohman, *The American Whaleman*.
10. Davis, Gallman, and Gleiter, *In Pursuit of Leviathan*, pp. 211–12; price per gallon by year as indicated in Starbuck, *History*, and Hegarty, *Returns of Whaling Vessels Sailing from American Ports*; Ommanney, *Lost Leviathan*, p. 57; Hohman, p. 144. For these calculations I assumed prices per gallon (annual prices from Starbuck and Hegarty), with forty gallons per barrel. Sperm whales averaged sixty barrels each, and other whales averaged eighty. The dollar value for the respective year's ships returned to port uses 2016 as the baseline with an online calculator used for the inflation-based dollar values; *U.S. Dollar Inflation Counter*, https://www.officialdata.org/1830-dollars -in-2016?amount=1 (1830 and/or year is a variable).

Chapter 1. Dynasty

1. Paul Cuffe, quoted in Mott, *Biographical Sketches and Interesting Anecdotes of Persons of Colour*, 1826, p. 36, http://www.americanancestors.org/features /paul-cuffe.
2. Thomas, *Rise to Be a People*, p. 16. Thomas is the source of much of the information about Paul Cuffe in this chapter.
3. Thomas; Armistead, *Memoir of Paul Cuffe*, p. 31.
4. Symposium: *Exploring Paul Cuffe: The Man and His Legacy*, Saturday, October 3, 2009, New Bedford Whaling Museum.

5. Shoemaker, *Native American Whalemen*.

6. Wiggins, *Captain Paul Cuffe's Logs & Letters*, p. 45; Schneider, *The Enduring Shore*, p. 156; Pierce and Segal, *Wampanoag Families of Martha's Vineyard*, vol. 2, pt. A, p. 197.

7. Cordeiro, "Paul Cuffe."

8. Karttunen, *The Other Islanders*, p. 68; Thomas, *Rise to Be a People*, pp. 5, 7; McKissack and McKissack, *Black Hands, White Sails*, pp. 32–33; Pierce and Segal, *Wampanoag Families*, pp. 200, 639–41.

9. Pierce and Segal, p. 1022; Thomas, p. 8.

10. Thomas, pp. 5–9.

11. Thomas, pp. 9, 10–12.

12. Barboza, "The Best Blockade Runner in the Business"; Armistead, *Memoir of Paul Cuffe*, p. 29.

13. Thomas, *Rise to Be a People*, p. 94; McKissack and McKissack, *Black Hands, White Sails*, p. 34; Grover, *The Fugitive's Gibraltar*, p. 72.

14. Bolster, *Black Jacks*, p. 173.

15. Bolster, p. 173; Wiggins, *Captain Paul Cuffe's Logs & Letters*, p. 515.

16. Sherwood, "Paul Cuffe."

17. Pierce and Segal, *Wampanoag Families*, p. 1019.

18. Shoemaker, *Native American Whalemen*, p. 169; Pierce and Segal, p. 1022; Thomas, *Rise to Be a People*, p. 8; Sandi Brewster-Walker, personal communication.

19. Thomas, pp. 13, 16, 25.

20. Pierce and Segal, *Wampanoag Families*, p. 1023.

21. Grover, *The Fugitive's Gibraltar*, pp. 70–72.

22. Thomas, *Rise to Be a People*, p. 24; Putney, *Black Sailors*, p. 163; Wiggins, *Captain Paul Cuffe's Logs and Letters*, p. 53.

23. Grover, *The Fugitive's Gibraltar*, notes to pp. 87–97, n. 53; Thomas, pp. 23–24, 43; Cuffe, *Narrative of the Life and Adventures of Paul Cuffe*, p. 5; Pierce and Segal, *Wampanoag Families*, p. 1023.

24. Malloy, *African Americans in the Maritime Trades*, p. 6; Grover, n. 53, p. 302.

25. Thomas, *Rise to Be a People*, pp. 26, 43; *New Bedford Mercury*, July 7, 1809; Wiggins, *Captain Paul Cuffe's Logs and Letters*, pp. 447–48, 461–62; Putney, *Black Sailors*, pp. 163, 171; Starbuck, *History*.

26. Pierce and Segal, *Wampanoag Families*, p. 1025.

27. McKissack and McKissack, *Black Hands, White Sails*, p. 90.

28. Putney, *Black Sailors*, p. 152; Shoemaker, NARA crew lists; Pierce and Segal, *Wampanoag Families*, p. 1024.

29. New Bedford Whaling Crew database, New Bedford Whaling Museum Library [hereafter cited as New Bedford crew list]; Lund et al., *American Offshore Whaling Voyages*, vol. 1; Putney, *Black Sailors*, p. 152; Malloy, *African Americans in the Maritime Trades*.

30. Lewis, "New Bedford/Westport, etc., Negro Ships Captains."
31. 1850 U.S. Census.
32. Putney, "Pardon Cook," pp. 28, 54; Putney, *Black Sailors*, p. 140; New Bedford Whaling Museum Research Library, May 1, 2014.
33. Putney, "Pardon Cook," p. 28; Putney, *Black Sailors*, 141; Grover, *The Fugitive's Gibraltar*, p. 90.
34. Putney, "Pardon Cook," pp. 54, 65; Putney, *Black Sailors*, pp. 79, 141; Obed Starbuck, the captain, was the only nonblack man on board; Starbuck, *History*; Haskins, his officers, and twelve of the twenty-two crewmen were black.
35. Malloy, "African Americans in the Maritime Trades," p. 7.
36. Lund, *Whaling Masters and Whaling Voyages Sailing from American Ports*, p. 3.
37. Stackpole, *The Sea Hunters*, p. 287.
38. Starbuck, *History*; Putney, *Black Sailors*, pp. 74, 156; Federal Writers Project, *Whaling Masters*, p. 307; Stackpole, p. 286; Lund et al., *American Offshore Whaling Voyages*, vol. 1, reports the *John Adams* at 296 tons.

Chapter 2. How Commercial Whaling Started

1. McKissack and McKissack, *Black Hands, White Sails*, p. xiv.
2. Davis, Gallman, and Gleiter, *In Pursuit of Leviathan*, p. 31.
3. McKissack and McKissack, *Black Hands, White Sails*, p. xiv; see also "History of the Basque People," http://www.bibliotecapleyades.net/ciencia/ciencia_basques04.htm; "Basque People," http://www.britannica.com/EBchecked/topic/55335/Basque; "A Brief History of Whaling," http://history1800s.about.com/od/whaling/a/histwhaling.htm; Hohman, *The American Whaleman*, p. 19; Davis, Gallman, and Gleiter, p. 31; "Discovery in Labrador: A 16th Century Basque Whaling Port and Its Sunken Fleet," *National Geographic*, March 1985.
4. Starbuck, *History*, p. 5.
5. Starbuck, p. 5; Federal Writers Project, *Whaling Masters*, p. 9.
6. Alisha Steindecker, "Shinnecock Indian History as Told through Photographs," *Southampton Press*, April 11, 2015; John Hanc, "Success and Struggles in Whaling," *Newsday*, February 7, 2016, p. E5.
7. Hanc, p. E8.
8. Julia Good Fox, *Historic Nantucket* 40, no. 3 (1992): 49–51; Stephanie Siek, "Who's a Native American? It's Complicated," www.inamerica.blogs.cnn.com/2012/05/14/whos-a-native-american-its-complicated; Cash, "African American Whalers," pp. 41–52.
9. Schneider, *The Enduring Shore*, p. 156.
10. Siek, "Who's a Native American?"

11. Ariel Levy, "Reservations," *New Yorker*, December 3, 2010.
12. Railton, *History of Martha's Vineyard*, pp. 333–34; Federal Writers Project, *Whaling Masters*, p. 9; Richmond Hill Historical Society, http://www.rich mondhillhistory.org/indians.html#IndianTribes.
13. New Bedford crew list; Starbuck, *History*; Shoemaker, *Native American Whalemen*, pp. 70, 72, 187.
14. Shoemaker, pp. 72, 86, 186–87; Strother, *Summer in New England 1860*, quoted in Shoemaker, pp. 448, 451–52; Todd, *In Olde New York*.
15. Shoemaker, *Native American Whalemen*, database.
16. Nancy Shoemaker, "The Lee Family and Nineteenth-Century Shinnecock Whaling," abstract, *Long Island History Journal* (2016), https://lihj.cc.stony brook.edu/2016/articles/the-lee-family-and-nineteenth-century-shinnecock -whaling/, p. 131 from the logbook of the *Abraham Barker* in 1872, p. 187; Shoemaker NARA database of crew lists.
17. Jennings, *The Invasion of America*, p. 298; Railton, *History of Martha's Vineyard*, p. 54; Karttunen, *The Other Islanders*, p. 53.
18. Railton, p. 64; "African Nantucketers," http://www.nha.org/pdfs/otherislanders /1bAfrican1o2.pdf.
19. Wampanoag tribal members refer to themselves as People of the First Light. Nancy Eldredge, "Who Are the Wampanoag?" Nauset Wampanoag, http:// www.plimoth.org/learn/just-kids/homework-help/who-are-wampanoag.
20. "The True Story of a Fugitive Slave," *Vineyard Gazette*, February 3, 1921; Shoemaker, *Native American Whalemen*, p. 167; Grover, *The Fugitive's Gibraltar*, pp. 49, 54.
21. Shoemaker.
22. "Was There a Real Moby Dick?" New Bedford Whaling Museum, http://www .whalingmuseum.org/learn/real-moby-dick; "They Collaborate on 'I Killed Moby Dick,'" *Vineyard Gazette*, May 31, 1957; "I Killed Moby Dick," as told to Max Eastman, *Reader's Digest*, June 1957; "Platina's Log Bears Out His Story of White Whale Capture," *Vineyard Gazette*, January 15, 1960; Tomahawk Fishing Charters, http://www.tomahawkcharters.com; Hoare, *The Whale*, p. 171; Davis, *Nimrod of the Sea*.
23. Railton, *History of Martha's Vineyard*, p. 64.
24. Shoemaker, *Native American Whalemen*, p. 171.
25. Railton, *History of Martha's Vineyard*, pp. 64–66; Farr, "Slow Boat to Nowhere," p. 162; Shoemaker, pp. 171, 176.
26. Pierce and Segal, *Wampanoag Families*, p. 407.
27. Pierce and Segal, pp. 414–15.
28. New Bedford crew list; Shoemaker, *Native American Whalemen*, p. 24.
29. Pierce and Segal, *Wampanoag Families*, pp. 65, 69, 575, 725; *New Bedford Standard*, October 20, 1926, New Bedford Whaling Museum Library

scrapbook collection, T 6, 7, 86; Shoemaker, *Native American Whalemen*; New Bedford crew list; Lund et al., *American Offshore Whaling Voyages*; "Pigeon from Sea Alights on Hearse," *Vineyard Gazette*, October 22, 1926.

30. Hegarty, *Addendum to "Starbuck" and "Whaling Masters"*; Pierce and Segal, *Wampanoag Families*, pp. 66–67; Shoemaker, NARA crew lists; Lund et al., *American Offshore Whaling Voyages*.

31. Shoemaker, NARA crew lists; Putney, *Black Sailors*, pp. 139, 155, 156.

32. Hough, "List of Vineyard Shipmasters Is Growing Longer."

33. Shoemaker, *Native American Whalemen*, pp. 206, 208.

34. New Bedford Whaling Museum Library scrapbooks T 6 7, 86; *New Bedford Standard*, October 20, 1926 (he died of myocarditis, a heart disease usually caused by a viral infection); Pierce and Segal, *Wampanoag Families*, p. 70; Hough, *Martha's Vineyard Summer Resort 1835–1935*, pp. 17–18.

35. Author's estimate.

Chapter 3. Nantucket to New Bedford

1. McKissack and McKissack, *Black Hands, White Sails*, p. 9.

2. Murphy, *Gone a-Whaling*, p. 59; Museum of African American History, Boston and Nantucket, maah.org; Stackpole, *The Sea Hunters*, p. 24.

3. *History of American Women: Colonial Women / 18th Century Women / 19th Century Women*, http://www.womenhistoryblog.com/2008/10/mary-coffin-starbuck.html.

4. Philbrick, *Away off Shore*, p. 209.

5. Grover, *The Fugitive's Gibraltar*, p. 21.

6. Grover, pp. 21, 36, 292, notes to pp. 32–36, 54; William Rotch Jr. to Frances Rotch-Bullard, in Grover, p. 263; New Bedford Whaling Museum exhibition, courtesy of a gift from Dr. Louise Clark.

7. Dolin, *Leviathan*, p. 208; Philbrick, *Away off Shore*.

8. Putney, *Black Sailors*; Karttunen, *The Other Islanders*; Lund et al., *American Offshore Whaling Voyages*; Starbuck, *History*; New Bedford crew list.

9. The Nantucket Historical Association's records suggest that Boston invested in this voyage (but did not sail), which had a white captain and an all-black crew, one of whom was Boston's friend Samuel Harris, the navigator and second mate; Stackpole, *The Sea Hunters*; 2,280 barrels sperm oil at 40 gallons per barrel at .65 per gallon (in 1830) times $23.91 (dollar in 2016) less $60,000 investment, divided by 20 (author's estimate).

10. Dolin, *Leviathan*, p. 208.

11. Dolin, p. 115.

12. Nantucket Historical Association, *African Nantucketers*, http://www.nha.org/pdfs/otherislanders/1bAfrican1o2.pdf.

13. *Historic Nantucket* 40, no. 3 (1992): 49–51.

14. The Museum of African American History, Boston and Nantucket, maah.org.

15. Karttunen, *The Other Islanders*, pp. 53, 55.
16. Museum of African American History, maah.org; http://www.afroammuseum .org/bhtn_site10.htm; Karttunen, *Nantucket Places and People*, p. 52; http:// www.afroammuseum.org/documents/higginbotham_preservation_release .pdf.
17. Karttunen, *The Other Islanders*, p. 68.
18. Karttunen; "Hidden History of Nantucket," http://www.unitarianchurch nantucket.org/wp-content/uploads/2011/07/Barbara-White-Presentation -Feb.-23–2014.pdf; Nantucket Historical Association, "African Nantucketers," http://www.nha.org/history/hn/HN-karttunen-boston.htm; Barbara Johnson/ Friends of Nantucket Historical Association MS Collection 381, 1766–1891.
19. Lewis, "New Bedford/Westport, etc., Negro Ships Captains prior to Civil War."
20. *Nantucket Inquirer*, "Shipping News," May 16, 1822; Starbuck, *History*, p. 243.
21. Putney, *Black Sailors*, p. 101.
22. Nantucket Historical Association, "African Nantucketers"; *CPI Inflation Calculator*, http://www.in2013dollars.com/1855-dollars-in-2016?amount=1.
23. Karttunen, *Law and Disorder in Old Nantucket*, pp. 124–29.
24. Interview, Frances Ruley Karttunen, January 30, 2016.
25. Nantucket Historical Association, http://www.nha.org/pdfs/otherislanders /1bAfrican1o2.pdf; Putney, *Black Sailors*, pp. 71, 80; Cohn and Platzer, *Black Men and the Sea*, p. 74.
26. Cohn and Platzer, p. 74.
27. New Bedford crew list; Hayden and Hayden, *African Americans on Martha's Vineyard and Nantucket*, pp. 237–38; Putney, *Black Sailors*, p. 101.
28. Nantucket Historical Association, http://www.nha.org/pdfs/otherislanders /1bAfrican1o2.pdf.
29. Beegel, "African American History on Nantucket," pp. 45–48.
30. Beegel, pp. 45–48.
31. Nantucket Historical Association records, January 1, 2015, nha.org.
32. Al Dorof, "James Forten (1766–1842)," *Queen Village Neighbors Association* (previously published at the Southwark Historical Society), https://qvna.org /2012/03/19/forten/; "James Forten: Inventor, Abolitionist, 1766–1842," http://gardenofpraise.com/ibdfort.htm; Logan and Winston, *Dictionary of American Negro Biography*, p. 234.
33. Wench, *A Gentleman of Color*; Sherwood, "Paul Cuffe."
34. Wench.
35. Pierce and Segal, *Wampanoag Families*, pp. 770–72.
36. Foner and Lewis, *Black Workers*, pp. 71–72, 75; Douglass, *Life and Times*, pp. 178–93.
37. Grover, *The Fugitive's Gibraltar*, pp. 143–48; Karttunen, *Law and Disorder in Old Nantucket*, p. 119.

38. *Vineyard Gazette*, November 27, 1857, and December 4, 1857.
39. Kaldenbach-Montmayor, "Blacks on the High Seas"; Morison, *The Maritime History of Massachusetts 1783–1860*, p. 333, courtesy Nantucket Historical Association Research Library.
40. Kaldenbach-Montmayor.
41. Lindgren, "Let Us Idealize Old Types of Manhood," p. 167.
42. Grover, *The Fugitive's Gibraltar*, p. 9; Hohman, *The American Whaleman*.
43. Baker, "Blacks in Whaling," p. 8; Grover, *The Fugitive's Gibraltar*, p. 9; *Local New Bedford, Ma History*, http://www.whalingcity.net/new_bedford_local _history_1900_1909.html.

Chapter 4. Whaling

1. McKissack and McKissack, *Black Hands, White Sails*, p. 101.
2. "What Is a Whale's Spout?," *National Marine Life Center,* http://nmlc.org /2009/04/what-is-a-whales-spout/.
3. Federal Writers Project, *Whaling Masters*, p. 2; Hohman, *The American Whaleman*, p. 157.
4. Hoare, *The Whale*, p. 18; Federal Writers Project, pp. 22–23.
5. Federal Writers Project, p. 23; Davis, Gallman, and Gleiter, *In Pursuit of Leviathan*, pp. 29, 214, 274–76.
6. Cuffe, *Narrative of the Life and Adventures of Paul Cuffe*, p. 7.
7. McKissack and McKissack, *Black Hands, White Sails*, pp. 88–89; Huntington, *Songs the Whalemen Sang*, p. 17. The *Catalpa* made six trips from New Bedford between 1852 and 1879. This particular voyage was led by Captain William F. Snow, and the logbook is in the Providence Public Library. Lund, *American Whaling Masters*, pp. 301, 421; Davis, Gallman, and Gleiter, *In Pursuit of Leviathan*, p. 87.
8. Logan and Winston, *Dictionary of American Negro Biography*, p. 555; Chatterton, *Whalers and Whaling*; Ellis, *Men and Whales*, p. 177.
9. Logan and Winston, p. 555; Chatterton.
10. Malloy, *African Americans in the Maritime Trades*, p. 8.
11. Kaldenbach-Montmayor, "Blacks on the High Seas"; Kaldenbach-Montemayor, "Black on Grey"; Hohman, *The American Whaleman*, pp. 231, 240; Federal Writers Project, *Whaling Masters*, p. 18.
12. *Morning Star*, 1912–14; quoted in Karttunen, *The Other Islanders*, p. 132.
13. Warrin, *So Ends This Day*, p. 269.
14. New Bedford Whaling Museum exhibit, May 2015.
15. Davis, Gallman, and Gleiter, *In Pursuit of Leviathan*; Hohman, *The American Whaleman*, p. 84.
16. Hohman.
17. Dolin, *Leviathan*, p. 258; Ellis, *Men and Whales*, p. 169; Mawer, *Ahab's Trade*, p. 166; Cheever, *The Whaleman's Adventures in the Southern Ocean*, p. 303.

18. Gomes, *Captain Joe*, pp. 12–14.
19. Gomes, pp. 12–14; Murphy, *Gone a-Whaling*, pp. 37, 70.
20. Busch, *Whaling Will Never Do for Me*, p. 5; Lund, *Whaling Masters and Whaling Voyages Sailing from American Ports*, p. 3.
21. New Bedford Whaling Museum exhibit, "Personal Stories," May 2015; Warrin, *So Ends This Day*, p. 274; Lund et al., *American Offshore Whaling Voyages*.
22. Warrin, p. 274; Old Whaler, "Captain and His Teacher," unidentified, from scrapbooks of the New Bedford Whaling Museum Library.
23. New Bedford crew list; Ships' Papers: Whaling Manuscripts, New Bedford Whaling Museum Library; log of the *Morning Star*, New Bedford Whaling Museum Library.
24. Warrin, *So Ends This Day*, p. 274. *Boston Herald*, December 7, 1909, from the Middleton "Spike" Harris Papers, Schomburg Library Collection, New York Public Library. *New Bedford Mercury*, November 29, 1909.
25. Warrin, *So Ends This Day*, p. 274; *Boston Herald*, December 7, 1909, from the Harris Papers, Schomburg Library Collection, New York Public Library; *New Bedford Mercury*, November 29, 1909.
26. *New Bedford Mercury*, April 7, 1910.
27. Unidentified newspaper article dated September 18, 1914, from New Bedford Whaling Museum Library scrapbooks: Ships Papers: Whaling Manuscripts, New Bedford Whaling Museum Library, visited May 5, 2014; *New Bedford Mercury*, November 29, 1909.
28. Lund, *American Whaling Masters*; New Bedford Whaling Museum exhibit, "Personal Stories," May 2015.
29. Crew list; Hegarty, *Addendum to "Starbuck"*; Lund, *Whaling Masters and Whaling Voyages Sailing from American Ports*; Mandly quote from New Bedford Whaling Museum Library scrapbook collection; Lund et al., *American Offshore Whaling Voyages*.
30. Putney, *Black Sailors*, pp. 83, 152, 157; age imputed from crew list; Finley, All Captains spreadsheet, www.skipfinley.com.
31. McKissack and McKissack, *Black Hands, White Sails*, p. 3.
32. McKissack and McKissack, p. 3; Sherman, *The Voice of the Whaleman*, p. 25; Starbuck, *History*, p. 5; *Cape Cod Whalers of Color: An Exhibit of Photographs and Artifacts-Materials*, collected by George Bryant, March 29, 1998, Cape Cod Community College; Stephen Borkowski; Hohman, *The American Whaleman*, pp. 148–52.
33. *A Personal Tour*, produced by Carol Pugliese, 2010, Provincetown Community Television; *Cape Cod Whalers of Color*; *Wooden Ships and Iron Men*, exhibit, Heritage Museum, Provincetown, Mass., 1994, http://www.provincetownhistoryproject.com/PDF/mun_001_852-wooden-ships-and-iron-men.pdf; *Provincetown Banner* (date unclear); Ancestry.com

/RootsWeb's WorldConnect Project: Nauset and Vicinity, obtained from Joan Barney, genealogist, New Bedford Public Library, April 9, 2015; Lund et al., *American Offshore Whaling Voyages*, indicates the 121-ton schooner was built in 1887 in Essex, Massachusetts.

34. Ancestry.com/RootsWeb's WorldConnect Project: Nauset and Vicinity.

35. "The Pilgrim Monument: Laying of the Cornerstone," Minutes of the King Hiram's Lodge; *Wooden Ships and Iron Men*.

Chapter 5. How Hard Was Whaling?

1. Dayan, *Whaling on Long Island*, p. 78; Lindgren, "Let Us Idealize Old Types of Manhood," p. 194.

2. Attributed to Isack Bray of Rockport, crewmember of the *Euphrasia*, 1849, in Huntington, *Songs the Whalemen Sang*, p. 49.

3. Federal Writers Project, *Whaling Masters*, p. 17.

4. Creighton, *Rites & Passages*, pp. 127–28; "Diary of Edwin Pulver," Columbus, August 9, 1852, Providence Public Library.

5. Mawer, *Ahab's Trade*, p. 173; Delano, *Narrative of Voyages and Travels*, pp. 377–78.

6. Mawer, p. 173; Delano, pp. 377–78.

7. Ellis, *Book of Whales*, pp. 178, 179; Poole, "Full Circle," p. 129; R. C. Murphy, *Logbook for Grace*, p. 18.

8. Ellis, pp. 178–79.

9. Busch, *Whaling Will Never Do for Me*, p. 101; Lindgren, "Let Us Idealize Old Types of Manhood," p. 194; Ellis, pp. 177–78; Poole, "Antone Fortes, Whaleman," p. 139; Dolin, *Leviathan*, p. 259; McKissack and McKissack, *Black Hands, White Sails*, pp. xvii, 71.

10. McKissack and McKissack, p. xvii.

11. Davis, Gallman, and Gleiter, *In Pursuit of Leviathan*, p. 197; Busch, *Whaling Will Never Do for Me*, p. 30; Dolin, *Leviathan*, p. 258.

12. Lindgren, "Let Us Idealize Old Types of Manhood," p. 175.

13. Warrin, *So Ends This Day*, pp. 28, 289.

14. Noice, *With Stefansson in the Arctic*; Warrin, p. 282.

15. Noice, p. 243.

16. Warrin, *So Ends This Day*, pp. 282–83.

17. Hohman, *The American Whaleman*, p. 162.

18. Philbrick, *In the Heart of the Sea*, p. 57; Smithsonian Institution, http://amhis tory.si.edu/onthewater/exhibition/3_7.html.

19. Busch, *Whaling Will Never Do for Me*, p. 104, remark quoted by the log keeper; Lund et al., *American Offshore Whaling Voyages*.

20. Kaldenbach-Montemayor, "Black on Grey"; Kaldenbach-Montemayor, "Blacks on the High Seas"; Morison, *Maritime History of Massachusetts*

NOTES TO PAGES 90–104 249

1783–1860, p. 323, courtesy Nantucket Historical Association Research Library.

21. Pierce and Segal, *Wampanoag Families*, p. 342; Shoemaker, "Mr. Tashtego," p. 128.

22. Shoemaker, *Native American Whalemen*; Pierce and Segal.

23. New Bedford Whaling Museum Library, visit on April 4, 2015. All five of Amos and Elizabeth P. Farmer Haskins' children (all daughters) died without issue; Pierce and Segal, pp. 343, 581, 415; Simmons, *Spirit of the New England Tribes*, pp. 13, 16.

24. Pierce and Segal, *Wampanoag Families*, p. 343.

25. Shoemaker, *Native American Whalemen*, p. 72.

26. Shoemaker, "Mr. Tashtego," p. 130; Shoemaker, *Native American Whalemen*, p. 72; Shoemaker, NARA crew list.

27. Shoemaker, "Mr. Tashtego," p. 131.

28. Pierce and Segal, *Wampanoag Families*, p. 343.

29. Pierce, "Sharper Michael," pp. 147–52; "Not Your Average Ahab," *Martha's Vineyard* magazine, May–June 2014, pp. 54–55.

30. Abrams, *Black and Free*, p. 68.

31. Hayden and Hayden, *African Americans on Martha's Vineyard*, p. 17; Railton, *History of Martha's Vineyard*, p. 193.

32. Pierce, "Sharper Michael," pp. 147–52.

33. "African American Whaling Captain," Providence Public Library, https://pplspcoll.wordpress.com/2009/10/09/african-american-whaling-captain/.

34. *Vineyard Gazette*, January 2, 1857, July 11, 1907; Pierce and Segal, *Wampanoag Families*, vol. 2, pt. A, pp. 81–82, 540.

35. Warrin, *So Ends This Day*, p. 197; log for the bark *Ohio*, Nicholson Collection, Providence Public Library, reel 524.

36. Busch, *Whaling Will Never Do for Me*, pp. 26, 30.

37. Warrin, *So Ends This Day*, pp. 199–200.

38. Lund et al., *American Offshore Whaling Voyages*.

39. Druett, *In the Wake of Madness*, p. 84.

40. New Bedford crew list; *Vineyard Gazette*, March 28, 1856.

41. Dolin, *Leviathan*, pp. 182–96.

42. Starbuck, *History*; the *Junior* departed New Bedford on July 21, 1857; *New Bedford Sunday Standard*, December 21, 1919; Dolin.

43. New Bedford Whaling Museum Library scrapbook collection.

44. Malloy, *African Americans in the Maritime Trades*, p. 16; newspaper article, New Bedford Whaling Museum Library scrapbook; Warrin, *So Ends This Day*, p. 324; notes from the 2008 Cape Verdean Museum (Providence) Hall of Fame Induction Program.

45. New Bedford Whaling Museum Library scrapbook.

46. Dolin, *Leviathan*, p. 365; Lund et al., *American Offshore Whaling Voyages*, vol. 1.

47. *New Bedford Standard Times*, June 1928–June 6, 2015; "The *Charles W. Morgan* Returns to New Bedford," p. 18; Stackpole, *The* Charles W. Morgan; Sao Nicolau, New Bedford Whaling Museum Cape Verdean Exhibit, "Personal Stories," May 2015.

48. Central Intelligence Agency, *The World Factbook*, https://www.cia.gov/lib rary/publications/the-world-factbook/geos/pp.html; Starbuck, *History*; New Bedford crew list.

49. Central Intelligence Agency; Starbuck, *History*; New Bedford crew list.

50. *Vineyard Gazette*, March 28, 1856.

51. Starbuck, *History*; New Bedford crew list; Lund et al., *American Offshore Whaling Voyages*.

52. Warrin, *So Ends This Day*, p. 216, log of the *Charles W. Morgan*.

53. New Bedford crew list.

54. Unidentified newspaper article recounting Captain John T. Gonsalves' record at sea, March 4, 1917, from New Bedford Whaling Museum Library scrapbook; *Nancy Ann* must have been a fictional name: there is no record of such a whale ship.

55. "In Many Species, a Family Dinner Means Something Else," *New York Times*, https://www.nytimes.com/2017/01/30/science/cannibalism-animal-biology .html?smid=nytcore-ipad-share&smprod=nytcore-ipad&_r=1; Burns, *A Year with a Whaler*, p. 16.

Chapter 6. Sometimes the Whale Won

1. Newell (b. 1906) was a former advertising executive who developed an interest in whaling in the 1940s. He built a museum in Norwalk, Connecticut, to display his collection and artworks and published works of maritime interest. See the New Bedford Whaling Museum website, https://www.whalingmu seum.org/.

2. Lund could not confirm the Captain Holmes/*Sea Fox* episode.

3. Stackpole, *The Sea Hunters*, p. 317.

4. Lund, *Whaling Masters and Whaling Voyages Sailing from American Ports*, p. 469; Murphy, *Gone a-Whaling*, p. 45; Stackpole, *The Sea Hunters*, p. 332.

5. Murphy, p. 114; Hohman, *The American Whaleman*, p. 185; Dolin, *Leviathan*, pp. 300–302; *Gledson's Pictorial*, 1853; Federal Writers Project, *Whaling Masters*, p. 21.

6. New Bedford crew list; Hegarty, *Returns of Whaling Vessels Sailing from American Ports*; Lund et al., *American Offshore Whaling Voyages*, vol. 2.

7. "Captain Mosher Writes of Wanderer's Thrilling Escape," unidentified newspaper article, September 27, 1912, New Bedford Whaling Museum scrapbooks.

8. Jeremiah N. Reynolds, "Mocha Dick: Or the White Whale of the Pacific: A Leaf from a Manuscript Journal, of the Pacific," New Bedford Whaling Museum; McKissack and McKissack, *Black Hands, White Sails*, pp. 102, 104; Stackpole, *The Sea Hunters*, p. 461; Hoare, *The Whale*, p. 167.

9. Marquardt, "Sag Harbor Whalers: Entombed at Sea"; Lund, *Whaling Masters and Whaling Voyages Sailing from American Ports*, p. 3, indicates there were forty-one.

10. Malloy, *African Americans in the Maritime Trades*, pp. 5–6.

11. Warrin, *So Ends This Day*, pp. 115–16.

12. Malloy, *African Americans in the Maritime Trade*, p. 18; Warrin, p. 200; Hegarty, *Returns of Whaling Vessels Sailing from American Ports*, p. 26; Lund et al., *American Offshore Whaling Voyages*.

13. Visit to New Bedford Whaling Museum Library, January 2, 2015.

14. Compilation: 83 barrels × 35 gallons per barrel × 69 cents each (then) × $28.57 (today) = $57,267.36. Murphy, *Gone a-Whaling*, p. 45.

15. The change in captains to Charles Brown is confirmed by Lund et al. in *American Offshore Whaling Voyages*.

16. Author's estimate based on the oil cargo returned versus average whale sizes.

17. Lund et al., *American Offshore Whaling Voyages*; New Bedford Whaling Museum Library, Captains Card Catalog: Foreign Language Logs. The *A. R. Tucker* had a second log on its 1901–3 voyage that was written by a Portuguese person attempting to write in English, resulting in a phonetic transcript; translation from Warrin, *So Ends This Day*, p. 201.

18. Warrin, pp. 272, 324.

Chapter 7. The Whale's Story

1. "1846: The Year We Hit Peak Sperm Whale Oil," *Gizmodo*, http://io9.com/5930414/1846-the-year-we-hit-peak-sperm-whale-oil.

2. Lacépède, *Histoire Naturelle des Cétacées*, 1804, quoted in Murphy, *Gone a-Whaling*, p. 19.

3. Davis, Gallman, and Gleiter, *In Pursuit of Leviathan*, p. 1.

4. Murphy, *Gone a-Whaling*, pp. 19, 181; Hoare, *The Whale*, pp. 7, 354, 356, and interview with the *Boston Globe*, January 24, 2010.

5. Murphy; Ommanney, *Lost Leviathan*; Davis, Gallman, and Gleiter, *In Pursuit of Leviathan*, p. 21; Ellis, *The Book of Whales*, pp. vi, viii; Mawer, *Ahab's Trade*, p. 261.

6. Samuel T. Pees, "Oil History," http://www.petroleumhistory.org/OilHistory/pages/Whale/whale_barrel.html; Ommanney, p. 57.

7. Dolin, *Leviathan*, pp. 77, 267–68; Hoare, *The Whale*, p. 65; Melville, *Moby-Dick*, pp. 384–85.

8. Oceanic Research Group, "Sperm Whales: The Deep Divers of the Ocean," http://www.oceanicresearch.org/education/wonders/spermwhales.htm; Ommanney, *Lost Leviathan*, pp. 141, 46.
9. Davis, Gallman, and Gleiter, *In Pursuit of Leviathan*, pp. 134, 138; Ellis, *The Book of Whales*, p. 2.
10. Stackpole, *The Sea Hunters*, p. 135.
11. Stevenson, *Aquatic Products in Arts and Industries*, Provincetown Museum exhibit, 2015.
12. Federal Writers Project, *Whaling Masters*, p. 24; Ommanney, *Lost Leviathan*, pp. 65–66; Stevenson.
13. Provincetown Museum exhibit, 2015.
14. Hegarty, *Returns of Whaling Vessels Sailing from American Ports*; New Bedford crew list; Lund, *Whaling Masters and Whaling Voyages Sailing from American Ports*; New Bedford Whaling Museum Library scrapbooks.
15. New Bedford Whaling Museum Library scrapbook, "Schooner *Whyland* Makes Rich Haul of Ambergris"; Hegarty, *Returns of Whaling Vessels Sailing from American Ports*.
16. Malloy, *African Americans in the Maritime Trades*, p. 8; Louis Lopes' passport application, October 31, 1921; from Lopes' death certificate; read by his granddaughter Rosita Lopes Silverman during a telephone conversation, June 23, 2015.
17. Captain William Hegarty was the father of whaling historian Reginald B. Hegarty. Lipman, *Medicine and Pharmacy aboard New England Whaleships*, p. 19; Hohman, *The American Whaleman*; Vogel, *Medicine at Sea in the Days of the Sail*.
18. From email obtained by William do Carmo from his cousin Rosita (Lopes) Silverman, May 12, 2011.
19. Lindgren, "Let Us Idealize Old Types of Manhood," p. 187, label on a busk (corset).
20. Murphy, *Gone a-Whaling*, pp. 24, 93; Busch, *Whaling Will Never Do for Me*, p. 3; Davis, Gallman, and Gleiter, *In Pursuit of Leviathan*, pp. 17, 62; Hohman, *The American Whaleman*, p. 334; Baker, ed., *Blacks in Whaling*, p. 31; Ellis, *The Book of Whales*, p. 237; Hoare, *The Whale*, p. 315.

Chapter 8. Whaling versus Slavery

1. *Bartlett's Familiar Black Quotations*, p. 114.
2. Horton and Horton, *In Hope of Liberty*.
3. Kendi, *Stamped from the Beginning*, pp. 16–18.
4. Oliver and Horton, *In Hope of Liberty*.
5. Spears, *The Story of the New England Whalers*, p. 359; McKissack and McKissack, *Black Hands, White Sails*, p. 5.

6. Coughtry, *The Notorious Triangle*, pp. 59–60; Malloy, *African Americans in the Maritime Trades*, p. 14.

7. Malloy, p. 14; Putney, "Black Merchant American Seamen of Newport," pp. 156–68; Coughtry.

8. Spears, *The Story of New England Whalers*, p. 362; Starbuck, *History*; Lund, et al., *American Offshore Whaling Voyages*.

9. Lund et al.; Creighton, *Rites & Passages*, p. 86.

10. Spears, *The American Slave-Trade*.

11. Malloy, *Black Sailors*, p. 10.

12. Hohman, *The American Whaleman*, p. 194; Cash, "African American Whalers," pp. 41–52.

13. Bolster, "To Feel Like a Man."

14. Bolster.

15. Foner and Lewis, *Black Workers*, p. 108.

16. Farr, *Black Odyssey*, p. 97; Verrill, *The Real Story of the Whaler*, p. 62; Krahulik, *Provincetown*, p. 65; *National Anti-Slavery Standard*, May 6, 1852; Foner and Lewis, pp. 109–10.

17. Foner and Lewis, pp. 109, 101–8; *The Liberator*, January 12, 1844.

18. Kaldenbach-Montemayor, "Blacks on the High Seas."

19. Grover, *The Fugitive's Gibraltar*, p. 292, notes to pp. 32–36, 54; William Rotch Jr. to Francis Rotch, in Bullard, *The Rotches*, p. 263.

20. Museum of African American History, Nantucket, Black Heritage Trail, October 2015; Kaldenbach-Montmayor, "Blacks on the High Seas," p. 12; May 18, 1727–28, town meeting, courtesy Nantucket Historical Association Research Library; Karttunen, *The Other Islanders*, p. 53; Wiggins, *Captain Paul Cuffe Logs and Letters*, p. 48; Lewis, "New Bedford/Westport, etc., Negro Ships Captains."

21. Kennedy, *Nigger*.

22. Langley, *The Negro in the Navy and Merchant Service*, p. 275, quoted in Rubin, Swift, and Northrup, *Negro Employment in the Maritime Industries*, p. 59; Druett, *In the Wake of Madness*.

23. Druett, p. 37.

24. Rubin, Swift, and Northrup, *Negro Employment in the Maritime Industries*, p. 59; Langley, "The Negro in the Navy and Merchant Service 1789–1860," p. 275.

25. Purrington, *Anatomy of a Mutiny: Ship* Sharon; Starbuck, *History*.

26. Busch, *Whaling Will Never Do for Me*, pp. 36–37; Shoemaker, "Mr. Tashtego," p. 121.

27. From Bolster, "To Feel Like a Man," pp. 147–48.

28. From Bolster, pp. 147–48; Noice, *With Steffansson in the Arctic*.

29. Kennedy, *Nigger*, p. 90.

30. Burns, *A Year with a Whaler*, pp. 52–53.
31. Burns.
32. Bolster, "To Feel Like a Man."
33. Rouleau, *With Sails Whitening Every Sea*, p. 112.

Chapter 9. Identity

1. Philbrick, *Away off Shore*, p. 207.
2. Horton and Horton, *In Hope of Liberty*.
3. Jackson, *Light, Bright and Damn Near White*, pp. 101, 143; Lund et al., *American Offshore Whaling Voyages*; Dixon, "Genealogical Fallout from the War of 1812."
4. New Bedford crew list database, https://www.whalingmuseum.org/online _exhibits/crewlist/search.php?reverse=DESC&order_by=&search_by =all&term=&page=4159.
5. McKissack and McKissack, *Black Hands, White Sails*, p. 24; New Bedford crew list, http://www.whalingmuseum.org/online_exhibits/crewlist/about.php; Creighton, *Rites & Passages*, p. 11.
6. Davis, Gallman, and Gleiter, *In Pursuit of Leviathan*, 1997.
7. Gomes, *Captain Joe*.
8. Farr, *Black Odyssey*, p. 79.
9. Malloy, *African Americans in the Maritime Trades*.

Chapter 10. The Whaling Captain

1. Smith, *The Provincetown Book*, pp. 72–73.
2. Davis, Gallman, and Gleiter, *In Pursuit of Leviathan*, p. 381.
3. Mawer, *Ahab's Trade*, p. 364; Stackpole, *The Sea Hunters*, p. 471.
4. Bullen, *The Cruise of the* Cachelot.
5. Bullen, pp. 68–69, 178–83; Busch, *Whaling Will Never Do for Me*, p. 30.
6. Creighton, *Rites & Passages*, p. 86; New Bedford Whaling Museum Library, September 22, 2016; Old Dartmouth Historical Sketch 81, "Published on the Occasion of the Opening of the Whaling Museum Library, New Bedford, Massachusetts, June 5, 1981."
7. Creighton, p. 86.
8. The *Alpha*, built in 1806 in Dartmouth, was 268 tons and 91 feet long overall; Thomas, *Rise to Be a People*, pp. 26, 50.
9. Unidentified newspaper article, Nantucket, Massachusetts, March 11, 1911, from a whaling scrapbook in the New Bedford Whaling Museum Library.
10. Starbuck, *History*; Stackpole, *The Sea Hunters*, p. 288; *CPI Inflation Calculator*, http://www.in2013dollars.com/1830-dollars-in-2016?amount=1; Philbrick, *Away off Shore*, pp. 188–89.

11. Dolin, *Leviathan*, p. 209; Stackpole, "Peter Folger Ewer."

12. Starbuck, *History*.

13. Lipman, "Medicine and Pharmacy aboard New England Whaleships," p. 8.

14. Druett, "Rough Medicine."

15. Lipman, "Medicine and Pharmacy aboard New England Whaleships," p. 23, Martha's Vineyard Museum Library; Vogel, "Medicine at Sea in the Days of the Sail"; Druett, "Rough Medicine."

Chapter 11. Innovators

1. Harold O. Lewis Papers, "List of Black Captains, Mates & Harpooners"; Lund et al., *American Offshore Whaling Voyages*, vol. 2; Putney, *Black Sailors*, p. 52; Grover, *The Fugitive's Gibralter*, p. 121.

2. Grover, pp. 88, 302, n. 49; Nell, *The Colored Patriots of the American Revolution*; Thomas, *Rise to Be a People*, p. 94.

3. Putney, *Black Sailors*, p. 79; Grover, p. 121; Nell.

4. New Bedford Whaling Museum Library, scrapbooks, no sources, undated newspaper article, "Old Time Shipbuilding"; Smithsonian Institution, "Commercial Fishers: Whaling," http://americanhistory.si.edu/onthewater/exhibition/3_7.html; Kaplan, "Lewis Temple and the Hunting of the Whale," p. 235; McKissack and McKissack, *Black Hands, White Sails*, pp. 58–59; New Bedford Whaling Museum, *Old Dartmouth Historical Sketches* no. 2, http://www.whalingmuseum.org/explore/library/publications/old-dartmouth-historical-sketches/odhs_no_2.

5. Smithsonian Institution; "Commercial Fishers: Whaling"; Shoemaker, "Mr. Tashtego"; Project Muse, University of Connecticut; Kaplan, "Lewis Temple," p. 235; *Vital Records of Dartmouth Massachusetts to the Year 1850*, published by the New England Historic Genealogical Society, at the Robert Henry Eddy Memorial Rooms, at the charge of the Eddy Town-Record Fund, Boston, Mass., 1929, http://dunhamwilcox.net/ma/dartmouth_marr_1.htm.

6. Hohman, *The American Whaleman*, p. 291.

7. Kaplan, "Lewis Temple," pp. 235–36; newspaper article, New Bedford Whaling Museum Library scrapbook, no source; Cash, "African American Whalers," p. 48.

8. Kaplan, Documents and Memoranda, "Lewis Temple and the Hunting of the Whale," p. 8; http://amhistory.si.edu/onthewater/exhibition/3_7.html; Dayan, *Whaling on Long Island*, p. 57. One-half of 13,000 voyages × 200 = 1.3 million, author's estimate.

9. Kaplan and Austin, *American Studies in Black and White*, pp. 229, 233, 237; Brown, *The Whalemen, Vessels and Boats, Apparatus, and Methods of the Whale Fishery*; Kaplan, Memoranda.

10. Kaplan and Austin, p. 234, and quote attributed to William H. Tripp, curator of the Old Dartmouth Historical Society and Whaling Museum.
11. Shoemaker, "Mr. Tashtego"; Kaplan and Austin, pp. 235–36.

Chapter 12. The Cape Verdeans

1. Al Vicente and I were owners of radio stations years ago and teammates during a Broadcasters Foundation of America fishing tournament. I think he could find and catch a fish in a swimming pool.
2. Almeida, "Cape Verdeans in the Whaling Industry."
3. Beleza et al., "The Admixture Structure and Genetic Variation of the Archipelago of Cape Verde," https://journals.plos.org/plosone/article?id =10.1371/journal.pone.0051103.
4. Martha's Vineyard Museum; Busch, "Cape Verdeans in the American Whaling and Sealing Industry," p. 106.
5. Martha's Vineyard Museum; Busch, pp. 107–8.
6. Haywood, "American Whalers in Africa."
7. Hohman, *The American Whaleman*, p. 243.
8. Krahulik, *Provincetown*, pp. 54–55, 65; Norling, *Captain Ahab Had a Wife*, p. 134; Jane E. Spear, "Cape Verdean Americans," *Countries and Their Cultures*, http://www.everyculture.com/multi/Bu-Dr/Cape-Verdean-Americans.html; https://www.census.gov/content/dam/Census/library/publications/2014/acs /acsbr12–16.pdf; Inmotionaame; African Immigration, http://www.inmotio naame.org/print.cfm;jsessionid=f83014740915716339678047migration=13& bhcp=1; James Brooke, "As Whalers They Left; as Yankees They're Back," http://www.nytimes.com/1989/02/16/world/fogo-journal-as-whalers-they -left-as-yankees-they-re-back.html.
9. Warrin, *So Ends This Day*, p. 21; Lindgren, "Let Us Idealize Old Types of Manhood," pp. 177–78.
10. Burns, *A Year with a Whaler*, p. 14.
11. Farr, *Black Odyssey*, p. 97; Verrill, *The Real Story of the Whaler*, p. 62.
12. Krahulik, *Provincetown*, p. 65.
13. Farr, *Black Odyssey*, p. 97; Verrill, *The Real Story of the Whaler*, p. 62; Krahulik, p. 65; *National Anti-Slavery Standard*, May 6, 1852; quote from Foner and Lewis, *Black Workers*, pp. 109–10; Cape Verdeans were often described this way because they spoke Portuguese.
14. Malloy, *African Americans in the Maritime Trades*, p. 8; New Bedford Whaling Museum exhibit, May 29, 2015; Murphy, *Logbook for Grace*.
15. Warrin, *So Ends This Day*, p. 291; Lund et al., *American Offshore Whaling Voyages*; Hegarty, *Returns of Whaling Vessels Sailing from American Ports*; Malloy, p. 8.

16. New Bedford crew list; Malloy, p. 8; Lund et al., vol. 2; Warrin, pp. 291, 305; Drewry, *Footsteps African American History*, May–June 1999 (Scrimshaw Soap), p. 22.

17. Bill do Carmo surprised me with the DVD he mailed after our visit in New Bedford in 2015. It is hand-titled "Capt. Manuel Domingoes, Son of Capt. Jose Domingoes, Brava, Cape Verde." I treasure it. I believe the video may have been recorded by the *New Bedford Standard Times* for a story dated August 4, 1987; Hegarty, *Returns of Whaling Vessels Sailing from American Ports*.

18. Interview at Mrs. Diane Havleton's home in Falmouth, Massachusetts, March 9, 2017; William T. Shorey also acquired a master's license from the U.S. Coast Guard.

19. Starbuck, *History*; Shoemaker, NARA crew list, ca. 2007; New Bedford crew list.

20. Almeida, "Cape Verdeans in the Whaling Industry."

21. Warrin, *So Ends This Day*, p. 325; Lund et al., *American Offshore Whaling Voyages*; Almeida, Meintel, and Platzer, *Cape Verdeans in America*.

22. Warrin, p. 251.

23. Lund et al., *American Offshore Whaling Voyages*; Hegarty, *Returns of Whaling Vessels Sailing from American Ports*.

24. Coli, "Cape Verdean Americans as Maritime Entrepreneurs," p. 16; Warrin, *So Ends This Day*, p. 266; Lund et al., vol. 1.

25. Almeida, "Cape Verdeans in the Whaling Industry"; New Bedford crew list.

26. Lund, *Whaling Masters and Whaling Voyages Sailing from American Ports*; New Bedford Whaling Museum Library, April 4, 2015.

27. Warrin, *So Ends This Day*, p. 171.

28. Almeida, "Cape Verdeans in the Whaling Industry," p. 26.

29. Lund, *Whaling Masters and Whaling Voyages Sailing from American Ports*, p. 212; Lund et al., *American Offshore Whaling Voyages*.

30. Warrin, *So Ends This Day*, p. 265; Lund; Murphy, *Gone a-Whaling*, p. 139; Cohn and Platzer, *Black Men of the Sea*, p. 24.

31. Reimers, *Other Immigrants*, p. 73.

Chapter 13. Whaling Moves to San Francisco

1. Hegarty, *Returns of Whaling Vessels Sailing from American Ports*.

2. Warrin, *So Ends This Day*, p. 283; Canadian Museum of History, *The Story of the Canadian Arctic Expedition, 1913–1918*, http://www.historymuseum.ca/cmc/exhibitions/hist/cae/peo614e.shtml; "Cape Verdean Had Hand in Canadian Arctic Expedition," *South Coast Today*, http://www.southcoasttoday.com/article/20060108/NEWS/301089992.

3. "Information: Captain William T. Shorey," *California Historical Quarterly* 51, no. 1 (1972): 75–84; Tompkins, "Black Ahab"; Conmy, "Captain William Thomas Shorey and Shorey Street"; Niven, "A Black Whaling Captain Escaped Prejudice at Sea," https://www.theroot.com/a-black-whaling-captain-escaped-prejudice-at-sea-1790858694; Beasley, *The Negro Trail Blazers of California*, pp. 125–27; *Cape Cod Whalers of Color: An Exhibit of Photographs and Artifacts*, March–May 1998, Cape Cod Community College, materials collected by George Bryant; handwritten notes from unfinished book by M. A. "Spike" Harris, Middleton A. Spike Harris Collection, Schomburg Center for Research in Black Culture, New York Public Library; Niven, Gates, and Higgenbotham, "William T. Shorey, Whaling Master"; Burns, *A Year with a Whaler*, p. 212.

4. Kentake Page, "William T. Shorey: The Black Whaling Captain," https://kentakepage.com/william-t-shorey-the-black-whaling-captain/; Niven; "William T. Shorey," https://en.wikipedia.org/wiki/William_T._Shorey

5. *Inflation Calculator*, http://www.davemanuel.com/inflation-calculator.php; Hegarty, *Returns of Whaling Vessels Sailing from American Ports*.

6. Burns, *A Year with a Whaler*, pp. 150–57.

7. Tompkins, "Black Ahab."

8. Tompkins, p. 80; *San Francisco Chronicle*, November 26, 1907; 1900 U.S. Census (Ancestry.com); Conmy, "Captain William Thomas Shorey and Shorey Street."

9. Harris, handwritten notes from unfinished book; Lund et al., *American Offshore Whaling Voyages*; "Gay Head Case Dismissed," *San Francisco Call*, November 20, 1895; "Whale Dives under the Ice, Smashing to Pieces the Boat of Its Pursuers," *San Francisco Call*, November 20, 1904; "Whaling Bark Brings Fair Catch: *John and Winthrop* Arrives from the Far North," *San Francisco Call*, November 21, 1905.

10. "Whaling Bark Brings Fair Catch."

11. Niven, "A Black Whaling Captain Escaped Prejudice at Sea"; "The Quest of the Whale Has Not Lost Its Lure," *Hawaiian Gazette*, February 25, 1908; "William Thomas Shorey (1859–1919)," *Black Past*, http://www.blackpast.org/aaw/shorey-william-thomas-1859-1919; "William T. Shorey," *Sea Captains: San Francisco 1800s*, The Maritime Heritage Project, http://www.maritimeheritage.org/captains/shoreyWilliamT.html; letter from John E. Peetz, director, Oakland Museum, dated December 7, 1970, to Mr. M. A. Harris (Middleton A. "Spike" Harris); Conmy, "Captain William Thomas Shorey and Shorey Street"; Lewis, "New Bedford/Westport, etc., Negro Ships Captains prior to Civil War: List of Black Captains, Mates and Harpooners."

12. "William Shorey," OaklandWiki, https://localwiki.org/oakland/William_Shorey; Abajian, *Blacks in Selected Newspapers, Censuses and Other* Sources, p. 377;

Charles F. Tilghman, *The Colored Directory*, https://localwiki.org/oakland/William_Shorey; Conmy, "Captain William Thomas Shorey and Shorey Street."

Chapter 14. So Ends

1. McKissick and McKissick, *Black Hands, White Sails*, p. 22.
2. For example, Valentine Rosa's *Canton II* had 14,982 square feet of sail; see Murphy, *Gone a-Whaling*, p. 139.
3. Hohman, *The American Whaleman*, p. 291.
4. Malloy, *African Americans in the Maritime Trades*, p. 7; Davis, Gallman, and Gleiter, *In Pursuit of Leviathan*, pp. 155, 191.
5. Abbey Schultz, "Captain Paul Cuffe, Portrait of a Remarkable Life," American Ancestors by New England Historic Genealogical Society; "Cuffee Clan Gathers to Remember a Remarkable Man," *Westport Shorelines*, August 9, 2005, http://ptatlarge.typepad.com/ptatlarge/2005/08/cuffee_clan_gat.html.
6. Hegarty, *Returns of Whaling Vessels Sailing from American Ports*.
7. Lund et al., *American Offshore Whaling Voyages*, vol. 2; Starbuck, *History*.
8. Starbuck; Federal Writers Project, *Whaling Masters*; Lund et al., *American Offshore Whaling Voyages*; New Bedford Whaling Museum crew list; New Bedford Free Public Library crew list.
9. Lund et al., *American Offshore Whaling Voyages*.
10. Lund et al., crew list; New Bedford crew list.
11. Lund et al., *American Offshore Whaling Voyages*.
12. New Bedford crew list; visit to New Bedford Whaling Museum, September 22, 2016.
13. New Bedford crew list.
14. Putney, *Black Sailors*, p. 160; Lund et al., *American Offshore Whaling Voyages*; New Bedford crew list.
15. Karttunen, *The Other Islanders*, p. 229; New Bedford crew list; Starbuck, *History*.
16. New Bedford crew list.
17. Karttunen, *The Other Islanders*, p. 229; Nantucket Historical Association Library; Starbuck, *History*; Lund et al., *American Offshore Whaling Voyages*.
18. Putney, *Black Sailors*, p. 160; ship names are from Lund et al., *American Offshore Whaling Voyages*.
19. Malloy, *African Americans in the Maritime Trades*, pp. 7, 8, and 20.

Selected Bibliography

Contemporary Professional Journals and Newspapers

Dukes County Intelligencer, Martha's Vineyard Museum

Vineyard Gazette, Edgartown, Massachusetts

Archival Sources

Abajian, James de T., comp. *Blacks in Selected Newspapers, Censuses and Other Sources: An Index to Names and Subjects, First Supplement*, vol. 2, p. 377. Boston: G. K. Hill, 1977.

Lewis, Harold O. "New Bedford/Westport, etc., Negro Ships Captains prior to Civil War: List of Black Captains, Mates and Harpooners." New York Public Library, Astor, Lenos, and Tilden Foundations, boxes 33, 34, 36.

Digital/Online Databases

Mystic Seaport: Integrated Statistics/Captains and Ships, https://research.mystic seaport.org/.

New Bedford Public Library and New Bedford Whaling Museum: Combined Crew List, https://www.whalingmuseum.org/online_exhibits/crewlist/search .php?reverse=DESC&order_by=&search_by=all&term=&page=4159.

Providence Public Library: Special Collections Department, Nicholson MSS, Nicholson Whaling Manuscript Collection, https://www.provlib.org/research -collections/historical-collections/nicholson-whaling-collection/.

Whalemen's Shipping List and Merchants' Transcript, 1843–1914, https://re search.mysticseaport.org/reference/whalemens-shipping-list/.

Published Primary Sources, Articles, and Memoirs

Federal Writers Project. *Whaling Masters*. Old Dartmouth Historical Society. Calif.: Borgo Press/Sidewinder Press, 1938.

Hegarty, Reginald B. *Addendum to "Starbuck" and "Whaling Masters" New Bedford Customs District*. New Bedford, Mass.: Reynolds Printing, Reynolds-DeWalt, 1964.

―――. *Returns of Whaling Vessels Sailing from American Ports: A Continuation of Alexander Starbuck's* History of the American Whale Fishery *1876–1928.* New Bedford, Mass.: Old Dartmouth Historical Society—New Bedford Whaling Museum, 1959.

Logan, Rayford W., and Michael R. Winston. *Dictionary of American Negro Biography.* New York: W. W. Norton, 1982.

Lund, Judith Navas. *Whaling Masters and Whaling Voyages Sailing from American Ports: A Compilation of Sources.* New Bedford, Mass.: New Bedford Whaling Museum, 2001.

Lund, Judith Navas, Elizabeth A. Josephson, Randall R. Reeves, and Tim D. Smith. *American Offshore Whaling Voyages, 1667–1927.* Vol. 1: *Voyages by Vessel.* Vol. 2: *Voyages by Master.* New Bedford, Mass.: Old Dartmouth Historical Society—New Bedford Whaling Museum, 2010.

Pierce, Richard A., and Jerome D. Segal. *Wampanoag Families of Martha's Vineyard.* Vol. 2, pts. A and B. Martha's Vineyard, Mass.: Wampanoag Genealogical History of Martha's Vineyard, Massachusetts, 2016.

Powers, Retha. *Bartlett's Familiar Black Quotations.* Boston: Little, Brown, 2013.

Rubin, Lester, William S. Smith, and Herbert R. Northrup. *Negro Employment in the Maritime Industries: A Study of Racial Policies in the Shipbuilding, Longshore, and Offshore Maritime Industries.* Studies of Negro Employment 2. Philadelphia: The Wharton School of the University of Pennsylvania, 1974.

Segal, Jerome D., and R. Andrew Pierce. *Wampanoag Genealogical History of Martha's Vineyard, Massachusetts.* Baltimore, Md.: Genealogical Publishing Co., 2003.

Sherman, Stuart C. *The Voice of the Whaleman—with an Account of the Nicholson Whaling Collection.* Providence, R.I.: Providence Public Library, 1965.

―――. *Whaling Logbooks & Journals, 1613–1927: An Inventory of Manuscript Records in Public Collections.* Rev. and ed. Judith M. Downey and Virginia M. Adams with Howard Pasternak. New York: Garland, 1896.

Starbuck, Alexander. *History of the American Whale Fishery from Its Earliest Inception to the Year 1876 (1878).* Waltham, Mass.: Kessinger Legacy Reprints 1878.

Books, Articles, and Dissertations

Abrams, Alan. *Black and Free: The Free Negro in America, 1830: A Commentary on Carter Woodson's Negro Heads of Families in the United States in 1830.* Sylvania, Ohio: Doubting Thomas Publishing, 2001.

Alexander, W. *Memoir of Captain Paul Cuffee, a Man of Colour: To Which Is Subjoined The Epistle of the Society of Sierra Leone, in Africa, etc..* London: C. Peacock, 1812.

Allen, Everett S. *Children of the Light: The Rise and Fall of New Bedford Whaling and the Death of the Arctic Fleet.* Boston and Toronto: Little, Brown, 1973.

Almeida, Raymond A. "Cape Verdeans in the Whaling Industry." Obtained from rleary@umassd.edu, University of Massachusetts, Dartmouth.

Almeida, Raymond, Deirdre Meintel, and Michael K. H. Platzer. *Cape Verdeans in America, Our Story*. Boston: Tchuba, the American Committee for Cape Verde, 1978.

Amaral, Pat. *They Ploughed the Seas: Profiles of Azorean Master Mariners*. St. Petersburg, Fla.: Valkyrie Press, 1978.

Armistead, Wilson. *Memoir of Paul Cuffe, a Man of Colour*. London: Edmund Fry, 1840.

Ashley, Clifford W. *The Yankee Whaler*. New York: Dover, 1926.

Baker, Charles F., ed. "Blacks in Whaling." *Footsteps African American History*. Cobblestone, May–June 1999.

Banks, Charles Edward. *The History of Martha's Vineyard: Dukes County Massachusetts*. 3 vols. Boston: George H. Dean, 1911.

Barboza, Robert. "The Best Blockade Runner in the Business: Paul Cuffe in the American Revolution." *South Coast Today*, October 16, 2013, http://www.southcoasttoday.com/article/20131016/pub02/310160345.

Beasley, Delilah L. *The Negro Trail Blazers of California*. Los Angeles: Times Mirror Publishing and Binding House, 1919.

Beegel, Susan F. "African American History on Nantucket." *Historic Nantucket* 40, no. 3, pp. 45–48, http://www.nha.org/library/hn/HN-n40n3-brotherhood.htm,https://nha.org/research/nantucket-history/historic-nantucket-magazine/african-american-history-on-nantucket/.

Beleza, S., J. Campos, J. Lopes, I Araújo, A. Hoppfer Almada, A. Correia e Silva, E. J. Parra, and J. Rocha. "The Admixture Structure and Genetic Variation of the Archipelago of Cape Verde and Its Implications for Admixture Mapping Studies." PLoS One 7, no. 11 (2012).

Bolster, W. Jeffrey. *Black Jacks: African American Seamen in the Age of Sail*. Cambridge, Mass.: Harvard University Press, 1997.

———. "To Feel Like a Man: Black Seamen in the Northern States, 1800–1860." In *A Question of Manhood: A Reader in U.S. Black Men's History and Masculinity*. Vol. 1: *"Manhood Rights": The Construction of Black Male History and Manhood, 1750–1870*, ed. Darlene Clark Hine and Earnestine Jenkins. Bloomington: Indiana University Press, 1999.

Braginton-Smith, John, and Duncan Oliver. *Cape Cod Shore Whaling: America's First Whalemen*. Charleston, S.C.: History Press, 2008.

Brewster-Walker, Sandi. *The Colored Girl from Long Island*. Champions Gate, Fla.: Lulu Publishers and Ram's Horn, 2007.

Brown, James Templeton. "The Whalemen, Vessels and Boats, Apparatus, and Methods of the Whale Fishery." In *The Fisheries and Fishery Industries of the United States*, vol. 6, by George Brown Goode. Washington, D.C.: U.S. Government Printing Office, 1887.

Bryant, George. *Cape Cod Whalers of Color: An Exhibit of Photographs and Artifacts, Materials Collected by George Bryant*. Cape Cod Community College, March 29, 2012.

Bullen, Frank T. *The Cruise of the* Cachelot. New York: Dodd, Mead, 1947.

———. *The Cruise of the* Cachelot: *Round the World after Sperm Whales*. F. T. B. Dulwich, 1897.

Bulloch, David K. *The Whale-watcher's Handbook: A Field Guide to the Whales, Dolphins and Porpoises of North America*. New York: Lyons Press, 1993.

Burkes, Betty. "A Little-Known Side to Whaling." *Cape Cod Times*, March 1992.

Burns, Ric. *Into the Deep: America, Whaling and the World*. Documentary DVD/video, July 6, 2010.

Burns, Walter Noble. *A Year with a Whaler: An Innocent's Journey to Manhood*. Warwick, N.Y.: 1500 Books, 2007.

Busch, Briton Cooper. "Cape Verdeans in the American Whaling and Sealing Industry." *American Neptune* 45 (spring 1985): 104–16.

———. *Whaling Will Never Do for Me: The American Whaleman in the Nineteenth Century*. Lexington: University Press of Kentucky, 1994.

Button, Emily. "A Family Affair: Whaling as Native American Household Strategy on Eastern Long Island, New York." *Northeast Historical Archaeology* 43, no. 6 (2014).

Cabral, Reginald, and James Theriault. *Wooden Ships & Iron Men*. Brochure. Provincetown Heritage Museum, June 12–July 31, 1994.

Cary, Lorin Lee, and Francine C. Cary. "Absalom F. Boston, His Family, and Nantucket's Black Community." Nantucket Historical Association, *Historic Nantucket* 25, no. 1 (1977): 14–23.

Cash, Floris Barnett. "African American Whalers: Images and Reality." *Long Island Historical Journal* 2, no. 1 (2013): 41–52.

"The *Charles W. Morgan* Returns to New Bedford." *New Bedford Standard Times*, June 28–July 6, 2014.

Cheever, Rev. Henry Theodore, and William Scoresby. *The Whaleman's Adventures in the Southern Ocean*. London: W. Kent, 1859.

Cohn, Michael, and Michael K. H. Platzer. *Black Men of the Sea*. New York: Dodd, Mead, 1978.

Coli, Walter Berger. "Cape Verdean Americans as Maritime Entrepreneurs: Whaling and the Packet Trade." *Revista Cabo-verdiana de Letras, Artes e Estudos Cimbão* 1, no. 1 (1996): 16.

Conmy, Peter Thomas. "Captain William Thomas Shorey and Shorey Street." Undated article by the Oakland, Calif., city historian, https://localwiki.org/oakland/Captain_William_Thomas_Shorey_and_Shorey_Street.

Connors, Anthony J. *Went to the Devil: A Yankee Whaler in the Slave Trade*. Amherst and Boston: Bright Leaf, 2019.

Cordeiro, Brock N. "Paul Cuffe: A Study of His life and the Status of His Legacy in Old Dartmouth." Master's thesis, University of Massachusetts, Boston, 2004, http://paulcuffe.blogspot.com/.

Coughtry, Jay. *The Notorious Triangle: Rhode Island and the African Slave Trade, 1700–1807*. Philadelphia: Temple University Press, 1981.

Creighton, Margaret S. *Dogwatch & Liberty Days: Seafaring in the Nineteenth Century*. Salem, Mass.: Peabody Museum of Salem, 1982.

———. *Rights & Passages: The Experience of American Whaling, 1830–1870*. New York: Cambridge University Press, 1995.

Creighton, Margaret S., and Lisa Norling. *Iron Men, Wooden Women: Gender and Seafaring in the Atlantic World, 1700–1920*. Baltimore, Md.: Johns Hopkins University Press, 1996.

Cuffe, Paul, Jr. *Narrative of the Life and Adventures of Paul Cuffe: A Pequot Indian: During Thirty Years Spent at Sea, and in Traveling in Foreign Lands*. Paul B. Cuffe.

Davis, Lance E., Robert E. Gallman, and Karin Gleiter. *In Pursuit of Leviathan: Technology, Institutions, Productivity, and Profits in American Whaling, 1816–1906*. Chicago: University of Chicago Press, 1997.

Dayan, Nomi. *Whaling on Long Island*. Charleston, S.C.: Arcadia Publishing, 2016.

Dean, Harry, with Sterling North. *The* Pedro Gorino. Boston: Houghton Mifflin, 1929.

Delano, Amasa. *Narrative of Voyages and Travels in the Northern and Southern Hemispheres: Comprising Three Voyages Round the World; Together with a Voyage of Survey and Discovery, in the Pacific Ocean and Oriental Islands*. Boston: E. G. House, 1817.

Dixon, Ruth Priest. "Genealogical Fallout from the War of 1812." *Prologue* 24, no. 1 (1992), http://www.archives.gov/publications/prologue/1992/spring/sea mans-protection.html.

Dodge, Ernest S. *New England and the South Seas*. Cambridge, Mass.: Harvard University Press, 1965.

Dolin, Eric Jay. *Leviathan: The History of Whaling in America*. New York: W. W. Norton, 2007.

Douglass, Frederick. *Life and Times of Frederick Douglass Written by Himself, His Early Life as a Slave, His Escape from Bondage, and His Complete History*. Hartford, C.T.: Park Publishing, Co., 1881.

Dow, George Francis. *Whale Ships and Whaling: A Pictorial History*. New York: Dover, 1985.

Drewry, Jennifer M. *Footsteps African American History*, May/June 1999 (Scrimshaw Soap)

Druett, Joan. *In the Wake of Madness: The Murderous Voyage of the Whaleship Sharon*. Chapel Hill, N.C.: Algonquin Books, 2004.

Druett, Joan. "Rough Medicine: Doctoring the Whalemen." *Dukes County Intelligencer* 30, no. (1988): 315.

Edwards, Everett J., and Jeanette E Rattray. *Whale Off! The Story of American Shore Whaling*. New York: Coward-McMann, 1932.

Ellis, Richard. *The Book of Whales*. New York: Alfred A. Knopf, 1980.

———. *Men and Whales*. New York: Lyons Press, 1991.

Esquemeling, John, *The Buccaneers of America*. London: George Allen; New York: Macmillan, 1911.

Farr, James Barker. *Black Odyssey: The Seafaring Traditions of Afro-Americans*. New York: Peter Lang, 1989.

———. "A Slow Boat to Nowhere: Multi-racial Crews of the American Whaling Industry." *Journal of Negro History* 68, no. 2 (1983): 159–70.

Finley, Skip. "Black Sea Captains of Provincetown Risked All for Acceptance and Wealth." *Provincetown Banner*, December 10, 2015.

———. "Not Your Average Ahab." *Martha's Vineyard* magazine, May–June 2014: 54–55.

Follansbee, Joe. *The Fyddeye Guide to America's Maritime History*. Lavergne, Tenn.: Fyddeye Media, 2010.

Foner, Philip S., and Ronald L. Lewis. *Black Workers: A Documentary History from Colonial Times to the Present*. Philadelphia: Temple University Press, 1989.

"Former Whaleman in City Dies at 93." Obituary, *New Bedford Standard Times*, February 26, 1975.

Fortin, Jeffrey A. "Paul Cuffe's Journey from Musta to Atlantic African, 1778–1811." In *Atlantic Biographies: Individuals and Peoples in the Atlantic World*, ed. Jeffrey A. Fortin and Mark Meuwese. Leiden: Brill, 2014.

"Full Sail: Heart of Whaling History Beats Again." *Vineyard Gazette*, June 20, 2014.

Gardner, K. Martin. *Rich Man's Coffin: The Legend of Black Jack White, an American Slave in New Zealand*. Bloomington, Ind.: Xlibris, 2002.

Gomes, Joseph, as told to Don Sevrens. *Captain Joe: Whaleman from New Bedford*. New York: Vantage Press, 1960.

Greene, Lorenzo Johnston. *The Negro in Colonial New England*. New York: Atheneum, 1971.

Grover, Kathryn. *The Fugitive's Gibraltar: Escaping Slaves and Abolitionism in New Bedford, Massachusetts*. Amherst and Boston: University of Massachusetts Press, 2001.

Hanc, John. "In the 1800's Blacks Found High-Risk Opportunity in a Vital Trade." *Newsday Life*, February 7, 2016.

Hayden, Robert C., and Karen E. Hayden. *African Americans on Martha's Vineyard and Nantucket: A History of People, Places and Events*. Boston: Select Publications, 1999.

Haywood, Carl Norman. "American Whalers in Africa." PhD diss., Boston University, 1967.

Hoare, Philip. *The Whale: In Search of the Giants of the Sea*. London: Fourth Estate/HarperCollins, 2008.

Hohman, Elmo Paul. *The American Whaleman: A Study of Life and Labor in the Whaling Industry*. New York, London, and Toronto: Longmans, Green, 1928.

Horton, James Oliver, and Lois E. Horton. *In Hope of Liberty: Culture, Community, and Protest among Northern Free Blacks, 1700–1860*. New York: Oxford University Press, 1997.

Horwitz, Tony. *A Voyage Long and Strange: Rediscovering the New World*. New York: Henry Holt, 2008.

Hough, Henry Beetle. "List of Vineyard Shipmasters Is Growing Longer." *Vineyard Gazette*, November 3, 1944.

———. *Martha's Vineyard Summer Resort 1835–1935*. Rutland, Vt.: Tuttle Publishing Company, 1936.

Huntington, Gale. *Songs the Whalemen Sang*. Mystic, Conn.: Barre Publishing Company, 1964.

Jackson, Michelle Gordon. *Light, Bright and Damn Near White: Black Leaders Created by the One-Drop Rule*. Atlanta: Jackson Scribe, 2013.

Jennings, Francis. *The Invasion of America: Indians, Colonialism, and the Cant of Conquest*. Chapel Hill: University of North Carolina Press, for the Institute of Early American History and Culture, 1975.

Kaldenbach-Montemayor, Ana Isabel. "Black on Grey: Negroes on Nantucket in the Nineteenth Century." Thesis, Princeton University, May 13, 1983. Courtesy of Nantucket Historical Association Research Library.

———. "Blacks on the High Seas: The Arrival of Negroes on Nantucket." Paper written for Princeton University, May 12, 1982. Courtesy of Nantucket Historical Association Research Library.

Kaplan, Sidney. "Lewis Temple and the Hunting of the Whale." *Negro History Bulletin* 17 (October 1953).

———. "Lewis Temple and the Hunting of the Whale." *New England Quarterly* 26, no. 1 (1955).

Kaplan, Sidney, and Allan D. Austin. "Lewis Temple and the Hunting of the Whale." In *American Studies in Black and White: Selected Essays 1949–1989*. Amherst: University of Massachusetts Press, 1991.

Karttunen, Frances Riley. *Law and Disorder in Old Nantucket*. North Charleston, S.C.: Book Surge, 2007.

———. *Nantucket Places & People 1: Main Street to the North Shore*. North Charleston, S.C.: Book Surge, 2009.

———. *Nantucket Places & People 2: South of Main Street*. North Charleston, S.C.: Book Surge, 2009.

———. *Nantucket Places & People 3: Out of Town*. North Charleston, S.C.: Book Surge, 2009.

———. *The Other Islanders: People Who Pulled Nantucket's Oars*. New Bedford, Mass.: Spinner Publications, 2005.

Kendi, Ibram X. *Stamped from the Beginning: The Definitive History of Racist Ideas in America*. New York: Nation Books, 2016.

Kennedy, Randall. *Nigger: The Strange Career of a Troublesome Word*. New York: Vintage Books/Random House, 2001.

Krahulik, Karen Christel. *Provincetown: From Pilgrim Landing to Gay Resort*. New York: New York University Press, 2005.

Langley, Harold D. "The Negro in the Navy and Merchant Service, 1789–1860." *Journal of Negro History* 52 (October 1967).

Lindgren, James M. "Let Us Idealize Old Types of Manhood: The New Bedford Whaling Museum." *New England Quarterly* 72, no. 2 (1999): 163–206.

Lipman, Arthur G. "Medicine and Pharmacy aboard New England Whaleships." American Institute of the History of Pharmacy, 1969.

Malloy, Mary. *African Americans in the Maritime Trades: A Guide to Resources in New England*. Kendall Whaling Museum Monograph Series 6, 1990.

Marquardt, Jim. "Sag Harbor Whalers: Entombed at Sea." *Sag Harbor Express*, http://sagharboronline.com/sagharbor express/tag/whaling, October 3, 2008.

Mawer, Granville Adam. *Ahab's Trade: The Saga of South Seas Whaling*. Singapore: South Wind Production, 1999.

McKissack, Tricia C., and Fredrick L. McKissack. *Black Hands, White Sails: The Story of African-American Whalers*. New York: Scholastic Press, 1999.

Melville, Herman. *Moby-Dick: The Whale*. New York: Macmillan Collector's Library, 1851.

Murphy, Jim. *Gone a-Whaling: The Lure of the Sea and the Hunt for the Great Whale*. New York: Clarion Books/Houghton Mifflin, 1998.

Murphy, Robert C. *Logbook for Grace: Whaling Brig* Daisy, *1912–1913*. New York: Macmillan, 1947.

Nantucket Historical Association. "African Nantucketers," https://nha.org/wp -content/uploads/PUB-Other-Islanders-1bAfrican1o2.pdf.

Nell, William Cooper. *The Colored Patriots of the American Revolution, with Sketches of Several Distinguished Colored Persons: To Which Is Added a Brief Survey of the Condition and Prospects of Colored Americans*. Electronic edition. Academic Affairs Library, University of North Carolina at Chapel Hill, 1999.

New Bedford Whaling Museum. *Exploring Paul Cuffe: The Man and His Legacy*. Symposium, New Bedford Whaling Museum, October 3, 2009.

———. "Groundbreaking of Captain Paul Cuffe Park." *New Bedford Whaling Museum Bulletin* (winter–spring 2017).

————. Map: "Whaleships Departing New Bedford."

Nicholas, Tom, and Jonas P. Akins. "Whaling Ventures." Harvard Business School case study, October 17, 2012.

Niven, Steven J. "A Black Whaling Captain Escaped Prejudice at Sea." *The Root*, February 5, 2015, https://www.theroot.com/a-black-whaling-captain -escaped-prejudice-at-sea-1790858694.

Niven, Steven J., Henry Louis Gates Jr., and Evelyn Brooks Higginbotham. "William T. Shorey, Whaling Master." Hutchins Center for African and African American Research, http://www.blackpast.org/aaw/shorey-william-thomas -1859-1919.

Noice, Harold. *With Stefansson in the Arctic*. New York: Dodd, Mead, 1925. Available online at https://archive.org/details/withstefanssonin017001mbp /page/n3.

Norling, Lisa. *Captain Ahab Had a Wife: New England Women and the Whalefishery 1720–1870*. Chapel Hill: University of North Carolina Press, 2000.

Ommanney, F. D. *Lost Leviathan: Whales and Whaling*. New York: Dodd, Mead, 1971.

O'Neill, Jenny. "New Insights into the Remarkable Life of Paul Cuffe and His Family." Westport Historical Society, February 22, 2017, http://www.wpt history.org.

Paine Smith, Nancy W. *The Provincetown Book*. Brockton, Mass.: Tolman Print.

Perdue, Heather. "Paul Cuffe." *Learning to Give*, https://www.learningtogive.org /resources/cuffe-paul.

Philbrick, Nathaniel. *Away off Shore: Nantucket Island and Its People, 1602– 1890*. New York: Penguin Books, 1994.

————. *In the Heart of the Sea: The Tragedy of the Whaleship* Essex. New York: Viking Penguin, 2000.

Pierce, R. Andrew. "Sharper Michael, Born a Slave, First Islander Killed in the Revolution." *Dukes County Intelligencer* 46, no. 4 (2005). Martha's Vineyard Museum.

Poole, Dorothy Cottle. "Antone Fortes, Whaleman," *Dukes County Intelligencer* 11, no. 4 (1970): 139.

————. "Full Circle." *Dukes County Intelligencer* 10, no. 1 (1968): 129.

Purrington, Philip E. *Anatomy of a Mutiny Ship*: Sharon 1842. New Bedford: Old Dartmouth Historical Museum, 1968.

Putney, Martha S. *Black Sailors: Afro-American Merchant Seamen and Whalemen prior to the Civil War*. New York: Greenwood Press, 1987.

————. "Pardon Cook: Whaling Master." *Journal of the Afro-American Historical and Genealogical Society* 2, no. 2 (1983): 65–74.

"The Quest of the Whale Has Not Lost Its Lure." *Hawaiian Gazette*, February 25, 1908.

Railton, Arthur R. *The History of Martha's Vineyard: How We Got to Where We Are*. Martha's Vineyard Historical Society, 2006.

Rankin, Hugh F. *The Golden Age of Piracy*. New York: Holt, Rinehart and Winston, 1969.

Rediker, Marcus. *Between the Devil and the Deep Blue Sea: Merchant Seamen, Pirates and the Anglo-American Maritime World, 1700–1750*. New York: Cambridge University Press, 1987.

Reimers, David M. *Other Immigrants: The Global Origins of the American People*. New York: New York University Press, 2005.

Reynolds, Jeremiah. "Mocha Dick, or the White Whale of the Pacific." *Knickerbocker* magazine, May 1839.

Robertson, R. B. *Of Whales and Men*. New York: Alfred A. Knopf, 1954.

Rouleau, Brian. *With Sails Whitening Every Sea: Mariners and the Making of an American Maritime Empire*. Ithaca, N.Y.: Cornell University Press, 2014.

Rubin, Lester, William S. Swift, and Herbert R. Northrup. *Negro Employment in the Maritime Industries: A Study of Racial Policies in the Shipbuilding, Longshore, and Offshore Maritime Industry*. Philadelphia: University of Pennsylvania Press, 1974.

Salvadore, George Arnold. *Paul Cuffe, the Black Yankee 1759–1817*. New Bedford, Mass.: Reynolds DeWalt Printing, 1969.

Schneider, Paul. *The Enduring Shore: A History of Cape Cod, Martha's Vineyard and Nantucket*. New York: Henry Holt, 2000.

Sherwood, Henry. "Paul Cuffe" and "The Will of Paul Cuffe." *Journal of Negro History* 8 (1923).

Shoemaker, Nancy. "Mr. Tashtego: Native American Whalemen in Antebellum New England." *Journal of the Early Republic* (spring 2013).

Shoemaker, Nancy. *Native American Whalemen and the World: Indigenous Encounters and the Contingency of Race*. Chapel Hill: University of North Carolina Press, 2015.

Simmons, William Scranton. *Spirit of the New England Tribes: Indian History and Folklore, 1620–1984*. Lebanon, N.H.: University Press of New England, 1986.

Sokolow, Michael. *Charles Benson: Mariner of Color in the Age of Sail*. Amherst: University of Massachusetts Press, 2003.

Spears, John R. *The American Slave-Trade: An Account of Its Origin, Growth and Suppression*. London: Bickers & Son, 1901.

———. *The Story of the New England Whalers*. New York: Macmillan, 1922.

Stackpole, Edouard A. *The Charles W. Morgan: The Last Wooden Whaleship*. New York: Meredith Press, 1967.

———. "Peter Folger Ewer: The Man Who Created the Camels." *Historic Nantucket* 33 (July 1985): 19–30.

———. *The Sea Hunters: The New England Whalemen during Two Centuries 1635–1835*. Philadelphia: J. B. Lippincott, 1953.

Stein, Douglas. "American Maritime Documents 1776–1860." *Mystic Seaport Research,* https://research.mysticseaport.org/item/l006405/l006405-c017/, 1992.

Stevenson, Charles H. *Aquatic Products in Arts and Industries*. Report of the Commissioner for the Year Ending June 30, 1902, part 28. U.S. Commission of Fish and Fisheries, Washington, D.C., 1904.

Strong, John. "Shinnecock and Montauk Whalemen." *Long Island Historical Journal* 2, no. 1, pp. 29–41.

Thomas, Lamont D. *Rise to Be a People: A Biography of Paul Cuffe*. Urbana: University of Illinois Press, 1986.

Todd, Charles Burr. *In Olde New York: Sketches of Old Times and Places in Both the State and the City*. New York: Grafton Press, 1907.

Toll, Ian W. *Six Frigates: The Epic History of the Founding of the U.S. Navy*. New York: W. W. Norton, 2006.

Tompkins, E. Berkeley. "Black Ahab: William T. Shorey, Whaling Master." *California Historical Quarterly* 51, no. 1 (1972): 75–84.

Verrill, A. Hyatt. *The Real Story of the Whaler: Whaling, Past and Present*. New York: D. Appleton and Company, 1923.

Vieira, João A. Gomes. *O Homem e o Mar (Man and the Sea: The People of the Azores and Long Distance Fishing in the Banks of Newfoundland and Greenland)*. Lisbon: Intermezzo-Audiovisuais, 2004. Printed in Portuguese and English.

Vogel, Karl. *Medicine at Sea in the Days of the Sail, Milestones in Medicine*. New York: Appleton-Century, 1938.

Warrin, Donald. *So Ends This Day: The Portuguese in American Whaling 1765–1927*. North Dartmouth: University of Massachusetts Press, 2010.

Wench, Julie. *A Gentleman of Color: The Life of James Forten*. Oxford and New York: Oxford University Press, 2002.

West, Captain Ellsworth Luce, as told to Eleanor Ransom Mayhew. *Captain's Papers: A Log of Whaling and Other Sea Experiences*. Barre, Mass.: Barre Publishers, 1965.

Weston, Beth. "Temple's Toggle: An Important Invention." *Cobblestone* magazine/*Whaling in America*, ed. Carolyn Yoder (April 1984).

"Whale Dives under the Ice, Smashing to Pieces the Boat of Its Pursuers." *San Francisco Call*, November 20, 1904.

"Whaling Bark Brings Fair Catch: *John and Winthrop* Arrives from the Far North." *San Francisco Call*, November 21, 1905.

Whitman, Nicholas. *A Window Back: Photography in a Whaling Port*. New Bedford, Mass.: Spinner Publications, 1954.

Wiggins, Rosalind Cobb. *Captain Paul Cuffe Logs & Letters 1808–1817: A Black Quaker's "Voice from within the Veil."* Washington, D.C.: Howard University Press, 1996.

Zonderman, Jon. *How They Lived: A Whaling Captain*. Vero Beach, Fla.: Rourke Book Company, 1994.

INDEX

American or black, 14–15, 31–32, 151–52; constitutional rights of, 6–7; derogatory views about habits and intelligence of, 34, 36; free blacks from interracial marriages, 12, 32–33, 38; harpooning skills of, 27, 58, 62; identity and opportunities for, 151–55; intermarriages between races, 12, 19, 31–32, 36, 37, 38, 151–52; involvement in whaling of, xii, 4; laws enacted to arrest and return slaves to owners, 6–7, 10, 52, 142, 144–45; merit-based promotion of, 6, 27, 66; opportunities for in New Bedford, 7, 59–60; population share compared to proportion involved in whaling, xii; safer occupation opportunities for, 8, 31; success of and money made from whaling by, 18–19, 43, 47, 50, 51, 196, 205; use of expression and groups included in, 4; whaling as better than slavery for, 4–5, 27, 66, 205

Micah, Thankful, 31, 48–49
Millard, Martin Van Buren, 125, 165
Mills, Henry, 148
Milton, 184, 207
Milton, Anthony, 114
Minerva, 67
Minerva II, 171, 189
Moby-Dick (Melville), 5, 37, 61, 110, 113
Mocha Dick, 113
Montreal, 89, 132
Morning Star, 68, 72–73, 75, 169, 183, 184, 231, 238
Moses, Ruth, 13, 17, 31
Mosher, S. A., 113
Munroe, John, 224
Murphy, Jim, xiii, xiv, 71
mutinies, 6, 101–2, 107, 148–49

Myrick, Seth, 27, 114, 224
Mystic Seaport, 69, 204, 205

Nantucket: anti-slavery conventions and riot on, 53–54; black population on, 58, 59, 146; blockade running supplies to, 15; end of slavery on, 12, 46, 48, 54, 145–46; fire in and destruction of records, 154; focus of whaling industry in, xii, 13, 38, 44–45, 58–59, 146, 162, 235; harbor sandbar and camel system to allow ships into harbor, 162–63; integration of school on, 50, 53–54; parade to celebrate *Loper* return, 162; Quaker congregation on, 44–45; Wampanoag tribe on, 32, 36–38, 48, 90; whalemen and masters from, 47–54; whalemen with Native American blood from, 37, 38, 44, 45
Nassau, 35, 208
National Anti-Slavery Standard, 56, 144–45, 147–48
Native American Whalemen and the World (Shoemaker), xiii, xiv, 94, 155
Native Americans: blacks escaping slavery, role in, 36–37; choices about identification as black or Native American, 12, 14–15, 31–32, 151–52; discrimination and racism endured by, 32–33, 34; diseases and deaths caused by settlers, 36, 48, 58, 59; fishing skills and expertise of, 44; free blacks from interracial marriages, 12, 32–33, 38; identity and opportunities for, 151–55; intermarriages between blacks and, 12, 19, 31–32, 36, 37, 38, 151–52; loss of culture, identity, and rights of, 12, 32; pay

Thomas, 47, 49
Thoughts on African Colonization
   (Garrison), 52–53
Thriver, 114
Timoleon, 24
Tisbury, 36, 38, 93, 235
Topping, Richard, 224
Traveller, 14, 16, 19, 21, 22–23, 24,
   25, 26, 49, 238
Triton, 149, 222
Two Brothers, 25

Union, 111
Unk, Industry, 224

Valkyria, 75, 126, 133, 184, 190–91
Vanderhoop, Edwin D., 39
Vanderhoop, Netta, 36–37
vermin, 83
Viola, 127, 132
Virginia, 52, 138, 139, 142
voyages/whaling trips: all-black crews
   on, 9–10, 16, 22–23, 26, 49, 52,
   146, 159, 166, 167, 238; dangers
   and boredom of, 3–6, 31, 65–66,
   83–84, 88–89, 109, 246n7; families
   of captains on, 23; last trips, 205–6;
   length of, 5; lost ships that never
   returned to port during, 6, 72;
   mileage covered by, xiii; mutinies
   during, 6, 101–2, 107, 148–49; net
   profits from, 7–8, 16, 43, 68, 72–
   73, 240n10; number made, xii, xiii;
   number made with replacement
   masters, xii; records about, xiii–xiv,
   16; seasickness on, 70–71; time
   of the year and timing of, 77;
   worldwide locations and map of,
   xii–xiii, 206

Wade, 168
Wainer, Asa, 23, 25, 171
Wainer, Gardner, 21, 25

Wainer, Jeremiah, 19, 20, 21
Wainer, John, 19, 25
Wainer, Mary, 21, 24
Wainer, Michael (Micah), xiv, 15, 16,
   18, 19–20, 24, 25, 145, 151–52, 217
Wainer, Paul, xiv, 19, 21, 23–24, 145,
   217
Wainer, Rodney, 25
Wainer, Thomas, xiv, 19, 20–22, 24,
   25, 145, 159, 217
Wainer family, 31
Wampanoag tribe: blacks escaping
   slavery, role in, 36–37; death of
   from epidemics caused by settlers,
   36, 48, 58, 59; end of with death
   of last members, 48; eradication
   attempts by the Puritans, 35–36;
   Martha's Vineyard and Nantucket
   home of, 32, 36–38, 48, 90;
   Massasoit tribe relationship to, 90;
   number of members of, 36; Paul
   Cuffe's mother as member of,
   10, 12, 13, 31; People of the First
   Light name for, 243n19; whaling
   by, 37–38; whaling talent and skills
   of, 37–38
Wanderer, 41, 113, 207
Warrin, Donald, xiii, 94, 100, 155
wars, xii, 203
Washington, 76, 167, 168
Washington Freeman, 114
Watchman, 132
Wave, 100
Waverly, 94, 225
weather: affect on whaling industry,
   xii; dangers associated with, 5;
   hurricane season, 77, 112; North
   Pacific weather, 194, 200–201;
   ships lost from storms, 75–76; time
   of the year and timing of whaling
   trips, 77; whale hunting at the end
   of winter, 100; wind, weather, and
   seasickness on whaling trips, 70–

ABOUT THE AUTHOR

Skip Finley spent family summers on Martha's Vineyard before his career as a well-known broadcasting executive. Often failing at staying retired, he joined the *Vineyard Gazette*, where for five years he wrote the weekly "Oak Bluffs Town Column." He remains a contributor to its many publications, along with historical and maritime-related articles for *Cape Cod and the Islands* magazine, *Dukes County Intelligencer*, *The Maritime Executive*, *Martha's Vineyard* magazine, *MVM Quarterly*, the *Provincetown Banner*, *Sea History* magazine, and *The Vine*.

Whaling Captains of Color: America's First Meritocracy won the Non-Fiction Regional History Award from the Afro-American Historical and Genealogical Society, and Finley was named Author of the Year by his publisher, the Naval Institute Press. His book was highly recommended by the Nantucket Book Festival, *Wooden Boat* magazine, and the *Northern Mariner*, and *Sea History* magazine selected Finley's story on a figure from the book ("John Mashow") for the Rodney Houghton Award as the best article of 2020–2021.

More information on Skip and his writing is available at www.skipfinley.com.

The Naval Institute Press is the book-publishing arm of the U.S. Naval Institute, a private, nonprofit, membership society for sea service professionals and others who share an interest in naval and maritime affairs. Established in 1873 at the U.S. Naval Academy in Annapolis, Maryland, where its offices remain today, the Naval Institute has members worldwide.

Members of the Naval Institute support the education programs of the society and receive the influential monthly magazine *Proceedings* or the colorful bimonthly magazine *Naval History* and discounts on fine nautical prints and on ship and aircraft photos. They also have access to the transcripts of the Institute's Oral History Program and get discounted admission to any of the Institute-sponsored seminars offered around the country.

The Naval Institute's book-publishing program, begun in 1898 with basic guides to naval practices, has broadened its scope to include books of more general interest. Now the Naval Institute Press publishes about seventy titles each year, ranging from how-to books on boating and navigation to battle histories, biographies, ship and aircraft guides, and novels. Institute members receive significant discounts on the Press's more than eight hundred books in print.

Full-time students are eligible for special half-price membership rates. Life memberships are also available.

For a free catalog describing Naval Institute Press books currently available, and for further information about joining the U.S. Naval Institute, please write to:

Member Services
U.S. Naval Institute
291 Wood Road
Annapolis, MD 21402-5034
Telephone: (800) 233-8764
Fax: (410) 571-1703
Web address: www.usni.org